G000122585

(take)

advantage of us

This is your own personal Smith membership card. The moment you register it online you will start receiving details of exclusive last-minute offers from the hotels featured, and lots more. The Smithcard provides members-only privileges at all of our hotels, such as a free bottle of champagne on arrival, upgrades, discounts on room rates – just mention it when you book, and show your card at check-in.

Look out for the **Smith** at the end of each review.

Activate your card today by registering online at www.mrandmrssmith.com. (It only takes a minute.)

A *Mr & Mrs Smith* membership card should be affixed here
If it has been removed, you can still buy the book and we will send you a replacement card. Please send proof of purchase, with a return address, to:
Spy Publishing Ltd
192 – 194 Clapham High Street
London SW4 7UD
United Kingdom

Register now

Activate your Smith membership today and you will also receive our newsletter the Guest Book – it's packed with news, travel tips, even more offers, and fantastic competitions. And we promise not to bombard you with communications, or pass on your details to third parties; this is strictly between you and us.

Small print: all offers are subject to availability and subject to change.

bon voya

We've stayed in some out-of-this-world hotels, soaked up vibrant cultures, met fascinating characters, sampled exceptional eateries and visited unforgettable attractions – all in order for you to do the same. And to make it even easier for all of your dreams to come true, we have created an online booking service at www.mrandmrssmith.com.

Europe is an exotic patchwork of sights, flavours, smells and sounds. Follow in our footsteps and you won't go wrong, as we highlight everything from the best places to eat and drink to activities unique to each destination. As well as the lowdown on our favourite cities and the hotels we love, thanks to the Smith card enclosed, you are also entitled to some incredible offers.

The established hotel-rating system has become outdated – a five-star property may have more conference facilities than you can shake a fax machine at, but what use is a meeting room on a romantic jaunt, when all you want is somewhere stylish? We give you addresses you'll be eager to get to and reluctant to leave. There are also tips on shopping, sightseeing, arts and culture – even the best viewpoints and a diary of what's on when.

We return with another distinguished line-up of reviewers, who all visited the hotels anonymously. Let Stella McCartney entice you to Florence, *The Sunday Times*' Tiffinie Darke take you to Venice and acclaimed food critic Giles Coren steer you to Amsterdam. Cities are big places, with one heck of a lot on offer, so we have even taken the headache out of booking your trip – find the perfect boutique hotel, check availability and reserve your room through our website now.

Enjoy your trips…

Best wishes,

Mr & Mrs Smith

Contents

SWEDEN

● TALLINN

ESTONIA

● STOCKHOLM

● EDINBURGH

● HAMBURG

● AMSTERDAM

NETHERLANDS

UK

● LONDON

GERMANY

● PRAGUE

CZECH REPUBLIC

● PARIS

FRANCE

● MILAN

● VENICE

ITALY

● MONACO

● FLORENCE

SPAIN

● ROME

● BARCELONA

(at a glance)

PRAGUE

CZECH REPUBLIC

PRAGUE
Hotel Josef
Design & Style Hotel Neruda

MTWTFSSMTWTFSSMTWTFSSMTWTFSSMTWTFSSMTWTFSS
CESKA REPUBLIKA

Prague

CITY LIFE   TRULY BOHEMIAN
CITYSCAPE   PICTURESQUE PAGES FROM HISTORY

'The persons I pity who know not the city… the beautiful city of Prague'
William Jeffery Prowse

M T W T F S S M T W T F S S M T W T F S S M T W T F S S M T W T F S S M T W T F

CESKA REPUBLIKA

PRAGUE

Europe's favourite weekend destination for cobblestoned romance, fringe culture and fantastic beer, Prague is a medley of architectural styles, where 10th-century chapels sit alongside post-modern monuments and Vienna-style coffee houses. The opera is still as cheap – and as excellent – as the ale, but modern Prague also means casinos, warehouse clubs and department stores. The Velvet Revolution saw the Gilded City paint over totalitarian grey with the revival of a rich and idiosyncratic arts scene and the enduring Bohemian enthusiasm for after-hours culture. Prague's oldest quarters lie on opposite banks of the River Vltava, linked by the famous Charles Bridge. High on a hill in the Hradčany district is Prague castle and its foreboding cathedral. Beneath is Malá Strana, where you'll find little pubs to warm up in on chilly nights; across the river is Staré Město and its famous square, next to the Jewish Quarter, once home to Franz Kafka. You'll be grateful for all that walking: the new Prague is a world-class restaurant capital, too.

GETTING THERE

Planes Ruzyně airport is about 20 mins from the city centre. Taxis cost around CZK 650 (about €22), but most hotels offer a free pick-up service if you phone ahead. Bus 199 will take you to Dejvická station, which is on the metro.
Trains International trains arrive at the art nouveau Wilson Main Station.
Automobiles Driving isn't easy, and parking is hellish: most areas are residents-only blue zones.

DO GO / DON'T GO

Winters can be freezing, summers scorching and busy – the best times are late spring and early autumn. If you don't mind the cold, and periodic smog alerts, the city is lovely in snow.

PERFECTLY PRAGUE

Join locals at Baráčnická rychta, a wonderful old beer hall on Tržiště in Malá Strana. Take in an opera at the Baroque Estates Theatre, where Mozart premiered *Don Giovanni*. Listen to live trad jazz at the art nouveau Café Imperial on Na poříčí.

LOCAL KNOWLEDGE

Taxis You can hail them from the street, but cabs can be hard to come by. Some drivers try and get away with not turning on the meter – insist they do.
Trams Buy tickets at tobacconists, or shops with a red and yellow DP sticker.
Tipping culture A small cover charge and extras for bread are normal, as is a tip – round up to the nearest CZK 10.
Packing tips Trainers (fancy shoes may not be able to negotiate the hills and slippery pebbles), opera glasses, paracetamol if you like beer.
Recommended reads *The Castle* by Franz Kafka; *Laughable Loves* by Milan Kundera; *On the Sky's Clayey Bottom* by Zdeněk Urbánek.
Cuisine Pork, dumplings and sauerkraut still reign supreme, but the new Prague offers far more than rib-stickers, fashionable international cuisine is available all over town. Veggies can have a hard time; book ahead.
Currency Czech koruna; CZK 30 = about €1.
Dialling codes Country code for Czech Republic: 420. Prague: no code.

DIARY

February Masopust, a street party for Shrove Tuesday. **April 30** Witches' Night celebrates the end of winter. **May 1** Day of Love, when Mr & Mrs Smiths climb Petřín Hill and kiss under the statue of a romantic poet. **May–June** Spring International Music Festival (www.festival.cz). **June** Festival of Puppet Theatre (www.puppetart.com). **October** Jazz Festival (www.agharta.cz).

WORTH GETTING OUT OF BED FOR

Viewpoint The best view is from the top of Petřín Tower; take the funicular to the top of Petřín Hill and then make the long walk up this mini Eiffel Tower. (Remember to take change for the ticket machine, or buy a ticket in the newsagent at the foot of the hill). The TV Tower is a winner; sip on a cocktail or have dinner here. The castle grounds have two spots from which to peer over red-roofed Prague: the Garden of Paradise on the ramparts, and the Castle Steps (Thunovská).

Arts and culture For information on theatre and art exhibitions pick up a *Prague Post*. The Jewish Museum and Cemetery is the largest of its kind, in Central Europe, with one of the most extensive collections of Judaic art in the world. Galerie Rudolfinium (www.galerierudolfinium.cz) is the best place in town to see contemporary art, and Galerie Jelení, operated by the Center for Contemporary Arts (www.fcca.cz), hosts the most experimental exhibitions.

Something for nothing A walk on Petřín Hill – the biggest and greenest of Prague's seven hills.

Shopping The pretty tree-lined street Pařížská in Josefov has been nicknamed 'French Street' as it means Paris and has so many fashionable boutiques and restaurants. We loved the shoes at Vicini, and Deco Interior on Štupartská. If you want decent souvenirs, head to Malá Strana.

And... Take a boat cruise or the metro out to the castle at Vyšehrad, a sprawling and rocky hilltop ruin whose gardens and panoramic views make it an unusual romantic day-trip. There is also the Slavin cemetery here which is Prague's answer to Père Lachaise in Paris.

Tourist tick box Prague Castle ❏ Charles Bridge ❏ Old Town Square ❏

CAFES

The coffees and cakes are divine at **Cremeria Milano** on Pařížská, an old-style tearoom that spills onto the street in the summer. **Nostress Café** on Dušní is one of our favourite places in Prague. Great for a quick stop-off, the inviting interior mixes Japanese and Vietnamese design.

BARS AND RESTAURANTS

Huge black and white photos of actors and models adorn the walls of **Barock** on Pařížská (222 329 221). The more relaxed, intimate candlelit restaurant specialises in Japanese and Asian cuisine with irresistible sushi. **Hot** on Václavské náměstí (222 247 240) is the newest addition to the city's ever-growing array of fashionable eateries. Designed in an art deco style, with a terrace area overlooking Wenceslas Square, it's the place to be seen, and enjoy Asia-meets-Europe cuisine. **La Perle de Prague** on the corner of Rašínovo nábřeží and Resslova (221 984 160) is located in the Dancing House, a building made entirely from glass; to eat here is an honour, so dress up. It's fun to perch at the bar of posh cocktail lounge **Bugsy's** on Pařížská (224 810 287) and watch Prague's rich set in action. **Kolkovná** on V Kolkovně (224 819 701) is an art nouveau pub always packed with people enjoying the traditional food and beer; the cellar turns into a nightclub at 22h. **Kampa Park** on Na Kampě (257 532 685) serves traditional Czech food as well as French and Italian delicacies. For a special occasion, book a table overlooking the river and St Charles Bridge.

NIGHTLIFE

Tretters on V Kolkovně (224 811 165) is a laidback but sophisticated New York-style cocktail bar which attracts both locals and tourists. **Radost FX** on Bělehradská (www.radostfx.cz) is a nightclub, cocktail bar and art gallery all rolled into one. It also has a vegetarian restaurant.

'Glass walls, shiny chrome and
an open-plan nature lend Josef
a design-heavy aura different
to anywhere else in Prague'

Hotel Josef

CITY	PRAGUE
STYLE	MINIMALIST COOL
SETTING	ANCIENT STREETS

MTWTFSSMTWTFSSMTWTF**SS**MTWTFSSMTWTFSSMTWTF

PRAHA

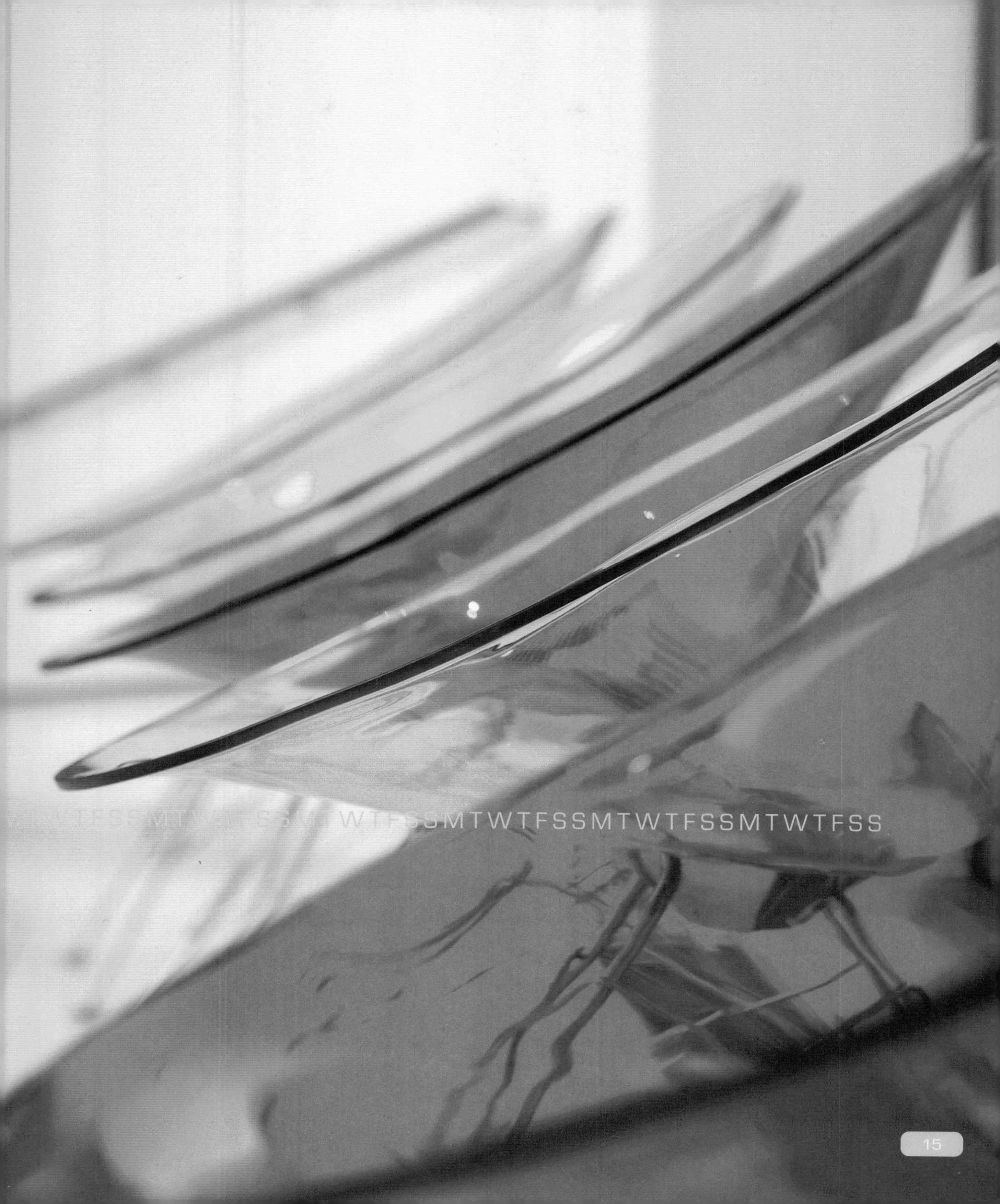
SMTWTFSSMTWTFSSMTWTFSS

We're slightly frazzled after a late arrival, so a friendly welcome with a nothing-is-too-much-bother attitude is just what we need. (A friend suggested this is a city where the inhabitants can be economical in the smile department – clearly he hasn't met the staff at Hotel Josef.) A chic white-on-white lobby, with a glowing glass-fronted bar and reception desk welcomes us to the seemingly sprawling hotel, and instantly instills calm. This uncluttered space designed by Eva Jiřičná, near the old Jewish Quarter, or Josefov, is to become our tranquil refuge in magnificent Prague.

We're escorted through a glass-lined corridor past chrome-covered doors with porthole windows, and are curious as to whether our room will be in the Pink or the Orange House. Mrs Smith wonders about the colour coding of Josef's two six-storeyed buildings – neither are fuchsia or tangerine as she'd envisaged, but a clean white. We discover the chosen shades apply only to the room numbers: I ponder whether the designer had synaesthesia; Mrs Smith opines it's more likely an imaginative alternative to simply referring to the buildings as the front and the back.

I'm no chartered surveyor, but as we enter our room decked out in muted taupes and greys, it seems more spacious than its square footage. They've made the most of every inch, effecting the architectural equivalent of a Wonderbra. The impression of openness is achieved by housing the pale-limestone bathroom in a glass box – smart thinking. Philippe Starck taps visible on the sink also suggest the designers had an exhibitionist streak; their if-you-got-it-flaunt-it mentality extends to an open wardrobe (so maybe leave the Hawaiian shirts at home). As modern as we consider ourselves to be, we're happy to see that's all that's geared to gawping eyes; the loo and walk-in shower are a no-voyeur zone, discreetly hidden behind opaque glass.

But Mrs Smith's final judgment is reserved for what she considers most important: the bed. Loads of pillows (you get three each, so if you're planning a night away with a giraffe, you know where to take them) and a huge fluffy white duvet, rather than the two single duvets so often the case on the continent, mean it passes with flying colours. And where interior-design purists might

choose to remark on the tasselled bed-throw and its textural contrast with the high-sheen of the lacquered headboard, I swoop to inspect something far more important: the mini-bar – this being the birthplace of real lager, after all. I'm not disappointed, and after quite enough analysis of the Czech lager, we hit the proverbial (and super-comfy) sack.

Morning glory for any technophile, opening the curtain the following day is a satisfying process that involves buttons to open the blinds and operate the automatic shutters. Having arrived at night, we're excited to see a jewel of bright-green grass revealed below, and we race down to join the multilingual babble of chattering tourists in the hotel's limestone courtyard, rustling maps and flicking through guidebooks over eggs Benedict.

Once we've refuelled on Bohemian crepes, it's time to explore Prague. We soon see why it's been dubbed 'the city of 100 spires'; you can't turn a corner without spotting a steeple or an ornamented palace. Having never been bombed or shelled in war, Prague's core is

a unique architectural treasure – mediaeval but especially Baroque. Even 40 years of communist proletarian functionalism left its wonders alone and during the course of our weekend we're determined to see as much as we can. Our strolls take us past cubist, modernist and constructivist architecture, the like of which no other city can boast. We even steal a fix of art nouveau in the Municipal House on Námestí Republiky where we dip into one of the small exhibitions to get a glimpse of the grandiose interiors. Next we're drawn to the bright lights of Prague's 'Prada Street', Na Příkopě. Grabbing an ice-cream at Cremeria Milano, we ogle the posers and window-shop alongside dressed-up nouveaux riches at the Versace, D&G and Dunhill stores. Who knew Prague-dwellers could give Florentines and Parisians such a run for their chi-chi-ness? ↓

Then the sanctuary of Hotel Josef draws us back; we cool down with a glass of wine on the terrace beside the emerald lawn. In such a beautiful city, you are obliged to get out and about, but wanting a relaxing weekend too, we find the hotel's lack of adornment a calming antidote to the sightseeing sensory overload. Glass walls, shiny chrome and an open-plan scheme lend Josef a design-heavy aura different to anywhere else in Prague. Furniture aficionados might arch an eyebrow in interest when they see the Marcel Breuer Cesca chairs (tubular chrome with beech frames, stained black to match the glass table tops) and Eileen Grey lookalike tables.

A freshen-up later and we're back down for an aperitif on the low-slung, hipster-style Bombo stools that front the bar at Josef. With no restaurant in the hotel, we explore the alternatives and discover several traditional and fine-dining options, all within walking distance. Pravda proves perfect, with quality food and friendly service from young international staff, but we return to Josef for a nightcap. Lounging around on the white furniture, we

flick through the Kodak moments from our day; as we scroll through our digital camera, we realise that our location in Josefov was ideal – even the nearby cemetery is a wonder of the world. As for the hotel, it's a living showroom of modern interiors – although chances are most guests might not even notice all the furniture and fittings, as they they're as practical as they are stylish. But our conclusion is that what we appreciate most isn't the hotel's visual impressions – it's simply the atmosphere; if only we could capture a little of that serenity and take it on every city break.

Reviewed by Mr & Mrs Smith

NEED TO KNOW

Rooms 110, including breakfast.

Rates €167–€348.

Check-out Midday; sometimes later for an extra charge.

Room service 09h–0h30: an international menu with snacks and main courses available.

Facilities Gymnasium, limousine service, indoor parking, free high-speed internet connection.

Children A bed or cot can be provided free of charge for children under six; babysitting services available.

Also Special rates at the local Toni & Guy hair salon.

IN THE KNOW

Recommended rooms Room 801 has fantastic views of the old town and 704 overlooks Prague castle; they both have terraces and are much larger than the other rooms; the price of these rooms includes an airport pick-up service.

Hotel bar A small but chic, minimalist setting for drinks, open 09h–01h.

Hotel restaurant Only breakfast is served 06h30–11h30 and until 12h30 at the weekend.

Top table It has a canteen-style layout, but try and grab seat near the window.

Dress code Casual.

LOCAL EATING AND DRINKING

Pravda on Pařížská (222 326 203) is a fine-dining experience split over two all-white contemporary levels. Service is impeccable, and the food delicious. The cavernous candlelit area downstairs is more suitable for dinner; ask for a window seat and dress up. Ask for a table on the terrace or by the window in winter. **Barock** on Parizská (222 329 221) offers a respite from usual Czech comestibles, as its cuisine is Japanese and Asian. The coffee and cakes are divine at **Cremeria Milano** on Pařížská, an old-style tearoom which spills tables onto to the tree-lined 'French Street' in the summer. **Kolkovná** on Kolkovne is an art nouveau pub, always packed with merrymakers enjoying the traditional food and beer; the cellar transforms into a nightclub at 22h. The fruits of the French and Thai kitchen at Nostress café on the corner of **Dusni** (222 317 004) are best enjoyed at lunchtime in the garden. It also specialises in fresh juices and Belgian chocolate cake. **Tretters** on Otevreno (257 811 165) is a popular New York-style spot.

 A free bottle of wine and free use of the DVD library. Register your Smithcard online, then show your card at check-in, to claim your offer.

Get a room! Use our free online booking service: check availability and make reservations through www.mrandmrssmith.com.

SMITH CONCIERGE Registered Smith cardholders can call +44 (0)20 7978 7333 and have Original Travel book everything from your flights to your day trips, at no extra charge.

Original idea We'll organise a visit to the State Opera House on the banks of the Vltava River, making sure you sit in the best seats in the house, and meet the cast afterwards.

Hotel Josef 20 Rybná, Prague 110 00 (+42 0 221 700 901)
office@hoteljosef.com; www.hoteljosef.com

'Nothing grand or overly fussy,
it's a comfortable marriage of
modernism and classicism'

Design & Style Hotel Neruda

CITY   PRAGUE
STYLE   SIMPLE, STYLISH COMFORT
SETTING   CLOSE TO THE CASTLE

M T W T F S S M T W T F S S M T W T F S S M T W T F S S M T W T F S S M T W T
PRAHA

MTWTFSSMTWTFSSMTWTFSSMTWTFSSMTWTFSS

The perils of talking up a romantic weekend to your Mrs Smith is that the pressure is on to deliver. Driving up the steep cobblestoned streets towards Hotel Neruda, I breathe a sigh of relief. Not only are we right under the magnificent castle walls (you couldn't get closer), but when the smiling manager, Petr, appears to help us with our bags, I know we've lucked out.

Hotel Neruda is as unpretentious a hotel as you could hope for. Nothing grand or overly fussy, it's a comfortable marriage of modernism and classicism. The lines of a contemporary townhouse are encased in a centuries-old shell. Sharp-looking stone steps meet glass balustrades, rough-end red granite, brushed aluminium uplighters, and the human touch of an antique copper coffee urn, gilt framed mirrors and a dream glass chandelier, which we're quick to covet. Lighthearted details abound; dark-wood block flooring is a witty echo of the street cobbles outside, and you can't help getting tactile with the weighty, sand-filled leather bags that double as key fobs. (I've always been scornful of jugglers, but their squidginess had me tempted to join the street performers on the Charles Bridge).

Adding intellectual gravitas, the warm-coloured walls are dotted with quotations from Jan Neruda, the beloved 19th-century Czech poet, writer and journalist who lived in the building for more than 20 years and after whom the street and hotel is named. (To the uninitiated, the hand-painted pearls of his wisdom may appear indecipherable. I assure Mrs Smith a few Pilsner Urquells will limber up my pronunciation. She is right to furrow her brow; when eventually I do try reading them out, my stab at saying 'úsměvné jitro zrcadlilo se…' translates not as 'a joyful daybreak mirrored…' (A blushing Czech lady next to me informs me I have somehow used the past tense of the verb to defecate.) The Czech language and its pronunciation are quite specific, and rather difficult for foreigners to conquer.

As you'd expect from an old building, all the rooms are different. Each is basic and contemporary, but we're delighted to discover ours is split-level. Rattan carpets, dark-wood cupboards and an ochre palette create a cosiness, and gold organza curtains float behind decadently heavy drapes, lending a romantic air. With a spacious bathroom, good-sized toiletries and a walk-in shower, it's the ideal base for a weekend away.

We've so much we want to see and do, but feeling peckish, we head to the hotel's café-restaurant Carolina, in the mezzanine lounge. The friendly Magda soon talks us into a glass of local wine, and wisely navigates us to the roof terrace. (Incidentally, if you thought Czech beer was good, the wine is also worth shouting about.) We find wooden deck furniture and vast umbrellas in a suntrap enclosed by terracotta-tiled gables, right on the castle's ramparts. How nice — we can soak up the history without moving an inch. Thanks to a hairpin bend in pedestrianised Nerudova Street, there are buskers a few metres above our

heads, treating us to classical, jazz and secret soft-rock Eighties favourites. (A burst of Dvořák on the viola ensures that when we walk up to the Hrad ourselves, we drop off a few coins to say thanks for our personal concert.) After three courses polished off with a delicious hot chocolate like a melted Galaxy bar, a post-lunch snooze is inevitable. A power nap later and we're ready for a whirlwind all-you-can-see exploration.

We're soon in Malostranské náměstí, the main square, in Malá Strana, or Lesser Town, beneath the castle and cathedral. It's a Baroque neighbourhood of narrow streets and lanes; and we pass embassies, galleries, cafés and souvenir shops as we make for the Kampa Park restaurant. I can tell by the narrowing of Mrs Smith's eyes that she's concerned whether we'll get a table. I smugly inform her that I've booked ahead and asked for a river view (remember, I was under pressure and leaving nothing to chance). ↓

We get a seat on the deck, usually a prime position, but at 21h on this particular Saturday, construction workers are hard at it – still, when the flood defenses are rebuilt and the cement-mixers gone, the view of Charles Bridge will be lure enough. The food is excellent, as is the wine list – although the service hardly ebullient (perhaps those who order the £2,000 Pétrus get a smile).

Not sure what to expect, we duck into Casino for a drink. Just as I'm admiring an exotic-looking waitress, one saunters over to take our order. I feel a pinch on my leg and recognise a glint in my other half's eye that usually means 'sober up, you're embarrassing me', or 'call us a cab'. What's she trying to tell me… has she asked for spritzer? Hardly the classiest of drink requests, but why the gritted teeth? Oh – stripper! I twig that the six-foot siren before us wants to entice us for a lapdance upstairs. With that Mrs Smith suggests a cocktail for the road. (I ask for an extra-strong one, hoping she'll pick up where the waitress left off, back at Neruda.)

Fast-forward to breakfast, and we're back on the rooftop. (This time with some Louis Armstrong followed by a classic strings selection.) A 'good morning' card arrives with our home-made strudel, outlining the city's cultural programme (strangely, Casino is absent) with a daily tip sure to motivate the most apathetic visitor. Not that Prague requires much motivation. It is one of the most beautiful and captivating capitals you could visit.

No Neruda guest can miss out on a wander around the Hrad and the huge St Vitus cathedral. We catch the changing of the guard – stern-faced troopers marching to the sounds of a military band – highly entertaining. There's more to see but sadly no time, so we return to check out. We leave with a gift of home-baked cake, happy in the knowledge we'll be back. I'm planning a return to a snow-covered Prague. I've found the winning weekend-away formula, so why risk changing it?

Reviewed by Guy Dittrich

NEED TO KNOW

Rooms 20.
Rates €220–€320, including breakfast.
Check-out Midday, but late check-out sometimes possible.
Room service 07h–22h. You can order from the café/restaurant menu.
Facilities Internet connection.
Children Childminder service available on request.
Also Breakfast is served on the upstairs terrace in summer.

IN THE KNOW

Recommended rooms 16, 18, 25 and 27 are the best rooms looking out on to the cobbled street that leads up to the castle. 17 and 26 have bathtubs.
Hotel bar/restaurant Café/restaurant Carolina is good for light lunches and home-baked pastries. Don't leave without trying the legendary home-made hot chocolate.
Top table Breakfast on the terrace, spring to autumn.
Dress code Relaxed.

LOCAL EATING AND DRINKING

The two-levelled **Hergetova Cihelna** on Cihelna (257 535 534) is a huge bar, Italian diner and pool hall rolled into one; a great place for lunch, it turns into a rocking bar at night. **The Three Violins** restaurant on Nerudova (257 532 062), a former violin workshop of the kind Prague was famous for, serves good fish and typical Czech dishes. One of Prague's most high-profile destination restaurants is **Kampa Park** on Na Kampé (257 532 685). Ten minutes away, right next to Charles Bridge and the Vltava River, it serves classic Czech dishes with as much finesse as fancy international recipes from fresh seafood to game (we loved the duck). Perfect for a special occasion; try and get a table overlooking the river. **Square Café** on Malostranske was the old haunt of poet Jan Neruda, and so an appropriate rendezvous for guests of Neruda. Newly renovated with a glass facade, it is a popular spot to enjoy a beer or a candlelit dinner of Italian, Mediterranean dishes or tapas.

 A traditional Czech cake (vanilla/chocolate) and a free bottle of wine. Register your Smithcard online, then show your card at check-in, to claim your offer.

Get a room! Use our free online booking service: check availability and make reservations through www.mrandmrssmith.com.

SMITH CONCIERGE Registered Smith cardholders can call +44 (0)20 7978 7333 and have Original Travel book everything from your flights to your day trips, at no extra charge.
Original idea Let us rent you a rowing boat and hand you a lantern for an evening so you can explore the Vltava River in the most romantic way possible. And as there is no commercial traffic allowed on the river, it's perfectly safe and wonderfully peaceful.

Design & Style Hotel Neruda 44 Nerudova, Prague 11800 (+42 257 535 557)
info@hotelneruda.cz; www.hotelneruda.cz

TALLINN ●

MTWTFSSMTWTFSSMTWTFSSMTWTFSSMTWTFSSMTWTF

ESTONIA

TALLINN
The Three Sisters

MTWTFSSMTWTFSSMTWTFSSMTWTFSSMTWTFSSMTWTFSS
EESTI

● TALLINN

Tallinn

CITYSCAPE   TURRETS ON THE BALTIC
CITY LIFE   MYSTERY AND MODERNITY

MTWTFSSMTWTFSSMTWTFSSMTWTFSSMTWTFSSMTWTF

EESTI

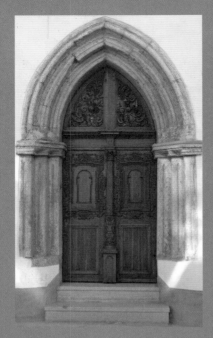

TALLINN

Tallinn is all contradictions: old/new, east/west, tradition/technology – and no right angles. A well-preserved maze of minarets, spires and red-tiled roofs, fringed by severe Seventies tower blocks that sprang up during the Soviet era, it's a living history book where wife-carrying championships take place alongside festivals of modern dance, cinema and contemporary music. Its people are text and email addicts, but you can still get an impression of bygone communism if you put your nose around the right doors. (The spire of St Olav's church, formerly the world's highest structure, was used as a receiver for KGB radio signals.) Explore 1,000 years' worth of churches, monuments and domestic architecture – the invading Danes, Swedes, Germans and Russians all left their mark. The Baltic is teeth-chatteringly cold in winter, so defrost in cockle-warming cafés with motherly service and flavoured coffee. In summer, swap hot chocolate for sandals and visit the beach, a 30-minute drive away, if for nothing other than its unconventional backward view of the city. By night, partake in up-for-it partying, lashings of vodka and Russian karaoke. Give Tallinn a few days and it'll give you crisp Baltic air, old-town atmosphere and all-singing, all-dancing Estonian fun.

GETTING THERE

Planes A taxi from the airport to the centre costs EEK80. Or take the number 2 bus from outside departures; it stops a short walk from the old town.

Trains Use as a last resort (the service in Estonia is poor), and stay away from the train station at night.

Automobiles Parking is tricky and/or expensive; however, if you're touring, a car is the best option.

DO GO/DON'T GO

Though it's very pretty in the snow in winter, it gets very cold – in February the temperature can drop to -25°C.

TYPICALLY TALLINN

Buy brooms and brushes for Walpurgis Night at the Estonian Folk Art and Craft Union (www.folk.ee). It's their equivalent of Halloween, and all the kids dress up.

LOCAL KNOWLEDGE

Taxis They are cheap; order one from the hotel, go to the taxi rank on Vabaduse Väljak, or hail one down on the main road.

Tipping culture Optional, but ten per cent is usually expected.

Packing tips An Estonian (Eesti Keel) phrasebook – although more and more people speak English. Warm clothing in winter.

Recommended reads *The Compromise* by Sergei Dovlatov; *The Conspiracy and Other Stories* by Jaan Kross; *The Autumn Ball* by Mati Unt.

Cuisine Cabbage or pea soup. Our favourite was served at the simple, traditional Eesti Maja (Estonian House) on Lauteri (645 5252).

Currency Kroon (EEK).

Dialling codes Country code for Estonia: 372. No city code.

DIARY

30 April Walpurgis Night sees a big Volbriöö party. **November** Jazzkaar, global jazz festival (www.jazzkaar.ee). **June** Eat, drink and dance at Grillfest (www.grillfest.ee) BBQ championship. **June–July** Old Town Days – mediaeval traditions, street markets and performers. **July** Beer Summer (www.ollesummer.ee), Nordic festival. **August** Modern dance festival (www.saal.ee). **December** Sip glöggi at the Christmas market.

WORTH GETTING OUT OF BED FOR

Viewpoint St Olav's church on Pikk; its spire offers the best view of Tallinn. Take the wobbly lift up Teletorn TV Tower (www.teletorn.ee) to the Galaxy restaurant for views of the city and beyond.

Arts and culture Visit Kadriörg Palace (www.ekm.ee) on Weizenbergi. An art gallery and a museum, open daily, it also hosts concerts.

Something for nothing Opposite the palace is Kadriörg Park. Folk come to watch concerts in the pagoda here in summer from a boat on the lake. The Old Town Square is the most famous and busiest part of the city; still, it's a great spot to sit in one of the many cafés and watch the world go by. But the biggest treat is Pirita Beach, about seven kilometres from the city centre, where you can swim and surf, or rent a boat and visit the islands.

Shopping You don't really hit Tallinn to shop, though on Viru, the main shopping street, you can pick up typical souvenirs – textiles, wooden crafts and vodka. Avoid buying in the old town where prices are hiked up; instead, visit traditional craftsmen in Kadriörg. Katariina Kaik is Tallinn's most enchanting alleyway, where you can watch artisans making jewellery, pottery and stained glass.

And… Naissaar is an island and nature reserve in the Gulf of Finland (639 8000; www.naissaar.ee) where you can take tours. Naissaare Reisid (www.naissaarereisid.ee) offer trips around the island in a revamped Soviet army truck. The best way to get to and from Naissaar is on a boat from Pirita harbour called Monica (052 55 363).

Tourist tick box The Old Town Square ❑ St Birgitta's Convent ❑ Pirita Beach ❑

CAFES

Café Anglais (644 2160), on the second floor of the Teachers' House on Raekoja Plats, has a warmer atmosphere than other cafés in Tallinn. A great place for a coffee and cakes, it also serves a divine hot chocolate made from real chocolate bars. Black and white photographs adorn the walls, and soft jazz and blues plays in the background.

BARS AND RESTAURANTS

Café Moskva (640 4694) on Vabaduse Väljak is a modern bar and restaurant, buzzing with Tallinn's most glamorous types in very cool, contemporary surroundings; it serves fusion food and stays open until midnight. **Bocca** (641 2610) on Olevimagi is a hip Italian bar and restaurant with good-looking staff, again popular with the fashionable crowd. Make sure you book at least ten days in advance. Near the port, the monochrome interior of **Restaurant Ö** (661 6150) is a stylish and airy environment to enjoy international and Japanese cuisine. The most fashionable folk flock here to look pretty over tasty soups and fresh sushi.

NIGHTLIFE

To seek out Tallinn's more cutting-edge scene, you have to make your way through a carpark in the port on Mere Pst, to find **Bon Bon Lounge and Club** (661 6080). Its wood carvings and mirrors give it an Asian theme, with a soundtrack of hip hop, global grooves and house. **Club Privé** on Harju (631 0545) is a cheesy club that's so naff it's fashionable, and the location for the said-to-be wild Vibe parties; there's live jazz on weekdays worth pitching up for. Nearby **Pegasus** (631 4040), also on Harju, is an extremely popular nightspot (having one a handful of awards), and is along the same lines as **Moskva** (see above in Bars and Restaurants).

'An intriguing puzzle of a hotel, with its secret staircases and the smell of passionflower in the air'

The Three Sisters

CITY   TALLINN
STYLE   NEW-SCHOOL, OLDE-WORLDE
SETTING MEDIAEVAL MERCHANTS' HOUSES

MTWTFSSMTWTFSSMTWTFSSMTWTF**SS**MTWTFSSMTWT
TALLINNAS

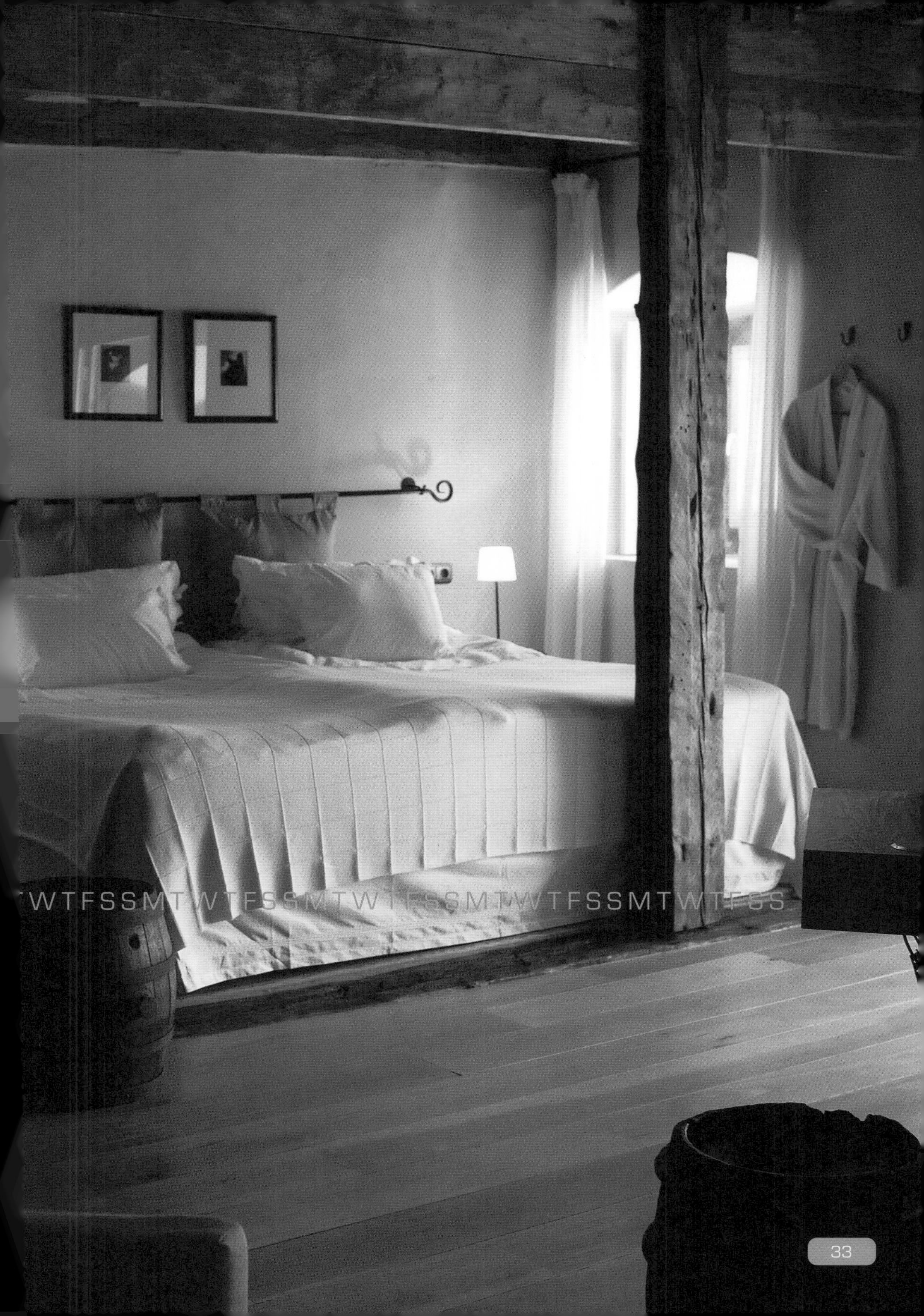
WTFSSMTWTFSSMTWTFSSMTWTFSSMTWTFSS

We arrive at 22h, just in time to see the first of three glorious red-gold sunsets on our way to the Three Sisters Hotel. At the end of a cobbled street in a corner of Tallinn's mediaeval walled old town, next to St Olav's church, three 14th-century former merchants' houses (the 'sisters') have been knocked together and renovated to form Estonia's first contemporary hotel. Outside, huge arched doorways and windows echo the shape of the roofs above. Inside, first impressions are good: sleek slate floors, high ceilings, chalky walls, modern washes of tangerine light, beautifully restored frescoes (discovered by the owners under 14 layers of paint and wallpaper), an old wooden staircase and 600-year-old beams. Young and very attractive (something of a theme in Tallinn) staff whisk our bags to our quarters at the top of the stairs.

The door opens to reveal three big rooms within. Hip Nordic touches such as blocky natural-wood window sills, a granite loo and low-slung sofas sit cleverly next to an antique sleigh bed and intricately carved French screen. That's not to mention the huge flatscreen telly that keeps me preoccupied while Mrs Smith splashes in a look-at-me way for half an hour in the tub.

It's 23h, and the hotel's cellar bar beckons. Tallinn has always been a party town. Even back in Soviet days, Finns would pile over by the boatload to go clubbing and get hammered on cheap Russian vodka. We weren't going to miss out. A dry martini and a Raspberry Collins later, I'm yanking the lady down a snaking cobbled street towards the town's main square. Her Helmut Newton-inspired stilettos, combined with the bumpy road, make this look like something police would describe as an 'incident'.

First stop is Pegasus, a moment from Raekoja Plats, the mediaeval town square. It is a simple bar, white with splashes of colour, packed with stick-thin blondes moodily sipping cocktails in repro Tulip chairs. This makes it an ideal location for practising the Italian cuddle (*leerus maximus*: the art of pulling a loved one to your chest, hence clearing a line of vision above their head).

Countless bars later, we stumble into the Moskva, an industrial-looking cocktail bar, to try the local tipple – a lemon vodka. Here, I learn a couple of lessons. One: it is, quite simply, paint-stripper. Two: no quantity of this poison will loosen your date into the idea of joining you for some lapdancing at nearby Club X, even if you ask repeatedly.

The following morning I am forgiven, once I have expunged my sins with the locals in one of Tallinn's spas. A 100°C-steam, plunge pool and massage at a local spa leaves me clean, fragrant and ready for culture.

There's a lot to see, and it's all pretty close together – ideal for a weekend. Mrs Smith has done admirable research and, despite fairly atrocious map-reading skills, has us hiking up Toompea Hill in no time. There's been a stone castle on the hill for more than 800 years, but it's the onion-domed Russian Orthodox Alexander Nevsky Cathedral that dominates now. Inside, it is intricately decorated with icons and mosaics imported from St Petersburg; at around 40 metres high, it's built on an awesome scale. Next door is the pink Baroque Palace, which was built in the 18th century for Catherine the Great. A short stroll further on, we stop to take in fantastic views of the city below.

Raekoja Plats is the perfect spot in which to have a beer in the evening sun. Tallinn is no shoppers' paradise and, 24 hours since her last retail hit, Mrs Smith starts seeing possibilities in unlikely places: in this case, an open-air folk market. I'm enjoying my beer, and heighten my pleasure by withholding our funds. The power is quite dizzying.

On Saturday night, we dine on delicious Italian food in a restaurant called Bocca, before hitting Club Privé. ↓

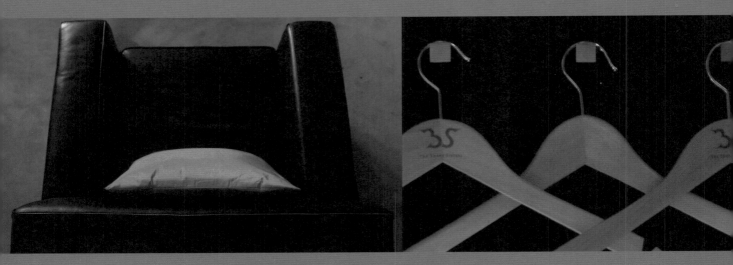

Beyoncé and 50 Cent pumps out of the speakers, while white, dreadlocked youths hold dancing competitions. If you don't like the sound of that, or locals' favourite Hollywood, with its split-level bars and caged dancers, there is Sigari Maja, a more gentlemanly affair with leather armchairs and cigars, on Raekoja Plats.

Back to the Three Sisters; where, we're happy to report, bar snacks are available throughout the night. During more civilised hours, the hotel's intimate restaurant, with more than 300 wines in its cellar (where you can also park your own booze), is one of Tallinn's finest. If you want to, you can eat a six-course meal in the kitchen, watching the chef cook by candlelight; in the summer months, the cobbled courtyard is romantic, too.

On Sunday, we dither between taking a look at Kadriörg Palace, commissioned by Peter the Great in 1718, which sits in parkland peppered with cherry trees near a huge lake; or seeing for ourselves how good the city beach is – we've heard lots about it. In the end, we counteract the excesses of Tallinn nightlife with some more wholesome wildness: just over an hour from Tallinn port by ferry is Naissaar, an island in the Gulf of Finland that has been turned into a nature reserve with beaches, woodland and, allegedly, deer and moose. There are Red Army trucks available, left over from Naissaar's days as a Russian military base, but we prefer to explore on our own by bicycle – invigorating yet exhausting.

I just want to clear something up. Tallinn is a very popular stag-weekend destination; you'll notice this as you wait to board the plane. But don't be put off. First, the majority of the population (six-foot-tall blonde ladies) redresses any imbalance that might concern male visitors at the outset of their journey; second, there wasn't a bachelor party in sight during our weekend. Like (or, perhaps, because of) Irish theme pubs, stag troops are easily avoided.

Before we leave, my soon-to-be wife and I opt for a cooling spritzer in the courtyard, where the summer smell of passionflower fills the air. We have explored, but there's more we haven't seen: the hotel is an intriguing puzzle, with its secret staircases, choice of different rooms and higgledy-piggledy layout, it must feel different every time you stay here. I mull over the possibility of having my own stag weekend in Tallinn. My arguments are good, strong ones: Estonia has recently joined the EU, so scheduled flights would be cheap (return tickets start at £36), and we have made local friends, who could show my friends a good time. Then a stunning blonde sashays in with our drink, and Mrs Smith vetoes the plan. Sorry boys.

Reviewed by Alex Proud

NEED TO KNOW

Rooms 23, all different, including five junior suites, two suites and the Piano Suite.
Rates €248–€590, including breakfast.
Check-out Midday.
Room service 24 hours.
Facilities Satellite TV, CD/DVD player, free internet connection, laptop available, shoe-cleaning service, free airport pick-up, laundry and valet service.
Children Welcome. Babysitting service available.
Also Beware of the ghost; the lady of the night has been known to sneak up when least expected and touch your shoulder. The hotel also has a wine cellar in which you can store your own favourites.

IN THE KNOW

Recommended rooms The Piano Suite, with a piano in its drawing room. Room 37, an attic room with an old-fashioned bath in the bedroom. Room 26 has a four-poster with white muslin drapes – very romantic.
Hotel bar Wine cellar bar, in the basement boasts fab wines at good prices (this is where you can also store your own). It is customary to have a pre-dinner cocktail either in Bar Cloud Seven or in the courtyard garden. No closing time: you can drink as late as you like.
Hotel restaurant Restaurant Bordoo is open for breakfast 07h–18h; lunch from 12h, and a candlelit dinner from 17h–23h. You can also eat a six-course dinner in the chef's kitchen.
Top table In summer, sit in the courtyard; indoors, choose a corner table.
Dress code Smart casual.

LOCAL EATING AND DRINKING

Bocca on Olevimägi (641 2610), is a stylish restaurant/bar in town, serving delicious Italian cuisine at lunch and dinner. Place-of-the-moment **Pegasus** on Harju (631 4040) is a minimalist bar and restaurant on two floors. The chic interior showcasing young artists and cosmopolitan cuisine give it a Manhattan feel, but the view over mediaeval buildings reminds you that you're in Tallinn. **Le Bonaparte** on Pikk (646 4444), is Tallinn's best French restaurant and **Troika** on Raekoja plats (627 6245) is fun if you want a Russian experience of stroganoff and folk music.

 An upgrade of your room, upon availability, and a complimentary glass of champagne. Register your Smithcard online, then show your card at check-in, to claim your offer.

Get a room! Use our free online booking service: check availability and make reservations through www.mrandmrssmith.com.

The Three Sisters 71 Pikk / 2 Tolli, Tallinn 10133 (+372 630 6300)
info@threesistershotel.com; www.threesistershotel.com

PARIS

MTWTFSSMTWTFSSMTWTFSSMTWTFSSMTWTFSSMTWT

FRANCE

MTWTFSSMTWTFSSMTWTFSSMTWTFSSMTWTFSSMTWTFSS
FRANCE

Paris

'To err is human. To loaf is Parisian'
Victor Hugo

MTWTFSSMTWTFSSMTWTWTFSSMTWTFSSMTWTFSSMTWT

S S

PARIS

WTFSSMTWTFSSMTWTFSSMTWTFSSMTWTFSS

PARIS

One mention of Paris, and into most thought-bubbles pop romance, culture, shopping, eating… could a city be more Mr & Mrs Smith? And, most welcome in a city that can be *très cher*, many of the best things in Paris are free. It is an urban walker's paradise: take in the unobscured architecture and ambience by foot; stroll *grands boulevards* off the Arc de Triomphe; wander the riverbanks of the Seine; take Rue St Dominique from Les Invalides lawns to the Tour Eiffel, then climb the lanes through the Montmartre of *La Bohème*… When you're tired of walking, Paris also has some of the loveliest parks in Europe to sit in. Home to the Louvre, the Musée d'Orsay and the Pompidou Centre, this art-lover's haven is also a treasure trove for those who like to stray off-piste. Once you've had your fill of designer boutiques and the more obvious beauty spots, one of the advantages of the French capital is that the tourist-riddled areas are small enough to avoid, leaving you to find tucked-away gems off the beaten track. Follow our lead, and we'll have you walking through your very own Cartier-Bresson photo story.

GETTING THERE

Planes A taxi from Charles de Gaulle airport to the centre will cost you about €50; buses run regularly into town at a fraction of the cost. RER/TGV trains run from CDG to Gare du Nord every 15 mins from 5h30–23h30 and take 35 mins.
Trains There are six main stations in Paris, all of which are central and link to the underground system. See www.sncf.com/indexe.htm.
Automobiles Parking is a challenge, and expensive – try to avoid it.

DO GO/DON'T GO

Paris grinds to a halt in August, the national holiday. We love springtime, when the blossom is out.

PERFECTLY PARISIAN

Rollerskate through town on a Friday night (www.pari-roller.com). Visit Musée Carnavalet on Rue de Sévigné for an engaging history of the 1789 revolution. Turn teatime into an elegant ritual at Mariage Frères on Rue du Bourg-Tibourg.

LOCAL KNOWLEDGE

Taxis Can be hailed in the street if you're more than 100 metres from a rank (these are all over Paris and have phones if no taxi is waiting). From about €8 you can get a multi-trip ticket (Paris Visite) for métro, buses and trams.
Tipping culture In bars, leave small change amounting to about ten per cent. Restaurants often state *service compris*; but it is polite to leave change.
Packing tips Sunglasses, silk scarf, cigarette-holder. Map – the taxi drivers can be clueless sometimes.
Recommended read *Les Fleurs du Mal* by Charles Baudelaire; *A Tale of Two Cities* by Charles Dickens; *A Moveable Feast* by Ernest Hemingway; *Paris: Capital of the World* by P L R Higonnet; *Down and Out in Paris and London* by George Orwell; *Perfume* by Patrick Süskind; *The Da Vinci Code* by Dan Brown.
Cuisine Still-walking steak; croque monsieur; chèvre salad, cheeses, wine.
Currency Euro.
Dialling codes France: 33. Paris: 1.

DIARY

21 June La Fête de la Musique – the start of summer sees streets lined with stages for live bands. **May–June** French Open tennis championship (www.fft.fr/rolandgarros/en). **June–July** Paris Jazz Festival – free concerts in the Parc Floral at weekends. **14 July** Bastille Day. **August–September** Open-air classical music festival, in the Parc Floral every weekend.

WORTH GETTING OUT OF BED FOR

Viewpoint The Eiffel Tower is open 09h30–23h; from mid-June to end August, 09h–midnight.
Arts and culture The Louvre (www.louvre.fr) houses some of the world's most famous art (open late on Mondays and Wednesdays; closed Tuesdays and some holidays). The Musée National d'Art Moderne is on level four of the Pompidou Centre (www.centrepompidou.fr). Musée National Picasso Paris is in an old house in the Marais, and is full of the artworks Pablo couldn't bear to part with; the venue is as alluring as the art itself (www.musee-picasso.fr), also the case for Musée d'Orsay, a converted train station (www.musee-orsay.fr).
Something for nothing Visitors can now make an excursion to the beach without leaving the city, thanks to the palm-tree-lined white sand of Paris Plage, a summertime addition to the right bank of the Seine (near the Pont Neuf and Hotel de Ville).
Shopping Rue du Faubourg Saint-Honoré is one of the city's famous long streets full of designer boutiques; our favourite is Colette, a very cool lifestyle shop with fashion, books and a café. There are lots of shops, cafés and restaurants in the Marais and Latin Quarters. Porte de Clignancourt market is a fleamarket for clothes and antiques; open Monday–Saturday until 19h.
And… Crazy Horse on Avenue George V (www.lecrazyhorseparis.com) is a cabaret performance in a small theatre where drinks are brought to your seat. Bonheur at the Lido Theatre on Avenue des Champs-Elysées (www.lido.fr) is a kitsch cabaret show which can be lots of fun.
Tourist tick tox Eiffel Tower ❑ Mona Lisa ❑ Notre Dame ❑

CAFES

The most famous are **Café de Flore**, **Les Deux Magots** and **Brasserie Lipp**, next to each other on Boulevard Saint-Germain. **L'Esplanade** overlooks the war museum in Place des Invalides.

BARS AND RESTAURANTS

Le Fumoir behind the Louvre on Rue de l'Amiral-Coligny (42 92 00 24) is a relaxed spot for lunch. **La Cantine du Faubourg** on Rue du Faubourg Saint-Honoré (42 56 22 22) is a favourite with celebs, serving Asian and French fusion in a stylish lounge. Also ideal for a drink. **Maison Blanche** on Avenue Montaigne (47 23 55 99) is a sleek all-white eatery with views over the city, and the Eiffel Tower from some tables. Book in advance. For more incredible views, try **Georges** at the top of the Pompidou Centre (44 78 47 99). The legendary **Buddha Bar** on Rue Boissy d'Anglais (53 05 90 00) is a must for Asian food in stunning surroundings. Book a table at a side booth in the main atrium, well in advance – avoid being put under the stairs. **Le Grand Vefour** on Rue de Beaujolais (42 96 56 27) is a beautiful, traditional French brasserie (closed at weekends).
Cristal Room Baccarat on Place des Etats Unis (40 22 11 10) is Philippe Starck's over-the-top bar and restaurant, in a crystal gallery-cum-shop; over the Kenzo store is another of his creations, **Kong** on Rue du Pont-Neuf (40 39 09 00). Request a table on the upper floor by the glass roof.

NIGHTLIFE

Le Cabaret on Place du Palais Royal has a contemporary Moroccan-style lounge, and the club stays open until 06h. If you want to rub shoulders with the stars, then head to **L'Etoile** on Rue de Presbourg or **VIP Lounge** on Avenue des Champs-Elysées. More gritty areas like Belleville, Oberkampf and around Ménilmontant are slightly shabbier, but bursting with character; romantic alleys and late-night bars along the canal will feel like your own discoveries.

Bourg Tibourg

CITY	PARIS
STYLE	MOROCCAN-MEDIAEVAL BOLTHOLE
SETTING	MIDDLE OF THE MARAIS

MTWTFSSMTWTFSSMTWTFSSMTWTFSSMTWTFSS

Hôtel Bourg Tibourg, Paris, France

We arrive to find Paris full of life: France is playing in a football tournament, and the city is buzzing with va-va-voom. We wind through back streets among throngs of supporters, until we reach our hotel on Rue du Bourg-Tibourg. It's in the heart of the Marais district, historically the Jewish quarter (great for bagels when you can't face another croissant aux amandes); more recently, the gay community have breathed extra energy into it. Parisian life unfurls before us like a scene from *A Bout de Souffle*, as a Citroën DS pulls up and deposits a Vanessa Paradis type. With a lingering smooch on her driver's lips, she skips into the hotel lobby, the rear lights of the vintage Citroën winking at us as it pulls away. We have arrived in one of the world's most romantic and beautiful cities, and Gallic cool washes over us.

The archetypal narrow Parisian street is dominated by the Hôtel Bourg Tibourg, the latest bijou property in the portfolio of the dynasty behind fashion-world favourite Hôtel Costes (and the music compilations of the same name). Hôtel Bourg Tibourg is as sartorially impeccable as its big sister, but the difference is that it is less of a destination hotel – more one defined by its locale. And, in contrast with the place-to-be-seen Costes, it feels like a beau-monde hideaway.

The entrance and lobby showcase designer Jacques Garcia's signature style, with decorative details and rich velvets transporting us to the belle époque. The sumptuous feel is amplified by contrasting patterns and colours, and details such as the outsized tassel on our keyring. The hotel has 31 rooms, accessed either by a spiral staircase in a mind-boggling shade of turquoise, or by the cheekiest lift ever. It's like stepping into an Hermès suitcase lined in coffee-coloured velvet: the car fits just two, and is perfect for pressing yourself against your date while making innocent eye contact – or for making new friends if you have to pop down to get your bags. (The receptionist usually helps you with your luggage, but there's no concierge as such. That's part of Bourg Tiborg's charm; when they hand you the key, you feel as if you're renting your own private Parisian pad, rather than checking into a hotel.)

Gothic wallpaper details, dark-blue cupboards with mediaeval-style panelling, mustard trim, leather-covered side-tables – we decide our new surroundings are sexiest when illuminated by the deep-red tasselled boudoir lights. Our instant impression is that the bedroom is not much bigger than the bathroom (plus ça change – Paris is celebrated for the dimensions of its buildings and petiteness of its rooms), but it's wonderfully intimate – and that's exactly what we want. To use the estate agent's adage, it's 'compact and bijou' – so what if you occasionally hear a shuffling from the corridor? The bathroom has a generously proportioned suite, and timber panelling

that creates a separate room for the bath. I'm the kind of girl who would choose where to stay according to whether the hotel's complimentary beauty products were tempting enough, and Hôtel Bourg Tibourg indulges me with crimson-packaged, cinnamon-scented, Costes-branded goodies. An aromatic shower and a Pernod later, we're ready to explore.

The hotel hasn't got a restaurant of its own, but it doesn't need one; the Marais is full of places for eating, drinking and voyeurism. We stumble on La Loir dans la Theière, which oozes that specific Parisian brand of bohemia; it's a world of rustic furniture, poster-covered walls and loud banter over home-made food. Wolfing down our giant fresh salads and quiche, we're convinced a French movie legend has just sashayed past. But little distracts us from our plates for long. For the finale, our frenetic waiter struggles over, weighed down by a breezeblock-sized ↓

slice of tarte tatin. A double espresso boosts our energy enough to allow us to duck into a small jazz club, 7 Lezards, on Rue des Rosiers, on our way home and the city becomes a blur to a sharp jazz score.

We wake the next morning with Sunday church bells tolling in the distance, our French windows open onto the balcony, and Paris starting slowly to come to life below. There is no pressure to take breakfast on the premises, but a decent spread can be had either in your bedroom or in the crypt-like basement. We descend the spiral stairs and find ourselves beneath a hidden-away vaulted ceiling that explains the design's mediaevalist leanings. The style is wild, with hanging tapestries, brocade-trimmed leopard-print baroque chairs and cast-iron chandeliers.

We don't have to stray far to find distractions both classic and unexpected: Bourg Tibourg, Pompidou, Place des Vosges, Picasso Museum, Berthillon… The hotel's central location allows you to dip in and out: a nap, a little love in the afternoon and, half an hour later, we're back among it all, checking out the artisan perfumers, hip independent boutiques, chocolatiers and galleries. Indeed, Hôtel Bourg Tibourg feels much less of a hotel in the traditional sense of the word, and more of a boutique pied-à-terre designed to let you grab your sunglasses and a packet of Gitanes and star in your own Parisian adventure.

Reviewed by Mr & Mrs Smith

Paris, France

NEED TO KNOW

Rooms 30.
Rates €150–€350.
Check-out Midday.
Room service Food is available 07h30–22h.
Facilities All rooms are air-conditioned. Rooftop terrace overlooking Paris.
Children Little ones are welcome, but it's better suited to hip young things.

IN THE KNOW

Recommended rooms Rooms 21 and 31 are quieter than others, with views of the garden. Every room on the fifth floor has its own balcony overlooking the lovely Bourg Tibourg street.
Hotel bar There is no bar, but guests are welcome to order drinks in the lounge or in their rooms.
Hotel restaurant There is no restaurant as such, but you can have breakfast in the subterranean lounge, or eat beneath a 17th-century vaulted ceiling.
Dress code Chic and cheerful.

LOCAL EATING AND DRINKING

There are lots of squares around Bourg Tibourg with cool boutiques, great cafés and restaurants; grab some falafel from one of the many Jewish stalls. **Place des Vosges** has a few places to choose from, including an amazing patisserie. **Pizza Sant' Antonio** on Rue Saint-Martin (48 87 34 22) is a great spot for pizzas, and **Feria Café** on Rue du Bourg Tibourg is ideal if you fancy tapas. **Chez Marianne** on Rue des Hospitalières (42 72 18 86) is a fantastic épicerie, traiteur and salon de thé, whose sweet and savoury comestibles call out to you through the window. We loved the boho vibe and poster-covered walls in **La Loir dans la Theière** on Rue des Rosiers (42 72 90 61); the brunch menu is especially enticing, and the salads and tartes irresistible. For a light lunch or supper and incredible views of Paris, head to the sixth floor of the Pompidou Centre, where you'll find **Georges** (44 78 47 99) on the fifth floor. Jazz lovers will find themselves among friends in Paris. If that includes you, head straight for the boho club **7 Lezards**, on Rue du Rosiers. It has a colourful musical calendar spanning all thing jazzy as well as Brazilian nights, French folk, theatre and poetry readings.

Free room upgrade or, if this is not available, a ten per cent discount. Register your Smithcard online, then show your card at check-in, to claim your offer.

Get a room! Use our free online booking service: check availability and make reservations through www.mrandmrssmith.com.

SMITH CONCIERGE Registered Smith cardholders can call +44 (0)20 7978 7333 and have Original Travel book everything from your flights to your day trips, at no extra charge.
Original idea We can book you a spot on the Friday-night mass rollerskate through Paris. The swarm of skaters leaves from Place d'Italie at 22h and follows a 25-kilometre circuit that changes weekly. There is a police escort to stop the traffic.

Hôtel Bourg Tibourg 19 rue du Bourg Tibourg. Paris 75004 (+33 (0)1 42 78 47 39) hotel@bourgtibourg.com; www.hotelbourgtibourg.com

'Its creators didn't design a guesthouse; they concocted a work of art with bedrooms and a great bar'

Hôtel Le A

CITY	PARIS
STYLE	ALL-WHITE AND ARTY
SETTING	CHI-CHI CHAMPS ELYSEES

MTWTF**SS**MTWTFSSMTWTFSSMTWTFSSMTWTFSSMTWT

PARIS

Hôtel Le A, Paris, France

Hôtel Le A is just like its name: diminutive and discreet. Located in an unremarkable street in the eighth arrondissement, it's round the corner from the Arc de Triomphe and the Champs Elysées. Our first impression is of a downtown SoHo gallery of the Seventies: definitely art scene, and more Right Bank sophistication than Left Bank boho. We half expect to find Leo Castelli in a corner, arguing over prices with Andy Warhol. This is all hardly surprising, considering Le A is a collaboration between architect/ interior designer Fréderic Mechiche, and Fabrice Hybert, artist, both contemporaries of Andy and Leo – and, thanks to their vintage, well versed in the nuances of classic Seventies chic. Mechiche is a devotee of 'minimalism lite'. Hybert's work is a very French intellectual hybrid of Claes Oldenburg and Cy Twombly, coloured by Morris Lewis. And it works.

The ground floor opens into a glassed-over central courtyard, which breaks the room into two natural areas that contrast beautifully. Dark hardwood floors, art-gallery white walls and chocolate velvet curtains are set off by a flood of natural light. It's an interesting space that Mechiche has used just so, for a discreet reception, cosy library, and intimate café bar. Three imposing works by Hybert enhance the area; unsurprisingly, they fit the space and the mood perfectly. A giant, loosely hung tapestry oversees the café bar, and two paintings are mounted flush into the walls of the library. Another piece of Hybert's is the scribblings on a wall by the lifts; very Left Bank (and not to be encouraged at home). The library, screened from the simple reception area, is what you'd expect of the backroom of a world-class art dealer. We could spend hours stretched out on the dark-brown velvet sofas researching lesser-known works of obscure artists, if we had more than a night in Paris. Instead, we only have time to drop our bags off. We have plans to eat, drink and merry-make the best we can in just one night in the French capital.

To reach the rooms, you brave a lift which is like stepping inside a Dan Flavin installation. A tiny white cubicle in white Perspex, it changes colour to indicate different floors. We get off at Red. Like all Parisian hotels with these kinds of dimensions, the hotel makes the most of limited space. Mechiche wastes as little as possible on corridors, behind-the-scenes functions and cupboards; so don't expect dinner, or pack too much. Once this Mr Smith's dusky maiden has emptied her suitcase into the one wardrobe I could forget unpacking my bag. The junior suite only manages one suitcase before everything starts to explode into the carefully balanced calm that has been so diligently created.

Each room is unique, with two works by Hybert; one declares the room's name; the other elaborates on the theme. We are in 'Desert d'Eau' (Ocean Desert), elegant and calming. We're curious as to how the room opposite, 'Oups', had been brought to life. Next time. The same colour palette is used throughout: white walls and loosely covered furniture; chrome; dark-chocolate wood veneers. Details echo Hybert's painting (in the case of our room, a striped green carpet). Double beds are just right, with sheets of the highest quality, and the whole hotel is lit perfectly. Technology is a forte; my laptop instantly detects the wireless broadband signal, and the hi-tech CD player and TV are impressive. Minimalist sensibilities extend to the in-room information, though, and a glance at the room service menu reveals endless variations on the cheese sandwich. We grab a bite to eat, before venturing out for our date at the Crazy Horse. ↓

A Parisian classic of cabaret, and nothing like the Moulin Rouge, the Crazy Horse is a small red-plush basement theatre that seats 150 – mostly tourists, but don't let that put you off. It's certainly a little crazy, though there are no horses; you are greeted at the door by a Canadian mountie, *sans cheval*. The curtains open and we're greeted by 20 identical ladies. It is reminiscent of that Robert Palmer video – they're naked but for flamboyant trimmings, performing (OK, miming) favourite showbiz melodies. Various kitsch city-scene sketches later, interspersed with comic displays, Mrs Smith admits she loves it.

So entertained are we, we don't roll in again until 03h. (Incidentally, reception can't change your sterling into euros, so when eventually find our way back, we have only Bank of England vouchers on us and have to borrow €20 from another guest. Sadly, we never find him again to pay him back. Was he on the green floor? Or was it yellow, next to the room called… Hmmm: no wonder all the room numbers are written on Post-it Notes under the little gems outside the doors. Staff confess they've resorted to this; it's unlikely that Hybert knows.)

Le A is not really a hotel. Its creators didn't design a guesthouse; they concocted a work of art with bedrooms and a great lounge bar attached. A great base if you want to be on the Right Bank and near the shopping, it's romantic, personal and an oasis of calm. It's for grown-ups who love art and know enough about it to appreciate the games designers play. Then again, even if you don't know who Warhol, Castelli, Flavin, Oldenburg, Twombly and Lewis are, it doesn't matter – just look them up in the library when you stay. Add a tour of a few of the amazing galleries and museums in this city, and Le A will have you leaving town an expert in art, with a capital A.

Reviewed by Rory Keegan

NEED TO KNOW

Rooms 26: nine junior suites, one classic room, seven superior rooms, eight deluxe rooms and one apartment.
Rates €320–€450.
Check-out Midday.
Room service Limited room service (snacks, salads, sushi) available 07h–22h30.
Facilities CD/DVD, satellite TV, car-parking service, 24-hour internet connection, laundry.
Children Not recommended for toddlers (too white for little fingers), but small babies are welcome. €50 charge for an extra bed/cot.
Also The lift to the rooms has different-coloured lights on every floor; helpful after a few of Le A's champagne cocktails.

IN THE KNOW

Recommended rooms The rooms all have the same facilities; only the size changes with price. From junior suites 502 and 503 you can see the tip of the Eiffel Tower.
Hotel bar The cool black-and-white lounge bar is open to the public, and usually buzzes until 01h.
Hotel restaurant A continental or hot breakfast is available as a buffet, or delivered to the rooms or the verandah, but there's no restaurant as such.
Dress code Style-savvy.

LOCAL EATING AND DRINKING

Accessible by a little boat, the **Chalet des Iles** is on the lake of the Bois de Boulogne in Porte de la Muette, on Chemin Ceinture (88 04 69). Eat on the terraces in the summer; in winter, a piano and open fireplace make it cosy indoors. If you feel like an Arabian night, head to **404 Restaurant** on Rue des Gravilliers (74 57 81), where you can enjoy belly-dancing with your spiced Moroccan tagine. Or head to the 'real pop art vs Moroccan pop art' **Andy Wahloo Lounge Bar** – part of the same establishment – and try the house speciality, 404 cocktail, not unlike a mojito, crammed full of fresh mint. **Toi** on Rue du Colisee (42 56 56 58) is bright red, fun and very chic. A delicious array of French and Italian dishes are available; it opens for dinner until late, and you can keep on drinking until 02h.

An Aphrodite – Le A's special champagne cocktail – for each of you. Register your Smithcard online, then show your card at check-in, to claim your offer.

Get a room! Use our free online booking service: check availability and make reservations through www.mrandmrssmith.com.

SMITH CONCIERGE

Registered Smith cardholders can call +44 (0)20 7978 7333 and have Original Travel book everything from your flights to your day trips, at no extra charge.
Original idea Why not take a 45-minute helicopter flight over Paris and Versailles? We can arrange for you to take off from Paris heliport, Toussus le Noble Airport or Longes Airfield.

Hôtel Le A 4 rue d'Artois, Paris 75008 (+33 (0)1 42 56 99 99)
info@hotel-le-a.com; www.paris-hotel-a.com

boules

How to play...

Pétanque, aka boules, is more than the Gallic equivalent of crown green bowling. It is an expression of supreme Frenchness, not to mention French supremacy. It is unspeakably competitive – and utterly nonchalant. Give a gang of French oldies a few square yards of grit or dirt and enough remaining daylight to see their feet, and they're off. If you want to join in, though, you'll need a spot of technique, not to mention a basic grasp of the rules. Play it on holiday, and you'll feel like a native; play it at home, and you'll feel like you're on holiday…

1

Start by drawing a circle in the dirt with your heel. Then toss the cochonnet, a small wooden ball that acts as a target for the boules, into the playing area, anywhere between six and 11 yards away.

2

You then take your first go, by lobbing one of your two or three iron boules towards the cochonnet, aiming to get it as near as you can.

3

The next player follows suit, trying either to nudge in more closely to the cochonnet than the first player, or to whack the other boule clear out of the way. A species of backspin, lobbed underhand as the player adopts a semi-crouched stance, seems to be the master's choice. Moving the cochonnet or hitting one of your previous throws in order to edge it closer are both allowed. Cunning is everything in this game.

4

Once the second player has either succeeded in getting one of his or her throws closest to the cochonnet or run out of boules, his/her go is over. And so it continues. For such a quiet sport, the jubilation you will feel when you are in the lead is quite something – but note that victorious cheering and football-style team hugs are frowned upon among veteran players.

5

Once all the boules have been tossed, the round is over. The winner is he or she whose boule is now closest to the cochonnet, and he/she gets a point for every boule closer than the nearest boule of the next most successful player. A new round takes place, usually played in the opposite direction, and so on, until one of the players has won 15 points. When it gets too dark to play any more, retire to the nearest bar and discuss semiotics till bedtime.

Flat caps, filterless Gauloises and bottles of pastis are unavailable in sports shops, but you should be able to buy a decent pétanque set for about €40. You'll see the game played *comme il faut* in squares and gardens around Paris, and along the banks of the Canal St-Martin.

Pershing Hall

CITY   PARIS
STYLE   LUXE A LA MODE
SETTING   EIGHTH ARRONDISSEMENT

MTWTFSSMTWTFSSMTWTFSSMTWTF**SS**MTWTFSSMTWTF

PARIS

'...it was back to the hotel for some more R&R on that cashmere blanket and a glass of bubbly from the complimentary mini-bar'

MTWTFSSMTWTFSSMTWTFSSMTWTFSSMTWTFSS

E veryone comes to Paris with expectations and preconceptions: it's the city for lovers, a gourmet's dream, a place brimming with culture and history… and fabulous for shopping. The great thing is that it lives up to all your hopes and desires. We even had glorious weather, from the moment we landed at CDG. In summer, you can pretty much guarantee you'll see the sun. You can also be sure to see crowds of Americans, who saturate the city during the season, but then, who am I to talk?

We'd heard that Pershing Hall, designed by one of the most talented interior designers in the world, Andrée Putman, is an übercool modern hotel. We weren't disappointed. A dramatic, brightly coloured stone tunnel takes you directly into the lobby, which features floor-to-ceiling columns of tropical plants. This 19th-century mansion, with hints of the Second Empire still apparent, has a sweeping staircase, splendid wrought-iron balconies and arched doorways, which all makes a powerful first impression.

The hotel's check-in time is 15h. We pitched up at 12h30 – but there are worse ways to kill time than over lunch in Paris. Particularly when you have the option to relax in a courtyard as incredible as theirs. With foliage climbing up an entire wall to the sky it's spectacular. Open air when it's nice, it's as though someone took the lid off the most elegant and exotic of living rooms. Here we were served a Modern European feast. White and green asparagus followed by lip-smacking black cod caramelised with sake for moi; a terrine of duck foie gras and then Chilean poached sea-bass with truffle juice and ginger for mon amour. By the time our suite is ready, we're more than satisfied with our stay so far.

Combining calm and serenity with understated luxury, each of the 26 rooms available is a design-conscious romantic's dream. We have a sumptuous supersize bed, deep bathtub, and sink-in armchairs. Everything is built with simple yet refined materials. It was clear the hotel wanted us enveloped in understated decadence; when I touched the blanket on the bed, I felt luxurious super-ply cashmere. I was sold.

Forgoing pudding in the hotel restaurant gave us the perfect excuse to make a trip to the celebrated patisserie La Durée, located on the Champs Elysées, a few minutes' stroll away. Dating back to 1862, it provides the good people of Paris with 14 types of croissants, and countless mouthwatering pastries. This is a city where dieting is not an option. Fortunately, walking around endlessly is irresistible. In addition to being the sexiest place you could rest your head, a great thing about Pershing Hall is that you are able to reach most of Paris's desirable spots comfortably by foot: the Left Bank, St Germain, the Latin Quarter, the Louvre, the Palais Royal and even Montmartre. In ten minutes we were at the Eiffel Tower, and couldn't resist going up, despite having lost count of how many times we've done so before.

Our evening adventure started off with a visit to the Cristal Room Baccarat: a must-see venue in an art gallery, designed by Philippe Starck. The restaurant is spectacular, decked out with 23 crystal chandeliers and velvet seating. It's just a shame the banquette seating, traditionally where the lady is seated, is positioned in the middle of the room. This little flaw in design leaves her with a view only of the restaurant wall; perhaps it's an artful way of allowing male eyes to survey the room. After just one course, we decided to move on to another Philippe Starck venue: Kong, a fun New-York-style Franco-Japanese bar and restaurant atop the Kenzo store. The restaurant has become legendary, thanks to a certain *Sex in the City* heroine having lunch with her Russian beau's ex-wife there. ↓

Having loved every minute of our first day of wining and dining, we treated ourselves to a lie-in the following morning, taking advantage of the hotel's 24-hour room service. Then we took some exercise. Walking in Paris is a joy not only because you can amble off a few calories, but also because, at some point, you're bound to indulge in some shopping. I loved Alexandre de Paris, two doors down from Pershing Hall, for its fabulous hair accessories and costume jewellery. (Gentlemen: if you really want to make her knees tremble, you couldn't do better than making a secret visit to Alexandre and then leaving the box under her pillow.) After a wander around Rue St Honoré and a nose around the epicentre of all things stylish, Colette, it was back to the hotel for some more R&R on that cashmere blanket and a glass of bubbly from the complimentary mini-bar.

Intoxicated by the joys of this charming city (and perhaps the free champagne), we headed for the Buddha Bar. World-famous thanks to its CDs, both the Asian restaurant and bar are extremely popular, so you need to book well in advance. It's a super-stylish environment that you have to experience first-hand, whether you want to relax over a delectable cocktail or let your hair down and armchair dance the night away. You could, of course, do both – or, as we did, take the third option and head back to our hotel after one drink. After all, this is a city for lovers and Pershing Hall the perfect hideaway.

Reviewed by Jori White

NEED TO KNOW

Rooms 26 rooms, including six suites.
Rates €390–€1,000.
Check-out Midday.
Room service The menu is that of the restaurant, when it's open; otherwise cold snacks are available (the club sandwich is very popular).
Facilities Fitness centre.
Children Babysitting is available. Children are welcome, but there are no other facilities.

IN THE KNOW

Recommended rooms The junior suites have balconies overlooking the terrace. We liked junior suite 54, and deluxe suite 55, but if the budget doesn't stretch, ask for standard rooms 41 or 42.
Hotel restaurant The chef comes from Nobu, and the cuisine is, logically, a fusion of French and Japanese.
Hotel bar Open 18h–02h, with a DJ supplying the tunes.
Top table The courtyard tables are the best.
Dress code Relaxed city chic.

LOCAL EATING AND DRINKING

Market on nearby Avenue Matignon (56 43 40 90) is a very fashionable restaurant for nouvelle cuisine. Sophisticated as it may be, it comes with prices to match. **Senso** on Rue de Tremoille (56 52 14 00) is a quiet spot a couple of minutes from Pershing Hall. **La Suite** on Avenue Georges V (53 57 49 49) is a hip place for dinner. **Cristal Room Baccarat** on Place des Etats-Unis (40 22 11 10) is a stunning, over-the-top bar and restaurant designed by Philippe Starck, set in a crystal gallery/shop. Sleek **Maison Blanche** on Avenue Montaigne (47 23 55 99) gives amazing views over the city: from some tables, you can see the Eiffel Tower. Book at least a week in advance. **L'Etoile Café** on Rue de Presbourg (45 00 78 70) is a great place near the Arc de Triomphe for drinks and a dance at the end of an evening.

 A free room upgrade if available; complimentary cocktail in the lounge. Register your Smithcard online, then show your card at check-in, to claim your offer.

Get a room! Use our free online booking service: check availability and make reservations through www.mrandmrssmith.com.

SMITH CONCIERGE Registered Smith cardholders can call +44 (0)20 7978 7333 and have Original Travel book everything from your flights to your day trips, at no extra charge.
Original idea An afternoon with a private shopper on the Rue St Honoré; or let us reserve you a table at exclusive nightspot Man Ray. Extend your trip with a few days skiing: we can reserve you a bed on a sleeper train so you'll be on the slopes by 10h the following morning.

Pershing Hall 49 rue Pierre Charron, Paris 75008 (+33 (0)1 58 36 58 00) info@pershinghall.com; www.pershinghall.com

HAMBURG

MTWTFSSMTWTFSSMTWTFSSMTWTFSSMTWTFSSMTWT

GERMANY

HAMBURG
25hours
Gastwerk

MTWTFSSMTWTFSSMTWTFSSMTWTFSSMTWTFSSMTWTFSS
DEUTSCHLAND

● HAMBURG

Hamburg

CITYSCAPE   LAKES, PARKS AND PORT VIEWS
CITY LIFE   COSMOPOLITAN AND QUIRKY

MTWTFSSMTWTFSSMTWTF **SS** MTWTFSSMTWTFSSMTWT
DEUTSCHLAND

'I didn't grow up in Liverpool – I grew up in Hamburg'
John Lennon

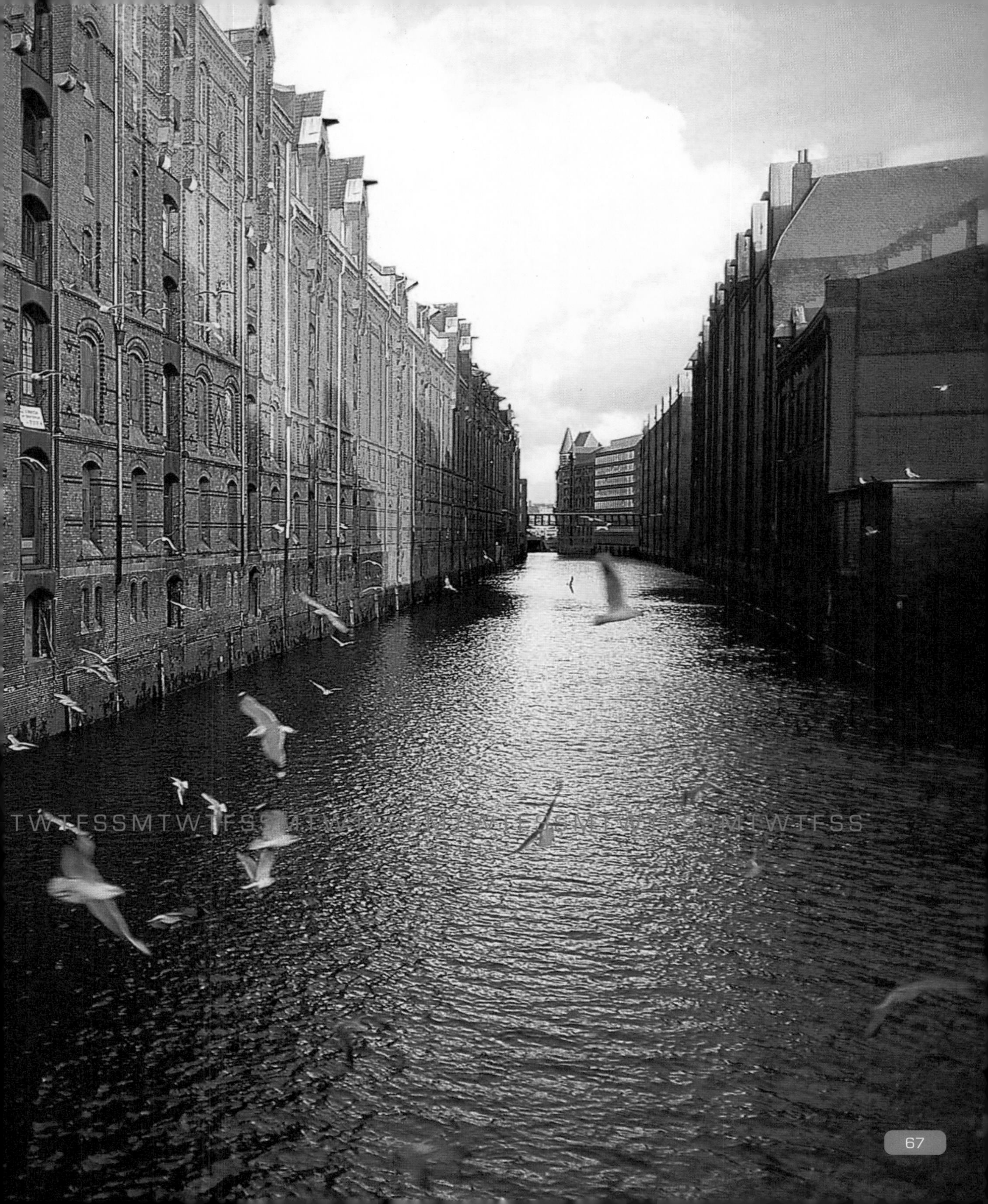

HAMBURG

Out there on its own among German cities, with its masses of green space, a lake with a beach, and young, contemporary hotels, Hamburg can definitely be described as a different kettle of fish. The extrovert energy of the archetypal sea port fuels the avant-garde scene around the Reeperbahn (where performance artists are starting to outnumber pimps, and you're just as likely to see young families as single guys), an ever-evolving network of bars and clubs, and world-class music-making: jazz, classical, hard rock, electro… The Sunday morning institution of the Fischmarkt offers clothing, trinkets and livestock alongside the fish, and elegant, intellectual urbanites mingle with creative types in the restaurants and cafés of Övelgönne. Immerse yourself in harbour history with a walk around the 19th-century warehouse complex, the Speicherstadt. Architecturally unusual, fashionably individual, still a backdrop for sailors, spice traders and working girls, Hamburg is rich in more ways than one. Missing out on one of northern Europe's most distinctive and forward-looking cities is a definite nein-nein.

GETTING THERE

Planes An express bus to the centre stops in front of terminals 1, 3 and 4.
Trains No direct connection to the centre. The S- and U-Bahn train networks are easy to navigate.
Automobiles A cab from the airport takes about 30 mins and costs around €20. For getting out of the city, a car is useful, and driving around is easy.

DO GO / DON'T GO

There's no golden rule. Hamburg's climate is similar to England's, with a few weeks of sunshine in the summer. July and August are fun months to visit: all the artificial beaches pop up; you can row on the lake; and everybody acts as though they're on holiday.

HIGHLY HAMBURG

Visit the private Roman garden in Blankenese, directly on the River Elbe. In the winter, go open-air ice-skating at central city park called Planten un Blomen. You can rent skates in the park itself.

LOCAL KNOWLEDGE

Taxis There are cab ranks on every street corner. If you can't find one, the nearest bar should be able to call one for you.
Tipping culture Ten per cent is the norm.
Packing tips An umbrella – it's an English-style climate. Swim wear in summer – then again public nudity is legal, common and (for some) fun.
Recommended reads *The World That Summer* by Robert Muller; *Buddenbrooks* by Thomas Mann.
Cuisine *Maischolle* (spring plaice), *aalsuppe* (soup with vegetables, ham and sweet prunes), *birnen, bohnen und speck* (pears, green beans and bacon).
Currency Euro.
Dialling codes Country code for Germany: 49. Hamburg: 40.

DIARY

February Carnival (www.germany-tourism.co.uk) is when the locals go crazy, with big parties, dressing up and lots of boozing in the streets. **April, August and November** Hamburg's Dom (www.hamburger-dom.de) is the biggest funfair in northern Germany, with show-booths, food tents and classic attractions. **July** Jazz in Hamburg sees big names performing in a marquee in front of the Deichtorhallen (www.jazzport.de). **September** The Hamburg Music Festival is a classical extravaganza (www.hamburger-musikfest.de).

WORTH GETTING OUT OF BED FOR

Viewpoint On a hill in Krameramtswohnungen stands the church of St Pauli next to Krameramtsstuben. Ascend the tower to a platform 82 metres up to see the city spread out.

Arts and culture The Kunsthalle, north of the Hauptbahnhof, is a museum in three interconnected buildings, with an impressive international collection. The Gallery of Contemporary Art (Galerie der Gegenwart) is housed here. You can also check out what's on at Deichtorhallen on Deichtorplatz, a converted flower market that puts on visiting exhibitions.

Something for nothing Go down to the Fischmarkt (fish market) on a Sunday morning, from 05h, and watch the circus of vendors. The show is accompanied by early-morning jazz, while shoppers and late-night survivors gather in the surrounding bars. Walk around Aussenalster Lake, where Hamburgers of note live in houses of worth.

Shopping Head to Marktstrasse for secondhand and trendy retro shops and unique designer boutiques. Chickiller on Bartelsstrasse sells funky womenswear. Portside, Stilwerk on Grosse Elbstrasse is great for interior design, including Bo Concept. The shopping centre overlooking the port is pretty impressive in itself. You'll find Armani and the like in the upmarket shopping area of Innenstadt.

And… Boat-spotters can get their thrills as the huge vessels come into port.

Tourist tick box Big ships ❑ Fischmarkt ❑ The Reeperbahn (red-light district) ❑

CAFES

Perfect for a coffee or lunch overlooking the water is **Alex Bar** on Jungfernstieg. Walk around Marketstrasse to find boho coffee shops hidden among the boutiques. In a pillared hall within the Kunsthalle complex, **Café Liebermann** is worth a visit to refuel after art.

BARS AND RESTAURANTS

Artisan on Kampstrasse (4210 2915) is informal at lunchtime, with tapas-style dishes prepared in front of you. It becomes more dressy by night, when white tablecloths and a seven-course menu come into play. Near the beach, **Das Weisse Haus** on Neumühlen (390 9016) is a small minimalist restaurant that does tasty German and international food. One of the most agreeable places to eat overlooking the port – alfresco in summer – is trendy **Au Quai** on Grosse Elbstrasse (3803 7730), near the Fischmarkt, which specialises in seafood. Nearby, **Turnhalle St Georg** on Lange Reihe (2800 8480) is another good tip. And **Indochine** on Neumuhlen (3980 7880) is a hit with both locals and visitors.

NIGHTLIFE

The fashionable **Au Quai** bar (next door to the above-mentioned restaurant) is popular with well-off Hamburgers. Another priority haunt is **Ciu** on Ballindamm, open from 15h till late, with its encyclopaedic cocktail list. **Bereuther Bar** on Klosterallee is the place to be on a Thursday, when easy-on-the-eye waiters mix cocktails to funky house tunes. Red-light Reeperbahn is a locale with some 'interesting' bars, among them some faintly undesirable ones. Clubwise, **Mandalay** on Neuer Pferdemarkt is probably one of the hippest places to drink/dance in Hamburg; at weekends, try to be there before 23h or after 02h if you want to avoid the crowds. **China Lounge** on Nobistor in Reeperbahn also gets filled with Hamburg's beautiful and fashionable types.

25hours

CITY   HAMBURG
STYLE   SIXTIES-RETRO
SETTING INDUSTRIAL-COOL QUARTER

MTWTFSSMTWTFSSMTWTF**SS**MTWTFSSMTWTFSSMTWT

HAMBURG

'accoutrements
include a Brionvega
TV, string-effect
curtains and bedside
lamps suspended on
taut chrome wires'

MTWTFSSMTWTFSSMTWTFSSMTWTFSSMTWTFSSMTWTFSS

25hours' aesthetic makes itself felt as soon as you walk in. It's a minimalist white space with flowing, organic curves, a splash of acid pink here, a shot of lime green there. Convex mirrors surround the circular leather-clad reception desk like a giant studded belt. There are shagpile rugs, sleek Sixties furniture, and lighting that changes hue as day turns to night.

It's an attractive brand of retro-futurism – as though the lovechild of Heidi Klum and Austin Powers had done a degree in interior design. Or maybe that should be *Barbarella*-era Jane Fonda and the members of Kraftwerk. As it happens, if your stay coincides with one of 25hours' big regular parties, you're likely to find yourself socialising with notables such as Ms Klum, who preceded us by a couple of weeks.

In our room, the accoutrements include a Brionvega TV, unusual string-effect curtains, and bedside lamps suspended on taut chrome wires from a rough concrete ceiling. Mrs Smith wonders whether the hotel is quite finished; I remind her of the popularity of the modern 'industrial' look. The bathroom is open-plan, with a powerful shower, and only a sliding door to the toilet: perhaps this isn't the place for a first-date weekend. But there is a heated lamp to keep you both warm if you're comfortable *au naturel* with your other half. And don't forget to take your own unguents; in keeping with 25hours' philosophy of keeping prices as low as possible, the only amenities supplied are a couple of shampoo sachets.

The 25hours bar Tageswandel is open tonight, but not on Sunday, so we take advantage of the opportunity to sample the sushi in which the hotel specialises. The chef sets to work with his knives, and quickly produces a beautiful platter that we snack on. The barman seems

a little reticent, but furnishes me with a perfectly executed caipirinha, and Mrs Smith with a piña colada that would make Del Boy blush. Stomachs lined with raw tuna and salmon, we grab a taxi into town.

As Hamburg virgins, we naturally find ourselves drawn to its infamous avenue of pleasure: the Reeperbahn. Joern, our mate on reception, has warned us it may not be to our taste, and recommends Hamburger Berg (Hamburg Hill), just off the main drag, where our taxi drops us. It's pretty seedy, so we press on through the back streets of St Pauli, looking for a suitable pitstop, until we hit Schulterblatt and strike gold. As soon as we come across Bok, we swivel round as one and walk straight in. Think Wagamama crossed with Soho's Busaba Eathai and you'll get the picture. It's a top stop for an Oriental-food fix, simple in design but exotic on the palate, with super-quick service. Further up the street we rub shoulders with media types and punks

alike in the standing-room-only Daniela Bar and Betty Ford Klinik, before slumping into a sofa at Le Fonque on Juliusstrasse.

Back at 25hours, we find the barman has cheered up considerably since earlier. It turns out he had been suffering the after-effects of a photo shoot for Captain Morgan rum (he models for the brand, and has to consume the product as he works). Over a few expertly mixed nightcaps, he gives us his lowdown on where to play out in Hamburg. It comes as some surprise to find that the city has spawned a number of Ibiza-style beach bars. The original, Strandperle (near the Museumshafen in Oevelgönne), has since been joined by four more, set along the banks of the River Elbe along Grosse Elbstrasse: Lago Bay, Hamburg City Beach Club, Hamburg del Mar, and Strandpauli. Each features all the requisites of a Balearic sunset spot: beach huts, hammocks, daybeds, swimming pool and, of course, chilled tunes. ↓

The next day, after revisiting the bar to get some breakfast (there is no room service, but you can take your continental back to bed in the lift) we depart in search of the U-Bahn. 25hours is in a quiet area, so you need to head into town to find things to do. We decide on the Kunsthalle art gallery for a bit of culture (OK then – *kaffee und kuchen*). Cafe Liebermann is the obvious choice but you have to pay for entrance to the museum to get there; our advice is to head straight for the Galerie der Gegenwart at the back: the modern wing, which has more interesting art and a bistro.

It's Saturday night, and we decide to spend it in the newly regenerated dockland area. At Au Quai, before a sublime if expensive dinner, we sip cocktails beneath the landmarks of Hamburg's industrial past, watching huge tankers coming into port. 'Great for cranespotting,' says Mrs Smith. It's a scene buzzing with well-heeled Hamburgers. Many of Germany's publishing powerhouses are based here, and it shows.

On Sunday morning, we make our discovery of the weekend. Tucked away between the docks, St Pauli and the Reeperbahn is the Portuguese quarter, evidence of Hamburg's heritage as one of the world's great ports.

Here, we find seafood so fresh it flips, ice-cold Superbock and piri piri chicken to match anything on the Algarve, all at cheaper prices than the trendy eateries along the dock itself. Our tip is the restaurant D.Jose on Ditmar-Koel Strasse, where the tables have their own beer pumps so you can help yourselves.

Hamburg is well worth exploring. We found a city of contrasts: bourgeois and seedy; cultured and commercial; leafy and gritty. With the port, the river, the great lakes and a major canal network, it's a marine marvel, and the warehouses and towering cranes of the docks make a change from the classical beauty of Europe's more obvious sexy destinations. 25hours is a relaxed base with funky design and excellent prices. The older and wealthier may find Gastwerk more suited to their tastes, but if you want to get to grips with Hamburg's young fashionable *szene*, 25hours is the place to be. Had the Beatles arrived 30 years later, this is where they would have stayed. The staff are the epitome of genuine laid-back friendliness, and their advice is worth listening to – just remember to ask them for directions to the Portuguese quarter.

Reviewed by Matt Turner

NEED TO KNOW

Rooms 65.

Rates €99.

Check-out Midday.

Room service There is no waiter service, but you can take sushi from the bar to your room until 23h. The hotel can also order takeaway for you.

Facilities There are drinks and snacks machines in the communal area on the third floor, where a giant screen shows films after 21h. Roof terrace. Use of fitness centre and pool for €13 each.

Children Older children will love it. Cots and babysitting can be arranged in advance.

Also The hotel also hosts house nights every so often, attracting 100 people.

IN THE KNOW

Recommended rooms The rooms are all similar, but you can choose between a blue or green colour scheme.

Hotel bar The Tageswandel Bar is a DJ bar, serving cocktails and snacks till 01h.

Hotel restaurant Breakfast is available at the bar, 06h30–midday. Sushi is available 17h–23h.

Top table A corner table.

Dress code Young, trendy, informal.

LOCAL EATING AND DRINKING

Brick on Paul Dessau Strasse (85 50 81 24) is a cool, contemporary restaurant, bar and lounge. Or head over to the Gastwerk and eat Italian in its **Da Caio**. **Einstein** on Bahrenfelder Chaussee (89 07 01 01) is an old-school spot with wooden tables and benches, serving typical German food . **Orchidee** is a Chinese, recommended for a takeway, on the same street (891972). **Mokka** bar, also round the corner on Bahrenfelder Chaussee, is an appealing place with lots of wood and good Turkish food (422 93 38). It is but a ten-minute cab ride to central Hamburg where you'll find all the bars and restaurants you could desire.

 A bottle of white Fonsina or red Giulin. Register your Smithcard online, then show your card at check-in, to claim your offer.

Get a room! Use our free online booking service: check availability and make reservations through www.mrandmrssmith.com.

SMITH CONCIERGE
Registered Smith cardholders can call +44 (0)20 7978 7333 and have Original Travel book everything from your flights to your day trips, at no extra charge.

Original idea We will arrange a seaplane flight from the waterfront, to give you an aerial view of one of Europe's great ports.

25hours 2 Paul Dessau Strasse, Hamburg 22761 (+49 (0) 40 855 070)
info@25hours-hotel.com; www.25hours-hotel.com

'In the hotel restaurant, the brickwork is enhanced by intelligent light projections'

Gastwerk

CITY   HAMBURG
STYLE   AS-YOU-LIKE IT ASIAN FUSION
SETTING REDBRICK FORMER GASWORKS

MTWTFSSMTWTFSSMTWTF**SS**MTWTFSSMTWTFSSMTWT
HAMBURG

MTWTFSSMTWTFSSMTWTFSSMTWTFSSMTWTFSS

Gastwerk, Hamburg

'Hamburg?' said one of our friends, trying to keep the surprise out of his voice. 'That's an, er, interesting choice for a romantic break.' The truth is, if you spend every weekend of every summer hightailing it along flight paths to put on parties or DJ at clubs and gigs all over Europe, every beach starts to look like a potential festival, rather than a location for kicking back with a daiquiri with the breeze on your face. So nothing could be more romantic than the prospect of somewhere new to explore together with our mobiles switched off.

We didn't know what to expect, and that was half the fun. The city of Hamburg turned out to offer a surprising breather of calm , culture and civility. Even the rashes of graffiti visible throughout the city look well thought-out. The architecture mixes modernism with tradition; the centre of town brings to mind Amsterdam and Stockholm, and the warehouses and cranes – it's a working port – give it an industrial, seafaring kind of atmosphere.

Housed in a redeveloped gasworks dating back to 1904, Gastwerk is a redbrick shell with original iron features and lofty ceilings that give it a grand and spacious feel. Upon arrival, you are greeted by a life-size stone gurkha; indeed, the whole vast reception, dotted with art, costumes and funky furniture, reminded us of London's Victoria & Albert Museum by way of Indonesia. The lovely Anna gave us our first indication that staff at the hotel, like Hamburgers in general, have your ultimate pleasure as their goal. This is a city populated by friendly, helpful and, frankly, lovely people.

Gastwerk's various bar and lounge areas are all beautifully decorated in warm reds and browns. It has a wonderful sense of peace and style, and we never felt overcrowded – it occurred to us that the building could just as easily have made an awesome gallery space. I immediately started planning the VIP bash my team and I would throw here.

On our first night, we had dinner in the hotel restaurant, Da Caio, where the brickwork is enhanced by intelligent light projections. The Italian-inspired food is fabulous, but we needed a hand from the waiter with the English translation of the German take on an Italian menu – 'nettle pesto' had us a bit stumped, but it tasted great with giant gnocchi. After dinner, we headed to the spa: we had it all to ourselves and the hotel will open it for you till 01h – perfect for night owls like us. The steam and sauna were as good as you'd expect in Germany, and the chill-out areas were heavenly, with Balinese statues and carvings, huge floor cushions, mirrored walls and a plasma TV.

On day two, we took a cab into town to hit the shops, heading for Marktstrasse, a road filled with one-off boutiques, many with workshops out the back and the clothes showcased up front. A seriously dented credit card later, after adding to my international collection of combat-style trousers (a must for us sad music-industry youth), it was time for a break. We had a light lunch at Alex im Alsterpavilion, overlooking Lake Alster, opposite Jungfernstieg shopping street. Most of Hamburg, young and old, seem to meet there for coffee and socialise. It's not far from there to the the centre of Hamburg, where you can find all the international designers and department stores, but vintage is more our thing (Mr Smith is partial to retro Adidas), so we found ourselves drawn back to Marktstrasse. ↓

After six hours of shopping and another spa session, a hearty meal was called for: dinner at Indochine on the docks, From our top-floor table, we had panoramic views of the city sparkling over the water. The restaurant offers an inspired menu from Laos, Cambodia and Vietnam, but in Texan portions. After dining according to our waiter's suggestions, we succumb to the call of music, and wandered 600 metres along the well-lit docks to Café Lago, allured by assurances that this is Hamburg's coolest music bar. More out of habit than necessity, we blagged our way in on the guestlist. It's a converted fish factory, happily sans aromatic afterlife. Great atmosphere, creative decor, deep-house music and an up-for-it crowd meant we had a great time. You can only keep a DJ in a club if the pull of the decks is greater than that of the wife, so we repaired to what we now considered our private spa, where the night manager of the hotel jovially delivered us a glass of wine in the steam room. Ah, self-indulgence.

In the morning, we ordered breakfast in our huge marshmallow-like bed. What arrived was nothing short of a banquet, so dragging ourselves from our lovely, airy room and spacious bathroom, and its views over the mini-lake with old factory settings set around it like pieces of art, took supreme effort. Nonetheless, we headed for the Kunsthalle art museum for a few hours; then after a short stroll along the river, it was time for a cold beer and a healthy debate on classic versus modern. My husband preferred the eclectic (and sometimes downright weird) modern stuff while I lost myself completely in Chagall, Degas and Liebermann. It could have seduced me all day, but work was calling. If Paris and Venice are your first responses to the romantic-weekend question, think again: Hamburg is industrial, alternative and exciting, and Gastwerk is an übercool, top-value port of call.

Rooms 135 rooms: 78 classic rooms, 54 individual lofts and junior suites; two penthouse suites with private roof terraces.
Rates €125–€360.
Check-out Midday.
Room service 06h–11h: a small selection from the Italian restaurant menu.
Facilities Asiatic-style wellness centre: sauna, steam room, relaxation area. Music room, parking. Use of nearby fitness centre and swimming pool for free.
Children Very welcome. Children up to 12 years of age stay free. Cots provided for babies. Babysitters available on demand.

Recommended rooms 321 and 341 each have two large bedrooms, stylish bathroom, comfy sofas and private roof terrace.
Hotel bar Black leather sofas and the mix of modern and old style is reminiscent of a gentlemen's club. The smart, black-aproned waiters will serve whatever takes your fancy – on the menu or not. A great place to chill out after a hectic day's ship watching, open until 01h.
Hotel restaurant Chef Renzo Ferrario serves great traditional Italian food in Da Caio, open 12h–15h and 18h–22h.
Top table Ask for a table by the window or the red wall.
Dress code Err towards smart.

Brick on Paul Dessau Strasse (8550 8124) is a cool contemporary restaurant/bar/lounge with a modern plush interior, right next to the hotel. The only other option within walking distance is the 25hours hotel bar. It also hosts a club night once a month – see www.25hours-hotel.com for details. For traditional German fare, head to **Einstein** on Bahrenfelder Chaussee (89 07 01 01). For Chinese takeaway, **Orchidee** is on the same street (891972). A simple Turkish cafe, **Mokka** bar is also on Bahrenfelder Chaussee (422 93 38). If you jump in a cab, it's only ten minutes to central Hamburg where you'll find restaurants galore.

A bottle of white Fonsina or red Giulin. Register your Smithcard online, then show your card at check-in, to claim your offer.

Get a room! Use our free online booking service: check availability and make reservations through www.mrandmrssmith.com.

Registered Smith cardholders can call +44 (0)20 7978 7333 and have Original Travel book everything from your flights to your day trips, at no extra charge.
Original idea For a tour of the city's highlights – while getting fit at the same time – try a jogging tour, lead by a fitness trainer with in-depth knowledge of the various sites along the route.

Gastwerk 3 Beim Alten Gastwerk, Daimlerstrasse, Hamburg 22761 (+49 40 890 620) info@gastwerk-hotel.de; www.gastwerk-hotel.de

MTWTFSSMTWTFSSMTWTFSSMTWTFSSMTWTFSSMTWT

MILAN

VENICE

FLORENCE

ROME

ITALY

FLORENCE
Continentale
Gallery Hotel Art
JK Place
MILAN
3Rooms
Bulgari Hotel
Straf
The Gray
Townhouse 31
ROME
International Wine Academy of Rome
VENICE
Ca Maria Adele
Charming House DD724

MTWTFSSMTWTFSSMTWTFSSMTWTFSSMTWTFSSMTWTFSS

ITALIA

FLORENCE

Florence

'A love affair between culture, commerce and good living'

M T W T F S S M T W T F S S M T W T F S S M T W T F S S M T W T F S S M T W T

ITALIA

MTWTFSSMTWTFSSMTWTFSSMTWTFSSMTWTFSSMTWTFSS

FLORENCE

For a city boasting more past glories than the average continent, the capital of Tuscany is excitingly forward-looking. A love affair between culture, commerce and good living, Florence has long been celebrated as the most aesthetically pleasing city in all Italy, if not the world. Between the fairytale squares, centuries-old churches and sprawling palaces run streets alive with sociability, style and irresistible shopping. Luxury goods a-go-go on roads such Via Tornabuoni, traditional artisan jewellers on the mediaeval Ponte Vecchio, and irresistible deli fare everywhere – the riches on offer are enough to tempt the toughest of anticapitalists out of their hair shirts. The city centre is architecturally breathtaking, and compact enough to stroll in an afternoon; follow glimpses of the Duomo and Campanile down narrow streets, soak up a quota of significant art (it's impossible not to, whether you spend hours in the Uffizi or not – Michelangelo's David stands proud outside, for all to admire), and eat Italian soul food in a simple trattoria. Then head a little further out to the Boboli Gardens, or San Marco for a heart-stirring view of the city. And pack light – Florence might be the birthplace of the Renaissance, but modern Fiorentinos were born to shop.

GETTING THERE

Planes The nearest airport is 20 mins' drive from the centre of town, and a taxi costs roughly €15. You can also fly into Pisa airport, from where a direct train takes 45 minutes and costs €5.
Trains The main station is behind Piazza Santa Maria Novella, for connections to the rest of Europe.
Automobiles Having a car in Florence can be a hindrance, but is essential if you want to explore the surrounding Tuscan countryside.

DO GO/DON'T GO

Florence is packed with tourists throughout the summer months, when it's also very humid.

FABULOUSLY FLORENCE

Go for a jog in Cascine Park. Browse the antiques market in Piazza dei Ciompi. Have lunch in a trattoria in Mercato Centrale. Rent a vintage car and explore the hills (www.bellinitravel.com).

LOCAL KNOWLEDGE

Taxis You can't hail a cab on the street; go to a designated *fermata di taxi*.
Tipping culture Five to ten per cent.
Packing tips A sketchbook, a sunhat, sensible shoes.
Recommended reads *A Room with a View* by EM Forster; *The Decameron* by Giovanni Boccaccio.
Cuisine *Pasta e fagioli* (beans), T-bone steak, game, Chianti. *Panforte nero di Siena*: a spicy confection of almonds, honey, cocoa and candied peel.
Currency Euro.
Dialling codes Country code for Italy: 39. Florence: 055.

DIARY

Florence hosts five major international fashion events yearly (www. pittimmagine.com). **May–June** Maggio Musicale Fiorentino, at the Teatro Comunale, is one of Europe's oldest music fests (www.maggiofiorentino. com). **11–24 June** The Festival of San Giovanni; highlights include the regatta, near Ponte Vecchio, and fireworks in Piazzale Michelangelo. **7 September** Rificolona festival, when children carry lanterns in a grand procession, and there are street performances and parties.

WORTH GETTING OUT OF BED FOR

Viewpoints Climb the 414 steps to the top of the Campanile or up the Duomo itself for a 360-degree view of Florence. Drive up to Fiesole and look down across the entire town.

Arts and culture Sixty per cent of the world's most important works of art are housed in Italy and half of these are in Florence. The Cathedral of Santa Maria dei Fiori, aka the Duomo, was built in 1434, and its dome is a celebrated feat of engineering. The Bargello contains an unrivalled collection of Renaissance sculptures (www.sbas.firenze.it/bargello). The famous Uffizi houses Botticellis, Michelangelos and da Vincis; reserve tickets (www.uffizi.com).

Something for nothing Stroll along the Ponte Vecchio; gaze at Michelangelo's David.

Shopping The market on Sundays around Piazza San Lorenzo is a little disappointing; try the fleamarket at Piazza dei Ciompi instead. For designer clothes, Luisa Via Roma on Via Roma is a high-fashion multi-designer boutique. Universo Sanchez on Via il Prato is a lifestyle shop with clothes, a bar and a barber. For interior design, try Flair on Lungarno Guicciardini.

And... Tea at the Villa San Michele hotel in Fiesole. A romantic day out to San Gimignano, a mediaeval town with towers, cobbled streets and very romantic views.

Tourist tick box The Duomo ❑ The Uffizi ❑ Ponte Vecchio ❑

CAFES

Overlooking Michelangelo's David in Piazza della Signoria, **Caffè Rivoire** is a people-watching hub. **Caffè Pitti** (239 9863) becomes a restaurant at night, specialising in truffle dishes. The Roberto Cavalli-owned **Giacosa** (277 6328), linked to his shop on Via della Spada, is a busy, fashiony place for breakfast, lunch, coffee and cocktails. Ask at **JK Place** about their sister eatery on Piazza Santa Maria Novella, which promises to be as fine as the next-door hotel.

BARS AND RESTAURANTS

Cantina Barbagianni on Via Sant'Egidio (248 0508) is in an ancient cellar; ideal for dinner à deux, or head there for their great value two-course lunch. **Cibreo** on Via de' Macci (234 1100) may be the most famous trattoria in Italy; it's formal and glamorous. **La Congrega** on Via Panicale (264 5027) is a quaint traditional trattoria for lunch or an informal but unforgettable dinner. Michelin-starred **Enoteca Pinchiorri** on Via Ghibellina (242 777) is set in a Renaissance palace, where Giorgio Pinchiorri himself helps you choose from his 150,000-bottle cellar; jacket and tie required. **Olio & Convivium** on Via Santo Spirito (265 8198) is a delicatessen and restaurant. **Capocaccia** on Lungarno Corsini is perfect for pre-dinner mojitos. Many restaurants close on Sunday or Monday; check first. **Il Latini** on Via Palchetti (210 916) can be hit or miss – but get there on a good night (ie: not full to the gills with tourists) and it's great fun. The kitchen decides what you'll be eating – you just name the colour of wine you prefer, and whether you want fish or meat.

NIGHTLIFE

Angels is a bar/restaurant on Via del Proconsolo, with frescos adorning its domed ceiling, but white muslin drapes, sexy lighting and modern furniture bring it crashing into the 21st century. Early on, tourists slurp fruity cocktails, while Florence's hipsters appear later. If you have to dance and want no more than a good ol' fashioned discotheque, try **Yab** on Via Sassetti.

Continentale

CITY   FLORENCE
STYLE   BRIGHT AND WITTY
SETTING   POLE POSITION BY PONTE VECCHIO

M T W T F S S M T W T F S S M T W T F S S M T W T F S S M T W T F **S S** M T W T
FIRENZE

'You'd never guess that
just steps from Florence's
iconic bridge lies this
monochromatic retreat'

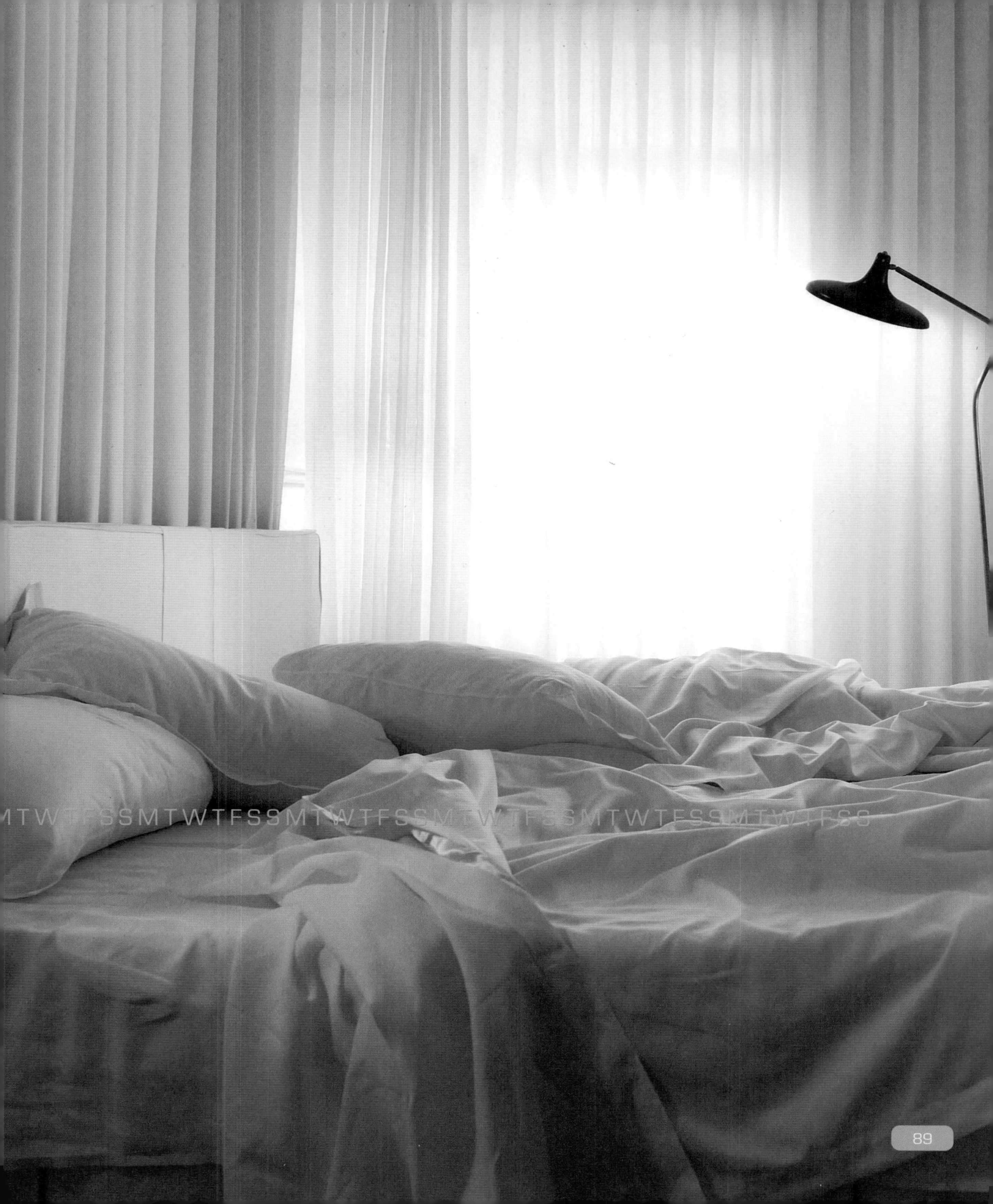

I first went to Florence with my mother when I was 18. I was in the middle of a full-on love affair with Renaissance art, and spent my days pounding the corridors of the Uffizi in search of Botticellis and Titians, seeking out obscure churches harbouring triptychs by Giotto and Mantegna, and scaling seemingly endless winding stone staircases in an attempt to fully understand the genius of Brunelleschi. My mother and I stayed in a crumbling palazzo on the outskirts of the city; behind the flaking wallpaper and fraying curtains lurked a glorious and no doubt decadent past. When I returned to Florence this time, I found myself in the throes of a very different love affair. The lure of da Vinci and co suddenly didn't seem quite so compelling. And the hotel the Continentale, the creation of Salvatore Ferragamo, while a far cry from my decaying palazzo, looked the perfect place for a weekend of dedicated romance.

With its sleek minimalist design, the Continentale is the very antithesis of the classic Florentine *Room With a View*-style pensiones, and it's a huge hit with those searching for a contemporary vibe. And then there's its location; it couldn't be more central. It almost sits right on the famous Ponte Vecchio, and is within a few minutes walk from, well, everywhere. You'd never guess that just steps from Florence's iconic bridge, lined with goldsmiths and stallholders selling all manner of 'ode to the Renaissance' paraphernalia, lies this monochromatic retreat. Sleek receptionists clad in black suits welcomed us into the cool white interior, where black and white fashion photographs line the walls. Classic European films run on a loop on a giant plasma screen in the foyer; or the hotel webcam delivers views of the human traffic on the bridge, bringing the outside in very cleverly.

From the moment we arrived, our every need was looked after by the Continentale's staff: from the charming bellboy who whisked us up in a vast glass lift complete with leather sofa, to the patient receptionist who spent hours tracking down my passport (which, to my embarrassment, I'd left in the lounge at Gatwick), smiling genuinely throughout.

The standard bedrooms are small but cleverly laid out. Our first thought was that the minimalist decor owed more to Habitat than John Pawson or even Conran, but such notions were quickly pushed to one side as the white cotton drapes around the bed fluttered seductively in the breeze. The bathroom boasted a spectacularly powerful shower, and the huge bottles of luxurious body products were a serious treat. But battling it out for Best Thing About The Room award, along with the fantastic bed, was the incredible view over the river: you can almost lean out and dip your little finger into the Arno. We sat for ages watching the early morning skullers meander down the river, bathed in Tuscany's unique soft golden light. Florence's beauty hasn't changed much since I was here as a girl, but I have. And somehow the Renaissance cityscape looked more beautiful than ever.

Breakfast is the only meal the hotel serves, and we opted for room service every time. When we did venture out of our modernist boudoir to explore the hotel's artfully designed communal areas, we discovered the relaxation room, with comfy day beds and stacks of magazines, and amazing views over the bridge. As a contrast to Florence's 'it's like the 19th century never happened' vibe, the aesthetic is really very refreshing. All that you could possibly desire lies minutes away, be it dusty old antique shops or chic boutiques, not to mention all that great art – though the studious 18-year-old in me was nowhere to be seen. ↓

204

Taking a respite from wandering Florence's answer to Bond Street – the superbly-heeled Via Tornabuoni, where Prada and Gucci have settled in next to Florence-based Salvatore Ferragamo – we settled on nearby Il Latini for lunch. Packed full of locals, with a commanding and eccentric maître d' who prefers to order for you and frowns if you don't get stuck in to one of the hefty bottles of house red provided on all the tables, this is the classic Italian restaurant at its best. Having drunk, laughed and sung (it was the man on the next-door table's birthday) far more than expected, we set off for the Santa Maria Novella apothecary, where we stared in wonder at the towering glass cabinets packed with giant bottles and jars, before stocking up on herbal potions and lotions made from recipes devised by 15th-century Franciscan monks. As editor of a fashion magazine, I am spoilt with beauty products at the best of times, but the old-school scents here – rose, iris, nothing faddy – are seriously sexy.

Unguents accomplished, we headed in the opposite direction of the crowds, who were now teeming menacingly around the Duomo and Uffizi, for the Boboli Gardens, behind the Pitti Palace, where we strolled and sat talking like teenagers for hours in the sunshine. It was only, however, when we climbed the steps up to the nearby Piazzale Michelangelo, which offers beautiful views over the Florence skyline (nearly as spectacular as those from Continentale's roof terrace) that my last vestiges of guilt about having not set foot in even one museum finally disappeared. As the setting sun enveloped the cathedral's famous dome in an Ready Brek glow, I finally grasped the real genius of Brunelleschi. More importantly, I realised that our weekend at the Continentale hadn't only meant falling in love in Florence – but also falling in love *with* Florence.

Reviewed by Lucy Yeomans

NEED TO KNOW

Rooms 43 rooms.
Rates €290–€1,050, including breakfast.
Check-out Midday.
Room service Until 23h.
Facilities Fitness centre with sauna.
Children Babysitting can be arranged.
Also Pets of the diminutive variety are welcome.

IN THE KNOW

Recommended rooms Deluxe tower rooms are spacious and have fantastic views.
Hotel bar Terrazza dei Consorti is a 'sky lounge', perfect for a cocktail under the stars.
Hotel restaurant Only breakfast is served, on the first floor.
Dress code Anything goes.

LOCAL EATING AND DRINKING

Pop across the road for some of the finest cocktails in town in the **Fusion Bar** in the Gallery Hotel Art, or book a table on the terrace if it's balmy, and enjoy unique French, Italian and Japanese cuisine. They will also wow you with the right wines to accompany each and every mouthful. **Olio & Convivium** on Via Santo Spirito (265 8198) is a deli and restaurant, specialising in olive oils, native wines and local cheeses. **Il Parione** is a cosy trattoria on Via del Parione (214 005), great for candlelit dinners. **Roses** on Via del Parione (287 090) is a café during the day and a sushi bar/Japanese restaurant in the evening. **Il Latini** on Via Palchetti (210 916) can be ridiculously popular for lunch and dinner, but if the queue looks bearable and you go late enough for it to be filled with locals and not tourists, it can be great fun. And choosing is simple – wine: red or white? Main course: fish or meat? They decide for you. Open since 1872, **Café Rivoire**, overlooking Michelangelo's David in Piazza delle Signorie, serves superb hot chocolate, cocktails and aperitifs and is great for watching the world go by. **Borgo San Jacopo** (281 661), within the Lungarno hotel on the San Jacopo, has a yacht-club feel. Home-made food ranges from fresh fish to meat dishes.

 A large-sized bottle of body product from the luxurious range by Lungarno Details for Mrs Smith, and a bottle of wine for Mr Smith. Register your Smithcard online, then show your card at check-in, to claim your offer.

Get a room! Use our free online booking service: check availability and make reservations through www.mrandmrssmith.com.

SMITH CONCIERGE Registered Smith cardholders can call +44 (0)20 7978 7333 and have Original Travel book everything from your flights to your day trips, at no extra charge.
Original idea A private shopping tour of the most exclusive shopping district of Florence: Via Tornabuoni, and Ponte Vecchio for jewellery.

Continentale 6r Vicolo dell'Oro, Florence 50123 (+39 055 272 62)
bookings@lungarnohotels.com; www.lungarnohotels.com

Gallery Hotel Art

CITY	FLORENCE
STYLE	CLASSIC-CONTEMPORARY COMFORT
SETTING	OASIS ON THE ARNO

'Contemporary but classical, it's the stuff that fairytales are made of – where everyone gets VIP treatment'

M T W T F S S M T W T F S S M T W T F S S M T W T F **S S** M T W T F S S M T W T
FIRENZE

TWTFSSMTWTFSSMTWTFSSMTWTFSSMTWTFSS

Florence can coax amazement out of the most jaded traveller. Snooty travellers who snigger at the more naive tourist's awed remark about how old everything is will find this is one place where they can't help but share those sentiments.

We are delighted to discover that our very stylish hotel, which comes courtesy of the Ferragamo family, is seconds from the 14th-century Ponte Vecchio. It's the stuff that fairytales are made of: tiny jewellery shops line the narrow cobblestoned bridge. As do tourists. Happily, in a city teeming with sightseers, the Gallery Hotel Art is all calm. On arrival, we wonder if word has sneaked out that we're here to review – our room has been upgraded, and staff are super-friendly. Then we realise that everyone gets VIP treatment.

Modern lines and a minimalist-inclined decor contrast with the flagstone streets and centuries-old architecture outside. On our visit the art du jour adorning the walls is black-and-white photographs of naked models: what does the middle-aged American couple next to us make of them? 'Those crazy Yurpeans,' chuckles the husband, as he sizes up an especially hirsute young lady.

The overriding impression of the Gallery Hotel Art is one of impeccable quality; furniture and fittings are all stylish but solid, eschewing gimmicks or novelties. It's through a heavy door that we enter our room. Cream, silver and dark wood – the perfumer Jo Malone would approve of the colour palette. The feel is contemporary but classical, and doesn't sacrifice comfort for whimsical design. As tempting as it is to stall here and savour our surrounds (and the petits fours left on the dresser), the sound of live jazz lures us down to dinner.

The only outdoor space at Gallery Art is its little terrace by the bar and restaurant: a delightful spot, particularly with a three-piece band providing the soundtrack. If you don't manage to bagsy an alfresco spot, inside is also appealing, whether you sit at the bar, on a sofa in the corner, or at a table for two next to the wall. Peopled by young and old, dressed-up and low-key, its biggest surprise isn't the clientele or the decor, but the Italian, French and Japanese fusion cuisine – best illustrated by the test tubes of flavoured oils and soy sauce on each table. The staff are very proud of the unique menu; Italians have been slow to embrace tastes even beyond the regional, each truly believing their own local cooking to be the best in the world. Mr Smith congratulates the waiter on his recommended red's harmony with the tender fillet; such is the Italian love of food, our sommelier says, in earnest: 'This is a beautiful moment for you.'

Though the cocktail selection in the hotel is exceptional, too, after dinner we're in the mood for a wander, and plump for a nightcap along the river at Capocaccia. We snuggle on a rattan sofa on the pavement, in prime position for seeing rather than being seen; there's a lot of coloured denim on the prowl, worn impressively tight. We're not in a country of big drinkers, and after two mojitos (speciality of the house) – and a lot of red Versace jeans – we feel ready to head home.

The value of a room where you can have such a wonderful night's sleep should not be underestimated. The windows keep out every peep of light, blinds stop the Tuscan sun from rousing you prematurely, and can you programme your desired room temperature. Breakfast is just how it should be: a spread of fantastic pastries, hams, cheeses – we could happily stay a few hours, grazing, especially as there is no clue that an outside world exists. Japanese blinds block out any views of the tiny alleys, cocooning you away in the library-style lounge and dining area. ↓

The queues for all the major sights are so enormous on this scorching day that we can't face broiling in a line only to be jostled along with a herd, however world-famous the art. You're guaranteed a fix of one masterpiece at least – a copy of Michelangelo's David is considerately placed outdoors for all to see at their leisure – so after a look at him we escape the crowd and head, predictably, to Boboli Gardens, south of the river, past Palazzo Pitti. It's deceptively enormous, and we get lost in lush green foliage. We're grateful for the work-out we get from its steep inclines, in anticipation of the mountains of pasta we plan to consume at lunch. Our destination for doing just that is at the other end of town, but Florence doesn't take long to traverse. It also gives us the opportunity to get some first-class window-shopping done en route. Prada, Salvatore Ferragamo, Gucci, Hermès line our path, and then appear again on the next street. Markets overflow with handbags, belts and jewellery. If you're someone who shares the sartorial sensibilities of Donatella Versace, you're especially in luck; glittering animal prints and tassels abound. So if you want to give Nancy Dell'Olio a run for her euros, you know where to head.

Bellies distended from the most incredible spaghetti vongole in Osteria la Congrega, we decide there's no better way to see the city than by horse-drawn carriage.

It may only be a step up from kiss-me-quick hats in the tourist stakes (and a heck of a lot less sympathetic to your wallet), but we get a memorable tour from the Duomo, round to Santa Croce, past the Uffizi and the Palazzo Vecchio. Despite the fact that the sun is nowhere near the yard arm yet, and our lunch is barely digested, Florence is home to such quality comestibles that we can't help thinking about our next meal. We pause for thought, and a glass of Chianti. Italians won't neglect any opportunity to feed or be fed; so antipasto is on offer where you'd be lucky to get a bowl of peanuts back home. After peeking at a few attempts at contemporary cool, we settle on family-run trattoria Buca Mario, where there are plenty of locals, affording us the best of both worlds: food that tastes home-made, and waiters well-practiced in playing both server and entertainer to English speakers. We end our night with an animated 'chat' with the matriarch of the trattoria; the fact that she speaks as little English as we do Italian doesn't impede our merry conversation over a limoncello. It's the fitting finale to a whirlwind stay at Gallery Hotel Art, into which we've still squeezed all that we craved. Rather like the power generation of drinks and medicines that fuels us these days, it's been Holiday Max Strength. And, boy, do we feel good.

Reviewed by Mr & Mrs Smith

NEED TO KNOW

Rooms 74.

Rates €260–€1,050 (plus ten per cent tax), including breakfast.

Check-out Midday.

Room service 07h30–23h. A snack menu is available until 12h, when the restaurant menu becomes available.

Facilities Private tour guide; chauffeured car service; golf-course agreement.

Children The hotel is not geared towards children, but it welcomes families.

Also Pets welcome, as long as they're on the small size.

IN THE KNOW

Recommended rooms Three penthouses on the seventh floor have amazing views; 701 has two terraces (with a super-comfy lounger on the deck); and 707 and 708 have terraces and a river view.

Hotel bar For the best cocktails in town, cosy up at the bar or on the terrace; between October and May you can sometimes catch live jazz in the evenings.

Hotel restaurant Fusion by name and by nature, serving unique Italian/Japanese cuisine.

Top table Go alfresco on the terrace when it's warm.

Dress code The clientele is as mixed as the cuisine; you'll fit in whatever your style.

LOCAL EATING AND DRINKING

Buca Mario on Ottaviani (214 179) is a friendly family-run trattoria that serves fantastic typical Tuscan cooking, in traditional surrounds. **Borgo San Jacopo** on Borgo San Jacopo (281 661) offers the timeless taste of Italian home cooking, overlooking the river Arno. At Michelin-starred **Enoteca Pinchiorri** on Via Ghibellina (242 777), Giorgio Pinchiorri himself advises on wines from the vast cellar in his Renaissance palazzo; it's worth the cab ride. **Il Parione** is a cosy trattoria on Via del Parione, (214 005), great for candlelit dinners. A café by day, **Roses** on Via del Parione (287 090) becomes a sushi bar/Japanese restaurant in the evening. Since 1872, **Café Rivoire** has served the best hot chocolate and superb cocktails and aperitifs, overlooking the replica of Michelangelo's David in Piazza delle Signoria.

A large-sized bottle of body product from the luxurious range by Lungarno Details for Mrs Smith, and a bottle of wine for Mr Smith. Register your Smithcard online, then show your card at check-in, to claim your offer.

Get a room! Use our free online booking service: check availability and make reservations through www.mrandmrssmith.com.

SMITH CONCIERGE Registered Smith cardholders can call +44 (0)20 7978 7333 and have Original Travel book everything from your flights to your day trips, at no extra charge.

Original idea Why not enjoy a tour of Florence by moped? A guide will collect you and lead the way. We can also arrange for you to venture out of town to go truffle-hunting in season.

Gallery Hotel Art 5 Vicolo dell'Oro, Florence 50123 (+ 39 (0)552 7263) gallery@lungarnohotels.com; www.lungarnohotels.com

'Surrounded by drawings, sculptures and photography books, we're in no doubt that we're in one of the world's most culturally stimulating cities'

JK Place

CITY   FLORENCE
STYLE   PRIVATE PERFECTION
SETTING   PERCHED ON THE PIAZZA

M T W T F S S M T W T F S S M T W T F S S M T W T F S S M T W T F **S S** M T W T

FIRENZE

MTWTFSSMTWTFSSMTWTFSSMTWTFSSMTWTFSSMTWTFSS

JK Place, Florence, Italy

U nlike most people, I am usually filled with a sense of dread by the thought of a few days in Italy. Not because I have anything against its people or their magnificent country, but because in my profession a three-day trip to Italy usually equates to a huge amount of hard work in a less-than-glamorous factory on the outskirts of Milan. Touching down in Pisa with nothing more than a romantic weekend on the agenda is a delightful novelty.

It's a warm and clear afternoon when my husband and I pull into Piazza Santa Maria Novella, one of Florence's many beautiful and bustling squares. Situated close to the train terminus, it's famed for its impressive Basilica and world-famous perfumery (a favourite place of mine, with ancient frescoes and implements, though it is the scents lingering in the air that make the strongest impression at Via della Spada). It's also, we discover, the perfect Florentine

bolthole. Tucked away on the corner of the piazza, between ordinary hotels and an Irish bar sits JK Place. It is unassuming and discreet – only a modest plaque indicates we are in the right spot and not at a private home.

This 20-bedroom boutique hotel exudes style, privacy and sophistication; it's a place where everything is whispered rather than shouted. On ringing the bell, we're met within seconds by an immaculately turned-out member of staff who offers a welcome you would expect from a friend you haven't seen for years. As the heavy doors close, screaming Vespas and constantly blaring car horns are locked out and a sense of calm descends. Surrounded by framed life drawings, sculptures, Fellini-esque images and books ranging from Helmut Newton to Umberto Eco, we are in no doubt that we're in one of the world's most beautiful and culturally stimulating cities.

The sense that you are staying not in a hotel but a private residence is most apparent at check-in, or rather lack of it. Our friends at JK Place have done away with the conventional bowl-of-boiled-sweets-style reception desk and have plumped for a more personal approach. We're handed our key in a small library, finished in dark wood, with mirrored doors that cleverly disguise the elevator. A refreshing glass of iced tea and a nibble on the torte of the day (served every afternoon in the courtyard), and we are shown to our room.

Having witnessed a very successful blend of modern and traditional downstairs, I'm glad to say our room doesn't disappoint. High-painted ceilings, panelled walls, a Louis XV fireplace and extremely well-edited modern pieces sit comfortably alongside every audio-visual requirement. While not enormous, the room is sufficiently spacious to accommodate a large sofa, two winged chairs, a writing desk, side table and a super-comfy modern four-poster bed. As someone who loves her fabric and is a sucker for detail,

I couldn't fail to be impressed by the perfectly pressed heavy damask curtains that are pleated into a fan-shaped 'puddle' on the floor. While wanting to avoid any clichéd reference to EM Forster's tale of romance, I'm finding it virtually impossible, confronted with three floor-to-ceiling windows, opening onto a small balcony in front of the Basilica. Our romantic weekend is afforded the full Merchant Ivory stage setting, and we have, without question, a room with a view.

Despite having polished off a generous piece of chocolate and Amaretto biscuit torte, my husband enquires about dinner. We'd planned to be lazy and eat in on our first night, only to discover it is but a basic bar-style menu – and when you've just arrived in Italy, a club sandwich doesn't cut it. Being in the heart of the city, we know fantastic restaurants must be only minutes away. We conclude it is probably a good thing that JK doesn't really do dinner as we would probably have never left the comforts of Room One. ↓

We feel in the mood to go rustico – or should I say, I am desperate for a real Italian pizza. L'Antica Porta is deemed by those in the know as the best place for it, so we take a cab off the tourist trail to an eatery full of locals. Having said 'ciao' to my health drive so far, I suggest a romantic stroll back across the Ponte Vecchio to work off a few of the calories.

The following morning my Mr Smith heads downstairs to take breakfast in the covered courtyard. There is only one large table, encouraging guests to chat over coffee and the papers. (Though they can't immediately oblige when *The Times* is requested, someone pops out to the local newsstand, quickly remedying the situation). I ask for some fresh fruit and a soya-based smoothie – a tall order in most hotels. But in true JK style they duly deliver one banana smoothie with soya milk – big brownie points from this vegetarian. Our Saturday lunch venue turns out to be another success. Cantinetta Antinori is owned by the famous family of Tuscan wine-producers of the same name and is only three minutes from JK. In a relaxed, buzzy atmosphere we enjoy pasta with zucchini flowers in a

light saffron sauce, which my husband deems one of the best he's ever had – and he knows his pasta). This was accompanied by a robust red from the family vineyard, which goes down all too easily. We feel content in the resignation we have left ourselves with little option other than to return to Room One, take out a DVD from the library and spend the remaining part of the afternoon enjoying the company of our new-found friend: the four-poster.

All too quickly the morning of our departure comes around. We're lying in our canopied crib, savouring the sun breaking through the curtains and the sound of the bells of Santa Maria Novella ringing out (the perfect backdrop to our final hours in Florence), when we realise that we still have no idea who our host for the weekend has been. Having spent the last two days enjoying JK's hospitality, it seems strange, somehow, that we haven't enquired. We eventually agree that it doesn't matter; whoever he or she is, we feel like we've known them for years.

Reviewed by Stella McCartney

NEED TO KNOW

Rooms 20.
Rates €285–€740, including breakfast.
Check-out Midday.
Room service Breakfast is available. The soft drinks in the mini-bar are free.
Facilities DVD and CD library; free internet access.
Children Beds available; babysitters can be arranged.

IN THE KNOW

Recommended rooms Room 9 has high ceilings and a staircase up to the bathroom. The penthouse has a 360-degree view. Room 1 has a canopied bed, and overlooks the square.
Hotel bar There's an honesty bar in the main lounge; and a rooftop lounge in summer.
Hotel restaurant No restaurant as such, but snacks are available in the lounge.
Top table In front of the fireplace.
Dress code Relaxed but elegant.

LOCAL EATING AND DRINKING

Enquire at reception about the restaurant next door, **JK Lounge** (264 5181), on Piazza Santa Maria Novella. **Cantinetta Antinori** on Piazza Antinori (292 234) is the restaurant in the 15th-century palazzo belonging to the Antinori family. Most ingredients used in their dishes come fresh from their estates, as does the fine wine. **L'Antica Porta** on Via Senese (220 527) is a casual trattoria beloved by locals for its pizza and pasta. If you can, book in advance. **Café Giacosa** on Via della Spada is a relaxed café, perfect for a cappuccino stop. **Buca Mario** on Ottaviani (214 179) is a friendly family-run trattoria where locals and tourists from every walk of life enjoy fantastic typical Tuscan cooking, in traditional relaxed surroundings. Closed at lunchtime on Wednesday and Thursday. **Il Latini** on Via Palchetti (210 916) is very popular for lunch and dinner; queues form, since you cannot book in advance. The service is all about traditional Italian flair and you don't get much choice. (Wine: red or white? Main course: fish or meat?) Can be touristy, but when it's not, it's great fun. **La Spada** on Via della Spada (218 757) is another traditional Italian restaurant ideal for lunch. For an evening drink, **Capocaccia** on Lungano Corsini is only a short walk away.

A glass of champagne, a basket of fruit and a Florence guidebook. Register your Smithcard online, then show your card at check-in, to claim your offer.

Get a room! Use our free online booking service: check availability and make reservations through www.mrandmrssmith.com.

Registered Smith cardholders can call +44 (0)20 7978 7333 and have Original Travel book everything from your flights to your day trips, at no extra charge.
Original idea Let us arrange a private viewing of the stunning Uffizi gallery, so you can walk peacefully around this former palace after the tourist hordes have left for the day.

JK Place 7 Piazza Santa Maria Novella, Florence 50123 (+39 055 26 45 181)
jkplace@jkplace.com; www.jkplace.com

With a little imagination and a decent selection of ingredients, you should be able to grab more than just a cold beer from the mini-bar. These cocktails are perfect for private time or to surprise your other half with.

If you are planning a small 'gathering' in the wee hours or just want a little privacy with your lover, preparation is the key. Cocktails must be cold, so a proper-sized champagne bucket filled with fresh ice is paramount. With that you'll also need a few lemons and limes, a couple of oranges, a sharp knife and some appropriate glassware. Check that you have lots of white-sugar sachets and that you have change to tip room service. Mini-bars are not well known for their vast array of choice, but here are a few great classics and a couple of contemporary cocktails from IP Bartenders that can be made easily from the basic ingredients.

mix a mini-bar cocktail

How to…

Tom Collins

The long, refreshing gin-based classic. Squeeze the juice of half a lemon into a tall glass. Dissolve four sachets of sugar into the juice and add a mini bottle of gin. Top up the glass with ice and sparkling mineral water or soda water. Stir well. If you have a lemon, garnish the drink with a wedge.

Cuba Libra

This is basically a dressed-up rum and Coke – but it comes from Cuba so it must be cool. Take a tall glass and fill it with ice-cubes. Pour in a mini bottle of rum (aged, if you have it) and fill with Coke. Then take a lime, cut it into wedges, squeeze them all into the drink, and drop them in. Give it a good stir.

Suite Sangria

It feels as though you're achieving some kind of greatness if you can knock up an impressive bedroom sangria. This is enough for two or three people. You will need to pour the following ingredients into an ice bucket: a small bottle of red wine (or two, ideally) half a brandy miniature, half a Cointreau miniature, the juice of half an orange, three to five sachets of sugar (depending on taste). Make sure all the sugar has dissolved by stirring, then add ice if you want it cold; otherwise just serve it up with slices of lime or orange.

Godfather

This is perfect after a satisfactory three-courser, and it couldn't be easier to make. In a tumbler half full of ice-cubes, add half each of a mini bottle of whisky and a mini bottle of Amaretto and stir.

Champagne Cocktail

If you manage to score some Angostura bitters from room service to make this glamorous classic, all the better. First, take a sugarcube and rub it firmly on the skin of an orange until the cube turns slightly yellow (picking up all those lovely bitter orange oils from the peel). Then place it in the bottom of a champagne flute and dash two drops of bitters over it. Pour half a mini bottle of brandy over the sugar and slowly top up with champagne.

Dandy Shandy

This is a contemporary take on the beer/lemonade combo. To a large glass full of ice-cubes, add half a mini bottle of Cointreau, then top it up with equal measures of lager and lemonade. Cut half a lime into wedges and squeeze and drop them into the drink. Give it a good stir.

Blockbuster

This is dead simple to make and even easier to drink. Pour a mini bottle of rum into a tall glass full of ice-cubes, almost topping it up with equal measures of Coke and ginger beer (ginger ale is a good second best). Then squeeze the juice of a lime into the glass and stir.

Dirty Martini

If you've got a jar of olives and some elegant glasses handy, this is a sophisticated tipple for two. Empty a gin miniature into a large glass or jug, and add a handful of ice and a splash of the brine from the olives. Give it a good stir and strain (perhaps with a fork) into the glasses. Pop an olive into each.

Gimlet

A refreshing alternative to the good old G&T, perfect for a hot-climate sundowner. Stir together two parts gin to one part lime juice or cordial; serve on the rocks with a splash of soda water.

Mrs Smith's Tea-Punch

Designed for larger social shenanigans, this refreshing punch will serve up to four people. It is tricky but rewarding to make. Measure two highball glasses of water into your kettle, and boil. Pour the boiling water over two teabags in an ice bucket, and leave to steep for a minute. Take out the teabags and squeeze in the juice of a lemon, then add two mini bottles of gin and a dozen or so sachets of sugar. Fill with ice to cool it down, and serve in small glasses garnished with slices of lemon.

Rusty Nail

One for the retro-lover, if you're lucky enough to find a little Drambuie in your mini-bar. After putting ice in two glasses, empty one whisky mini into each, then divide the Drambuie. Add a twist of lemon, et voilà.

Milan

CITYSCAPE   ULTRA-URBAN
CITY LIFE   ONE LONG CATWALK

M T W T F **S S** M T W T F S S M T W T F S S M T W T F S S M T W T F S S M T W T

ITALIA

'Arguably the fashion
capital of the world,
it's trendy yet friendly,
international yet elitist'

TWTFSSMTWTFSSMTWTFSSMTWTFSSMTWTFSS

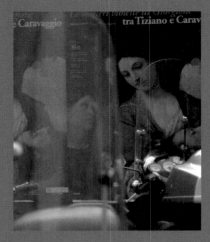

MILAN

Milan is Italy at its most urban and party-loving. Arguably the fashion capital of the world, it is trendy yet friendly, international yet elitist. With no major waterway, and sparse green spaces, its focal point is the huge Duomo. Attending mass is an atmospheric way to get under the city's skin or, at La Scala – the opera house where *Madame Butterfly* premiered, lavishly restored in recent years – you can witness the most critical (and sometimes tearfully adoring) audiences known to prima donna. Cutting-edge galleries such as the Prada Foundation compete for attention with Old Masters: da Vinci's *Last Supper* is housed in Santa Marie delle Grazie, though you'll get a less crowded view of wonderful Titians and Raphaels in the Pinacoteca di Brera. Fashion, furniture and football are Milan's other obsessions. The hub of the designer shopping area around Via Montenapoleone is gold-card nirvana, where you'll find local heroes Missoni, Armani and Etro, fantastic vintage, and highly covetable design and kitchenwares. Eating and partying here are as stylish as you'd expect, with bars and clubs designed to appeal to the crème de la cognoscenti, an organic gelateria (where else?) and sushi fit for the fussiest supermodel. It might not be the most beautiful city, but it's not looks that count in this hip metropolis – it's attitude.

GETTING THERE

Planes There are two airports: a taxi from Malpensa to the centre costs about €70; the fare from Linate is €18.

Trains The Malpensa Express runs every 30 mins, connecting Terminal 1 and Milan's Cadorna railway station in about 40 mins.

Automobiles A car can be a good idea, especially in summer when the lakes beckon, 40 mins away. Driving in Milan is not too challenging.

DO GO/DON'T GO

Everybody heads out to the lakes in high summer, so it can feel deserted. The best times are the January sales, or spring, when it's warm and buzzing.

MAJORLY MILAN

Find a bargain at the antiques fair in Navigli, 08h30–18h30, on the last Sunday of every month except July and August. Have a treatment at the Gianfranco Ferré spa (7601 7526). Rent a car and visit the lakes (Como, Garda, Maggiore).

LOCAL KNOWLEDGE

Taxis Taxis are dear, and you'll need to ring one, or find an elusive cab rank.

Tipping culture In restaurants, the cover charge represents your tip.

Packing tips Your most fashionista outfits; huge, extra-dark sunglasses.

Recommended read *Insider's Guide to Shopping* by J.Fairchild, G.Gallagher.

Cuisine *Risotto alla Milanese*, tomato-and-mozzarella-filled *panzerotto*.

Currency Euro.

Dialling codes Country code for Italy: 39. Milan: 02 – code always required.

DIARY

February Carnevale Ambrosiano, with floats and crowds processing to the Piazza del Duomo, ending on the first Saturday in Lent. Fashion week (autumn/ winter collections). **April** International Salone del Mobile, the giant furniture fair, recently renamed Milan Design Week to reflect its broad appeal. **May** Pittori sul Naviglio: an outdoor art show along Alzia Naviglio Grande canal. **July/August** Summer concerts, Thursday evenings in Wilson Park. **September** Fashion week (spring/summer). **December** Opera season starts.

°C

J 5
F 8
M 13
A 18
M 22
J 26
J 29
A 28
S 24
O 18
N 10
D 5

WORTH GETTING OUT OF BED FOR

Viewpoint It's a good climb to the top of the Duomo – 166 steps, or there's a lift – but worth it for the eyeful.

Arts and culture A tour of La Scala (www.teatroallascala.org) is no substitute for a performance, but diverting nonetheless. Santa Marie delle Grazie houses da Vinci's *Last Supper* (open until 18h45; closed Mondays; ring 8942 1146 to book). La Pinacoteca di Brera (722631) is a fine-art must.

Something for nothing At aperitivo time, 18h–21h, many bars lay on free canapés. Il Cimitero Monumentale (Tuesday–Sunday till 17h15), where Giuseppe Verdi lies, is an amazing open-air museum in its own right.

Shopping Via Montenapoleone, Via della Spiga and Via Sant'Andrea house the showrooms of the major designers, including Gucci, Prada, Versace, Dolce & Gabbana and Bottega Veneta. The Armani empire has its multi-concept store on Via Manzoni. For more affordable purchases (MaxMara, Bruno Magli, Pollini, H&M, Zara), head for Corso Vittorio Emanuele. The area around Porta Ticinese is good for street style (Diesel, Miss Sixty, Fornarina) as well as second-hand shops, handmade clothes and intriguing homewares. The Fiera di Senigallia market, every Saturday, sells ethnic handicrafts, records and bicycles along the Darsena dockyard. Mercato dell'Antiquariato di Brera, on the third Saturday of the month, has stalls selling books, jewellery, antiques and so on.

Tourist tick box Duomo ❑ La Scala ❑ Armani/Bulgari/Gucci/Prada ❑

CAFÉS

Marchesi, Via Santa Maria alla Porta, is legendary for its coffee and cake. An institution for breakfast and aperitivi, **Taveggia** on Via Visconti di Modrone, appeals for its original furnishings and great panini. **Cova** on Via Montenapoleone is famous for its rice pudding – stop here for some post-shopping star-spotting.

BARS AND RESTAURANTS

Chandelier on Via Broggi (2024 0458) is a place you'll either love or hate, with red-velvet decor, chandeliers, crucifix-covered drapes and dressed-up mannequins; the food comes second but is tasty. Open for dinner, **La Libera** on Via Palermo (805 3603) calls itself a beer cellar, but the food is also very good. Claudio Sadler prepares seafood with a nouvelle approach at **Sadler** on Via Troilo (5810 4451). **Giulio Pane e Ojo** on Via Muratori (545 6189), is good for Roman cuisine. **Nobu** on Via Pisoni (7231 8645) does Japanese-Peruvian fusion like its global siblings, in a corner of the Armani mini-mall. **Chatulle** on Via Piero della Francesca (342 008) is a sparkling-white restaurant, serving imaginative Italian cuisine. **Gioia 69** on Via Melchiorre Gioia (66710180) is a super-trendy combination of sombre Michelin-starred restaurant and black-velvet lounge bar. **Osteria dell'Operetta** on Porta Ticinese (8940 7426) serves some of the best *risotto alla Milanese* in the world. The food is also recommended in **Antica Trattoria della Pesa** on Viale Pasubio (655 5741). **360°** on Via Tortona (835 6706) is a great brunch stop for help-yourself salads, pasta and pudding.

NIGHTLIFE

In the early evening, the **Porta Ticinese** area gets packed out; a few hours here is a quintessential Milanese experience. **Roialto** on Via Piero della Francesca is 700 square metres of restaurant, cocktail bar and cigar bar, with a rooftop pool. **Executive Lounge** on Via di Tocqueville is a candlelit Indonesian-style bar with cushions and low wooden tables, open until 02h. By the entrance to Parco Sempione on Via Luigi Camoens, **Just Cavalli Café** is as flamboyant and sexy as one of designer Roberto Cavalli's clinging mini-dresses, all oriental fabrics and antelope furs, open until 02h. Open until 04h, **Il Gattopardo Café** on Via Piero della Francesca is a former church that converted in 2001. Its imposing chandelier and marble columns give it a fantastic ambience. The all-white **G Lounge** on Via Larga plays the best music on the nightlife scene.

3Rooms

CITY   MILAN
STYLE   FASHIONISTA PADS
SETTING   ART/DESIGN/FASHION SCENE

M T W T F S S M T W T F **S S** M T W T F S S M T W T F S S M T W T F S S M T W T
MILANO

'The shop and gallery are beloved
of international fash-mag folk,
though its restaurant and bar
are pleasingly unflash'

TWTFSSMTWTFSSMTWTFSSMTWTFSSMTWTFSSMTWTFSS

At the risk of offending a whole nation – or of stoking Italian national pride beyond what is proper – I must say that ducking into the entrance of 10 Corso Como, the complex where 3Rooms is situated, felt like a relief. The communicative manners of the Milanese seemed almost shocking, three hours away from head-down, eyes-front north London; on our short walk (Corso Como is pedestrian-only) between cab and hotel, restless eyes threatened to burn the very sleeves from Mrs Smith's shoulders. But it's only natural that the people of Milan should be avid to check out what you're wearing. After all, it would be rude to ignore how beautifully turned out they are. We admire everyone: the slinky-midriff brigade; the 'no socks, please – we're Italian' Eurohunks; shamingly chic sixtysomethings; expert fashionistas.

10 Corso Como is the creation of Carla Sozzani, one-time editor of Italian *Vogue*. Its shop and gallery are beloved of international fash-mag folk, though its restaurant and bar are pleasingly unflash. Our quarters take up the middle floor of one side of the squarish courtyard, and they're wonderful. The floor throughout is a burnished, swirly amber resin; both sitting room and bedroom are big, white-walled cubes, filled with Sixties furniture, artworks and chic home comforts: shelves of design and architecture books, Finnish and Belgian towels (the rough and the smooth), audio-visual-internet everything, and fresh blackberries and raspberries. We are given a set of keys and several mobile numbers; breakfast time aside, 3Rooms is virtually unmanned. It doesn't provide a scene or lobby life in the usual sense: just privacy, constant access to the buzz of the courtyard and the peace of the bookstore and gallery, and a very cool place to spend some time. I've seen hotel rooms full of design books before, but this weekend we actually feel moved to stretch out on the Eames bedcovers and read one or two or them.

Once Mrs Smith has taken command of the walk-in wardrobe and made sense of the spoils (including a 10 Corso Como cardboard camera – everything else is for sale, including the more tempting goods in the bathroom and, film for the camera), we decide to join

the scene downstairs. After a warm welcome from the hotel people, the waiters seem somewhat regal, but the crowd is neither scary nor starry. The restaurant is spread between an indoor dining room, a covered terrace, and half of the courtyard, opposite the bar. We decide to sit out among the olive trees, jasmine and palms, looking up at the rear of the façade, with its beautifully lit iron balconies dripping with creeping plants. Mrs Smith swears that one of our slightly snooty waiters is a double of Manolo Blahnik. I am surprised, because for some reason I had imagined the adored maestro of toe cleavage as a mustachioed seducer. I also think it unlikely Mr Blahnik would go undercover in order to seek inspiration beneath the tables of chic eateries. The variety of footwear on display is quite something, now we start paying attention. We realise we must look like members of the fashion police doing a little undercover work of our own, and bring our eyes back to the swordfish carpaccio.

After bespoke breakfast at 10h in our sitting room, we go in search of Milan. It is a completely unknown quantity to us both – we are aware of its status in the 'Paris, London, New York…' axis of fashion, but know nothing of its monuments, its feel, its pace. We walk south towards the centre, waiting for things to get hectic, but they don't. The city must still be waking from its summer shutdown; there are more cyclists than scooters, and precious few table-filled piazzas to stop for a beer in. We decide that Milan is more a cabbing-it place, where you head to a particular bar or area, than one in which you happen upon fun back streets by foot. We do make one accidental discovery: a very Italian sushi stop at Da Claudio on Via Ponte Vetero. We pay up front, €8 each, to stand at a bar in the middle of this giant fishmongers, where we drink prosecco and eat the freshest, sweetest raw tuna, salmon, bream and scallops (*cappesante*): it is sashimi Med-style, without the chopsticks or the intricate presentation, and with olive oil as well as soy sauce – amazing.

Later, a quick walk away from our base, even in heels, we find Light, a former wood workshop that has been made over most elegantly. We sit at the long alabaster ↓

bar as impossibly well-dressed women and men arrive in waves. The restaurant is a temple to modernism, but we're in the mood for something old-school, so we walk back around the corner to the Antica Trattoria della Pesa for our supper. It's the real thing: great food, no music, and pricelessly good, avuncular service.

On Sunday, brunch in the canal district, i Navigli, is worth the trek. At our destination, 12 Via Tortona, we find a closed door. We're stumbly-hungry, and Mrs Smith fears the worst, but we're soon buzzed in. Across a courtyard where laundry and *Pace* flags hang out, we see a twinkling sign: 360°. Inside, past a greenhouse area with digital waterfall wallpaper, is a contemporary canteen in bubblegum colours where thirty- and forty-something gangs are chatting over a delicious, fresh, salady buffet. There is a room off the side for shiatsu, but this is no hippie hang-out – it's a laidback Sunday social for some very lucky locals. And – the first time we've seen this particular phenomenon in Milan – there are even a few people sitting quietly and reading.

Back at 10 Corso Como, we explore Carla Sozzani's restrained pleasuredome. The art gallery is a pair of good-sized white boxes; we were expecting something fashiony, but we were impressed by the show we saw. It feels funny to be sleeping next-door; it reminds me of living beside an artists' collective years ago; one minute you're in a creative public space; the next, you close your door, watch telly and brush your teeth. Mrs Smith browses among the inspired cornucopia of the boutique, while I cherrypick from the incredible design bookstore. It's as impressive as any major gallery shop I have seen. 3Rooms is nothing like any other hotel, but a world away from fending for yourself in a villa. With our bedroom and sitting room in beautiful 3Rooms, the 10 Corso Como gallery and bookstore for a playroom/study, and its restaurant and cafe to meet all our other needs, this harmonious corner of Milan has been a joy to make ourselves at home in. And may the tourist board strike me down, but next time this twosome does 3Rooms, we're going to put ourselves under house arrest.

Reviewed by Mr & Mrs Smith

NEED TO KNOW

Rooms Three suites.
Rates €295, including breakfast.
Check-out Midday. Late departure is possible, but subject to an additional charge.
Room service 07h–01h: full restaurant menu.
Facilities Each suite has a balcony and private entrance. Bang & Olufsen entertainment systems (CD/DVD/video), 24-hour internet. Daily newspapers, mineral water and fruit are complimentary. Parking available for guests.
Children Are welcome.
Also 'Slow breakfast' involves a choice of fine foodstuffs. Guests can take it in their suite until 11; after that, in the tea room or garden. 10 Corso Como is a boutique complex, with art galleries, and shops selling fashion, books, CDs and homewares.

IN THE KNOW

Recommended rooms Each is uniquely decorated, so it comes down to personal taste, but our favourite is Room 3.
Hotel bar In summer, coffee and cocktails are served in the cobbled courtyard. There is also a very smart bar/restaurant.
Hotel restaurant The modern, art-decked restaurant serves Italian and sushi.
Top table An intimate corner position.
Dress code Intellectual chic.

LOCAL EATING AND DRINKING

Great for home-cooked fare is **Fabbrica Pizzeria con Cucina** on Viale Pasubio (655 2771). Five minutes further up the road, **Antica Trattoria della Pesa** (655 5741) does a mean osso buco in an authentic traditional interior. Bar/restaurant **Light** on Via Maroncelli (6269 0631) is better known for its chic decor and clientele than its food; it is a favourite with the fashion set where you can sit back and outfit-watch. **Executive Lounge** on Via di Tocqueville (6261 1617), open till 02h, is a big, candlelit, Indonesian-style bar with sofas, cushions and low wooden tables. Cocktails aren't up to much but it's very chilled. On the way towards the Duomo quarter, stand at the zinc bar at fishmongers **Da Claudio** on Via Ponte Vetero (805 6857), and enjoy Italian-style sushi.

Get a room! Use our free online booking service: check availability and make reservations through www.mrandmrssmith.com.

SMITH CONCIERGE Registered Smith cardholders can call +44 (0)20 7978 7333 and have Original Travel book everything from your flights to your day trips, at no extra charge.
Original idea We'll reserve you a table for a 12-course degustation menu at Ristorante Gualtiero Marchesi, a half-hour chauffeur-driven trip from Milan.

3Rooms 10 Corso Como, Milan 20154 (+39 02 626163)
info@3rooms-10corsocomo.com; www.3rooms-10corsocomo.com

'The interior is a chocolate box of browns, blacks and whites, with an expensive, soft-minimal feel'

Bulgari Hotel

CITY   MILAN
STYLE   REFINED AND PRESTIGIOUS
SETTING   PRIVATE GARDENS

M T W T F S S M T W T F **S S** M T W T F S S M T W T F S S M T W T F S S M T W T

MILANO

MTWTFSSMTWTFSSMTWTFSSMTWTFSSMTWTFSS

Bulgari Hotel, Milan, Italy

We'd heard a lot about the Bulgari from friends in fashion, even though it only opened in May 2004. We were expecting something upscale and sexy, and we weren't disappointed. The hotel is tucked away in a very quiet private street near the prime credit-card sweat zone of Via Montenapoleone, and has a sense of space rare in a city-centre site. Our first impression was of a grand, almost imposing building: a perfect backdrop for the many Italian designer labels for sale around the corner, and of course Bulgari jewellery. Sometimes these chic fashionista hotels are staffed by people who resent not being customers themselves. Not the Bulgari: from the moment we were allowed through the plate-glass door, we knew the service was going to be as good as the best anywhere in the world.

The interior is a chocolate box of browns, blacks and whites, with an expensive, soft-minimal feel. Staff are uniformed, and you'll never see a loose end or a scuff mark; even the flower-delivery boys looked super-sharp, though half obscured by the enormous green hydrangea heads they were positioning in the lounge. Here, there are design books to browse, and a fireplace for winter. It has a slightly masculine appeal; the Bulgari would make the ideal seduction scene for the sort of young man who gets upmarket mens monthlies for the girls and the gear, and sharp-witted current affairs weeklies for the gossip.

Our room was pared-down but luxurious, with teak, oak and quintessentially Italian furniture, designed by Citterio. (Architects Citterio and Partners are responsible, in fact, for the whole hotel.) The bathroom was so wildly to our liking that we decided to spend a couple of hours before dinner ensconced in there. We raided the mini-bar of house champagne, lit the candles, and took a long soak in the tub. The rooms are loaded with indulgent items, from the soap and huge bath towels, to the two flatscreen TVs. Luckily, our room

overlooked the garden and bar, or we would not have
been able to pull ourselves together to leave it at all.
The allure of the scene downstairs was too great and
we decided to take a closer look.

The bar was buzzing with smart locals hanging out
after work (a good sign for an international hotel).
In the evening sun, we sat among voguish business
people, several Japanese couples and a handful of
yummy-mummy types, looking out over the hotel's
mini-Versailles garden. Inside, on the other side
of an oval spaceship of a bar, the restaurant feels
something like an auditorium. The food is ambitious,
and the service impeccable. After our vain attempt
to walk off suckling pig and a bottle of wine, the
downy bed was a friend indeed.

Milan isn't an obvious choice for a typically Italian
lovers' jaunt, but you can't say you've seen Italy if you've
only experienced Florence and Venice. This is a living
city; there's nothing museumlike about it. And if you like

shopping, you'll love it. We entertained the idea
of strolling though areas of town we hadn't seen
before, but the pull of the shops was too great.
10 Corso Como is the benchmark lifestyle store.
It is a must-see – a must-browse – even though it
is expensive. It sells clothes, rare books, music,
even household goods. The café is an ideal
lunchtime spot, where you can eat simple food
made with very high-quality ingredients, in
a courtyard dappled in sunlight.

After more shopping along exclusive Via della
Spiga, we went back to the hotel for a well-earned
rest. My wife decided on a rebalancing chakra
stone therapy and facial in the spa, while I set off
to pound the treadmill. She came back feeling
completely refreshed, rejuvenated and rebalanced,
which was a delightful surprise for both of us, and
worth every penny. The spa is a major selling point:
it is utterly private and the pool is well-sized,
mosaic-tiled and romantically lit. ↓

It was late when we finished, and we wanted to eat good food somewhere casual. We'd booked at the Roman trattoria Giulio Pane e Ojo on Via Ludovico Muratori, not far from Porta Romana, where we ate extremely good pasta e fagioli and chicken with rosemary.

We decided on a very lazy last morning, moving very slowly from bed to bath and back to bed. We had left our children behind and wanted to make the most of it. When we did emerge from the hotel, it was only to visit the greatest delicatessen in the world, Peck on Via Spadari. No trip to Milan is complete without a pilgrimage here; in fact, its own-label olive oil is something you must bring back with you. There are many more things to tempt the tastebuds – we filled our bags and emptied our pockets. Maybe the faintly ascetic vibe at the Bulgari (well, it was a monastery a few hundred years ago) inspired us to indulge in a spot of greed. Actually, come to think of it, its super-sleek spaces are perfect for almost any kind of sin you can think of. And if your kind of seduction involves a spot of shopping, so much the better.

Reviewed by Oliver Peyton

NEED TO KNOW

Rooms 52 rooms: 33 deluxe; seven superior; five special rooms; six suites; one Bulgari suite.
Rates €560–€3,500 (plus ten per cent tax).
Check-out 13h.
Room service Everything from contemporary Italian to Iranian caviar available 24 hours.
Facilities Hotel spa, extensive private gardens with meditation area, unpacking and packing services, personal shopper, hair and make-up services, valet parking.
Children An extra bed can be provided for children under 15, free of charge.
Also Some of the rooms have meditation corners, complete with tatami mat.

IN THE KNOW

Recommended rooms The Bulgari suite is luxurious to the extreme, with its own front door from the lift, but at a high price. All the rooms except the four smaller rooms have teak balconies with fabulous views of either the gardens or classic Milanese villas.
Hotel bar The oval-shaped bar serves great juices and cocktails on an outside terrace with chocolate-brown sofas and candles.
Hotel restaurant The very modern restaurant serves contemporary Italian food over two levels. Open 07h–11h, 12h30–14h30, 19h30–23h.
Top table Any on the second floor.
Dress code Sophisticated and elegant.

LOCAL EATING AND DRINKING

If you fancy a cappuccino, have a roam around the university area of Brera; there are great cafés to be found in the narrow streets. **Gioia 69** on Via Melchiorre Gioia (667 10180) is a chic minimalist restaurant and lounge bar with a Michelin-starred kitchen, and a lounge filled with black velvet sofas; it's great for either dinner or a drink. Simple **Giulio Pane e Ojo** on Via Muratori (545 6189) has just eight tables where lovers of Roman cuisine come to sample *pajata* (offal), *pasta all'amatriciana*, or Jewish style artichokes (fresh, fried whole). **Cucina Economica** on Via Guicciardini (783 256) is a simple trattoria serving a few quality dishes with style (closed Wednesdays). **Trattoria Trinacria** on Via Savana (423 8250) is a fantastic Sicilian restaurant that opens for dinner. **La Libera** on Via Palermo (805 3603) calls itself a beer cellar but the seasonal food is delicious. (Only open for dinner.)

 A copy of the Bulgari book. Register your Smithcard online, then show your card at check-in, to claim your offer.

Get a room! Use our free online booking service: check availability and make reservations through www.mrandmrssmith.com.

SMITH CONCIERGE Registered Smith cardholders can call +44 (0)20 7978 7333 and have Original Travel book everything from your flights to your day trips, at no extra charge.
Original idea Watch a Serie A football match live – see AC Milan or Inter Milan play at home.

Bulgari Hotel 7b Via Privata Fratelli Gabba, Milan 20121 (+39 02 805 805 1)
bhr.milbg.reservation@bulgarihotels.com; www.bulgarihotels.com

Straf

'A celebration
of bona fide
cutting-edge
minimalism,
with black-clad,
very friendly staff'

CITY	MILAN
STYLE	INDUSTRIAL-COOL INSTALLATION
SETTING	DOORS DOWN FROM THE DUOMO

M T W T F S S M T W T F S S M T W T F S S M T W T F **S S** M T W T F S S M T W T
MILANO

TWTFSSMTWTFSSMTWTFSSMTWTFSSMTWTFSS

As we taxied off the runway at Milan's Linate airport, we were greeted by a colossal Emporio Armani logo, big enough to dwarf the terminal buildings. This seemed to soothe Mrs Smith's flying phobia, and the anxiety that had wracked her in the air melted into excitement as she began to fully comprehend that we had just touched down in one of the fashion capitals of the world.

Her excitement reached a crescendo as we entered Straf. Its unassuming façade masks a modern-elegant interior: raw-concrete walls and cocoa-brown chaise-longues give the lobby an air of hushed grandeur. It struck us as a destination for fans of the out-of-the-ordinary, the style-conscious and the arty.

Vincenzo de Cotiis' design has made the place almost an art installation in itself. If some of us have taken the odd lesson from hotel design, assimilating it into our own living spaces, this was the definitive masterclass. Straf is a celebration of bona fide cutting-edge fashionista minimalism, with black-clad, very friendly anglophone staff, distressed fabric under glass along its stylish corridors, and scuffed-satiny walls. We might have started off scratching our heads when we were looking for the secret entrance to our room but, once we got inside, all we could say were two things: 'Where's the bathroom?' and 'Wow!'. Once we had got over the shocking, austere colour scheme and the acres of bare concrete, we decided that this exoticism, this complete difference from Chez Smith in south London, was just the sort of out-of-the-ordinary we approved of.

Settling in was a sequence of gratifying discoveries: the bathroom, with a couple-sized shower within oxidised-brass walls, was revealed when we pressed part of the wall to release another secret door; our mini-bar and wardrobe were exposed when we slid back one of the many mirrored walls. We also discovered matching sets of robes and slippers, which helped soften the edges. I was happy to note that the seamless expanses of mirror looked like the perfect environment

for Mrs Smith to try on her new Myla kit. This homage to minimalism was only flawed when I emptied the contents of my man-bag into a pile onto the desk. My thoughtless act was followed by a distinct bleep emitted from somewhere in the room. Surely we weren't being given a subtle warning from an anti-clutter device? No messy men allowed!

Our first glimpse of Milan's number-one architectural/ historical attraction came from our very own balcony. Right next door, towering above everything in its vicinity, was the north face of the Duomo, the world's largest Gothic cathedral. We nipped round to buy tickets for the lift (stairs were out – heels, don't you know), so we could ascend to the level of the saints. It was here, among the intricate statues and 135 spires, that Mrs Smith summed up the cathedral's design: 'It's bit of a mess, really'. It's true that the gargoyles weren't troubling Straf in terms of designer minimalism, but a monument begun in 1385 and completed in 1965 was never going to aspire to 'pared-down'.

Snacking from the aperitif buffet and sipping icy mojitos in the Straf Bar, we decided to go for traditional Italian food at La Libera, in Brera, the Milanese equivalent to Montmartre. A working-class area that became a haven for avant-garde artists, it is now a nest of alternative cafés and boutiques. A beer cellar on the edge of its boho enclave, La Libera sums up what Italy does best: simple dishes, made to order with flavourful fresh ingredients, served to a cosmopolitan mixture of actors, musicians, families and tourists, by charming waiters running around under the watchful eye of Signor Italo.

The next day, Mrs S's dedication to all things Italian drew us to the local branches of Gucci and Prada, in the opulent shopping arcade Galleria Vittorio Emanuele II. Beneath its glass dome, we took the opportunity to bless ourselves with good luck by following local custom and standing on the testicles of the bull in the central mosaic. Such good advice should clearly have been heeded by the gallery's designer, Giuseppe ↓

Mengoni, who fell from the roof to a messy end a few days before the arcade was due to open in 1865. We wondered if Mr Mengoni forgot to stand on the bull's balls that day.

Luck did, indeed, seem with us – or our credit cards, anyway. A pleasant stroll through the designer-shopping district of Quadrilatero d'Oro taught that most of the shops are shut on Sundays. But what's a new handbag or another pair of shoes when you can head towards Porta Ticinese and hang out with Milan's hip young things? We observed the cool crowd at play before making grateful use of the aperitif buffets at bars around Piazza della Vetra. It's an irresistible way to pick at delicious Italian dishes for free, but be warned: you pay for it in the price of the cocktails.

Did this stop us dining in one of the swankiest joints in town? No – of course not. In the name of research we sought out Chatulle, a gleaming-white restaurant full of people who must were either models or representatives of a genetically superior race. Either way, they were a bit moody, but the food was divine, darling.

From there it was a short hop to the Cavalli Café, a chic hang-out set on the edge of Parco Sempione owned by designer Roberto Cavalli that has a lot in common with Ibiza's wonderful KM5. We gassed the balmy night away among the beautiful people, oblivious to the fact that we were the buffet for one hungry mosquito – and 1,000 of his friends. The next day, the lovely staff at Straf informed us that Milan was built on a giant swamp. No matter: what it lacks in classical beauty compared to Florence and Rome, it makes up for in thrilling hustle and bustle, and plenty of drop-dead style. Our weekend was a great insight into the milieu of the serious fashionista, and our base at Straf gave it sexy savoir-faire.

Checking out, we half-watched a fashion shoot taking place on the other side of a smoky-glass wall in reception. Before the supermodel in her threw a tantrum at the thought of returning to reality, I guided Mrs Smith firmly towards the door.

Reviewed by Rob Wood

NEED TO KNOW

Rooms 66.
Rates €235–€770, including breakfast.
Check-out Midday.
Room service 07h–22h30.
Facilities Fitness room (with some gym facilities).
Children Welcome, but the hotel isn't necessarily child-friendly.
Also Small pets welcome.

IN THE KNOW

Recommended rooms There is an executive room (bigger and it has a terrace), and two suites. Five Cromo rooms have a 'wellness corner' which includes massage chairs. If you are particular about bathrooms, choose one that is brass with a big shower or black stone with a tub.
Hotel bar The cosy, laid-back bar officially closes at 01h30, but it often stays open later.
Hotel restaurant What was previously the restaurant, is now their breakfast area. Lunch and dinner are available in the bar at the front. The menu is pizza, panini, focaccia, salads, sandwiches and a simple à la carte menu. There is a happy hour at 18h with hot and cold buffet.
Top table All are good.
Dress code As directional as the decor.

LOCAL EATING AND DRINKING

The **Marchesi Café** on Via Santa Maria alla Porta is legendary for cappuccini. **Taveggia** on Via Visconti di Modrone (602 1257) is a delightful café for breakfast and aperitifs among original historic furnishings. Visit **L'Orangerie** on the sixth floor of Hotel Duomo, Via San Raffaele (8833), for nouvelle cuisine. **Santani** on Via San Marco (655 5587) serves traditional, but not cheap, Italian cuisine to a cosmopolitan crowd. Milan's **Nobu** on Via Pisoni (7231 8645) serves the same delicious Japanese-Peruvian fusion as its international siblings. **G Lounge** on Via Larga (805 3042) is a fashionable gay-friendly club playing house and disco in a sleek white interior. **Just Cavalli Café** on Viale Camoens (311 817) is a great late-night bar/fusion restaurant set in a glass building with a views over gardens. The is the work of designer Roberto Cavalli. Open until 02h; weekends 04h. It's not particularly close to the hotel, but it's worth seeking out.

 A free drink at Bar Straf, and upgrade, upon availability, to a Cromo room with a 'wellness corner': Japanese automassage armchair, chromotherapy and aromatherapy facilities. Register your Smithcard online, then show your card at check-in, to claim your offer.

Get a room! Use our free online booking service: check availability and make reservations through www.mrandmrssmith.com.

SMITH CONCIERGE Registered Smith cardholders can call +44 (0)20 7978 7333 and have Original Travel book everything from your flights to your day trips, at no extra charge.
Original idea We'll ensure VIP treatment at the hippest clubs in Milan, and book you a table.

Hotel Straf 3 Via San Raffaele, Milan 20121 (+39 02 805 081)
reservations@straf.it; www.straf.it

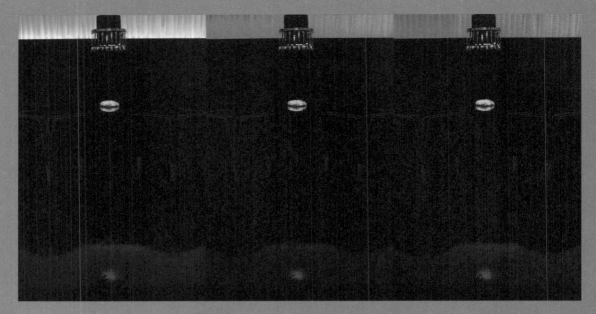

The Gray

CITY   MILAN
STYLE   PLAYFUL DEN FOR MODERN LOVERS
SETTING CENTRALISSIMO

M T W T F S S M T W T F S S M T W T F S S M T W T F **S S** M T W T F S S M T W T

MILANO

'The inner sanctum of our weekend is vast, with a seven-foot
leather bedhead, Egyptian cotton bedlinen and duckdown pillows'

MTWTFSSMTWTFSSMTWTFSSMTWTFSSMTWTFSSMTWTFSS

The Gray, Milan, Italy

W hat do you take to wear on a two-day trip to Milan? Black, obviously: arriving at Malpensa airport, we encounter a sleek army of northern Italians, milling about, talking, embracing and looking stylish. Apart from the odd Missoni stripe and Marni floral, they're dressed in black. At least we'll blend in – don't you hate looking like a tourist?

The Gray looks glossy, with a solid, mirrored rectangle as an awning. On our left as we enter is a small cocktail lounge, boudoirish, with velvet banquettes. We're greeted by the friendly black-clad staff in a reception area replete with a giant fuchsia-upholstered swing and, without too much messing about, we're taken up to our room for the unveiling.

Blimey. It's perfect. The white walls are broken up with two-tone wood veneer. The ivory silk curtains are button-operated, as is the lighting. The first thing we notice, as we play with the curtains twice, is the scene outside. The Gray is precisely central, with the Duomo at the end of the street, La Scala and the Galleria Vittorio Emanuele round the corner, and all the fun bits of town – Via Montenapoleone, La Brera, Porta Ticinese – a walk away. So we're perfectly positioned for playtime.

After the view, the bathroom: there's a huge, round Jacuzzi bath with a TV, and if you haven't got time for the tub (you'll need 20 minutes to fill it), there's the option of a big shower room, all marble, wood and glass.

Back in the bedroom, we look around to see what other buttons are worth pressing. The stereo has the *Kill Bill Vol 1* soundtrack sitting next to it. As the dulcet tones of Nancy Sinatra ring out, we survey the plasma TV, DVD player and fully stocked mini-bar. Finally, the bed. The inner sanctum of our weekend. It's vast, with a seven-foot leather bedhead, Egyptian cotton bedlinen and duckdown pillows. You could say we're up and running. I can't see myself leaving this room for the next two days.

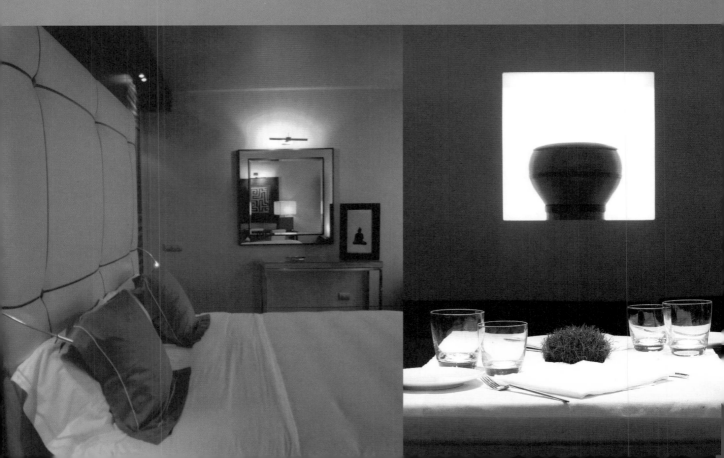

No such luck. Not even time to check out the stripping housewives on Italian TV. Maybe later, I am promised; we have a supper reservation in the hotel restaurant, Le Noir, so we just have time to splash about in the rock-star bath. Interesting. Let's hope Le Noir will be half as good. With the name, we imagine it might be a little pretentious, which isn't the case. It could have been a Quentin Tarantino set in a past life: it's a black box with opium-den lighting, and black velvet chairs round tables sporting squares of grass (the green, growing stuff). As in reception, with its *Alice in Wonderland does Dallas* swing seat, the feel is two parts opulence, one part humour. There are spoons and forks hanging from the light fittings: strange, but it looks bold and quirky rather than contrived. The staff are dressed in black. So are we.

The menu takes a firm Italian stance: we kick off with a Barolo, octopus carpaccio and lobster spaghetti. It was all excellent, as was the service – as was the second bottle of Barolo. Waking up the next day, we both feel like a million lira, ie: the price of a second-hand Vespa, and probably both look it. How can wine be legal? With a bathroom like this one, though, surely we can sort out our hangovers. Within an hour, we're out on the streets of Milan, having power-showered ourselves better, breakfasted in the hotel and dressed again in his 'n' hers black. The hotel is superbly positioned for a couple of hours of culture at the cathedral.

The Piazza del Duomo is basically Trafalgar Square with no Nelson's Column, just loads of pigeons and conspicuous, non-black-wearing tourists. The Duomo, on the other hand, is truly breathtaking: a vast gothicky pile with spires and flying buttresses, which towers over the piazza. It has to be seen. There is a steep winding staircase leading to the rooftop, where the 360-degree view gives our newcomers' eyes a sense of Milan's topography. We walk among the stone saints freely, ponder the merits of bringing a picnic, as some others have done, and take the lift down. We decide not to explore inside, but instead join the throngs of shoppers worshipping at the temples of Via Montenapoleone, ↓

Milan's premier shopping thoroughfare, and the surrounding stylish streets. Prada, Gucci, Hermès, Louis Vuitton – retail doesn't get more serious or spend-spend-spend than this.

We cross back past the Duomo and stop at Zucca, just inside Galleria Vittorio Emanuele, a great place for a Campari and soda. It's weird: Milan is full of men buying shoes for the women in their life. Sitting next to us is a couple who must have done just that. Hmmm – he's in his fifties and she can't be older than 25. Father and daughter? Husband and wife? Or a forbidden liaison – there are at least two shoe boxes visible at their feet. I suppose we'll never know…

After the cosy contemporary of Le Noir, we decide to go traditional for our last evening. There's an incredible array of choice in Milan; they love the 'next big thing' thing. At Il Coriandolo, the decor is very simple, unlike the food, which is sophisticated and delicious. One thing overshadows the menu, though. Believe it or not,

the man we saw earlier near the Duomo, entertaining a very young lady, walks into the restaurant with his companion. But this time, she belongs to his own age group, and is obviously his wife. Her shoes are great. They sit next to us, and he recognises us. He glances over at us again and again, shifting in his seat. I can't bring myself to wink. Maybe he thought I was a private investigator. He'll never know.

We've had a funny, free-flowing, easy time in Milan. The Gray is a sexy, intimate-opulent place to hang out, and the city is fantastic for eating and shopping (and drinking). It's a great escape from all the nonsense we put up with at home. Final thoughts: it's a small world, but I wouldn't like to paint it. Don't cheat on your wife. Oh, and keep buying shoes for the one you love. It certainly works for the Italians. Finally, I believe they're about to bring in a law that bans people from public places if they're not smoking.

Reviewed by Jason Alper

NEED TO KNOW

Rooms 21 individually designed rooms; two with private gyms.
Rates €300–€900 (plus ten per cent tax).
Check-out Midday.
Room service The restaurant à la carte menu is available 12h30–2h30 and 19h–22h30; otherwise, snacks such as smoked salmon and *insalata caprese* are available until 01h.
Facilities High-speed internet connection, hydro shower and/or hydro tub, valet parking. A personal shopper can be arranged.
Children A babysitter can be provided with 24 hours notice. Beds are available for small children at no extra cost.

IN THE KNOW

Recommended rooms 101, 201 and 301 have kingsize beds, round hydro tubs, and views of the Galleria Vittorio Emanuele.
Hotel bar Il Bar, the jewel-like cocktail lounge in a corner of the ground floor, is open until 01h.
Hotel restaurant The international clientele favours the cosy Le Noir for its Italian food and fantastic fish; last orders 22h30.
Top table Choose a round table for two.
Dress code Informal, but A-list.

LOCAL EATING AND DRINKING

Milan's **Nobu** on Via Pisoni (7231 8645) is as swanky as its siblings around the world, and serves the same Peruvian/Japanese fusion food to a cocktail-sipping crowd. **Cova** on Via Montenapoleone (7600 0578) is recommended for post-retail coffee and cake, and its celebrated rice pudding. **Marino alla Scala** on Piazza della Scala (8068 8295) is well worth popping into for a cocktail and a bite of Italian food either in the restaurant, or in the café. The minimalist decor is a suitable backdrop for the fashionable folk who frequent it. You can even take a little of its cool home with you, after a visit to the adjoining lifestyle boutique; there's also a bookstore. For those of you who want to shake your thing with a well-dressed mixed/gay crowd, hotspot **G Lounge** on Via Larga is open late.

A luxury fruit and chocolate basket in your room. Register your Smithcard online, then show your card at check-in, to claim your offer.

Get a room! Use our free online booking service: check availability and make reservations through www.mrandmrssmith.com.

SMITH CONCIERGE Registered Smith cardholders can call +44 (0)20 7978 7333 and have Original Travel book everything from your flights to your day trips, at no extra charge.
Original idea A day of Italian cookery, kicking off at a café, where you'll discuss what's in season and plan your menu. You will then shop at the superb outdoor markets for your ingredients. After the cooking lesson itself, you can relax and enjoy the fruits of your labour.

The Gray 6 Via San Raffaele, Milan 20121 (+39 02 7208951)
info.thegray@sinahotels.it; www.hotelthegray.com

Townhouse 31

CITY   MILAN
STYLE   GLOBAL LOOKS, HOMELY FEEL
SETTING   COLOURFUL PORTA VENEZIA

MTWTFSSMTWTFSSMTWTFSSMTWTFSSMTWTFSSMTWT
MILANO

'We enter via a carpeted walkway with
colonial furniture and boudoir pieces in
vivid pinks and lipstick reds'

MTWTFSSMTWTFSSMTWTFSSMTWTFSSMTWTFSSMTWTFSS

We've just spent a few days on the Amalfi coast, so we're comfortable with Italian ways by the time we reach Milan. Having only visited Italy's fashion capital once, many years ago, I have no particular expectations. Milan is handsome rather than beautiful, with a stunning Gothic cathedral, famously good restaurants and all the clothes boutiques you could reasonably want. I guess that covers all our bases, since our main aims are a little culture and a lot of eating and shopping.

Townhouse 31 gives quite a surreal first impression. It's on a quiet, typical Milanese street, but we entered via a carpeted walkway with a bright-red awning, adorned with both colonial furniture and boudoir-type pieces in vivid pinks and lipstick reds, as well as Oriental and African artefacts. If anything is eclectic, this is. It led us to a terrace bar and sunken lounge with similar decor, sheltered by a giant domed canopy.

Sunday evening, 19h: the courtyard was quiet, though I imagine that it hums with activity at weekends and during fashion week and furniture-fair times. It resembles a stage set, with its vivid tones and uplighters: the perfect backdrop for the smartly dressed Milanese in their dark suits and little black numbers. The accommodation is approached from the courtyard, giving rooms at the back a bird's-eye view of the 'stage'. The spacious reception with inviting cream sofas and high tables and stools, where guests take breakfast, looked more understated but equally relaxed.

That seems to be the point of Townhouse 31; it is exceptionally laid-back. There's no over-fussing, and no rules; it's a bit like, dare we utter the cliché, staying at the house of a well-travelled, artistic friend. We were expected, warmly welcomed and shown to our room. It had the same clean appeal as the reception, with cream and white tones, a generous bed with linen sheets, and pieces of feature furniture from the Orient: a running theme. The bathroom was rather glamorous in butterscotch marble, with a deep tub and a shower.

Making our entrance into the red and pink symphony of the outdoor lounge gave me a little frisson of exhibitionism. I am sure my quirky attire clashed a little with our surroundings – in a good way. It was now dark, and the place was lit with candles; it felt comfortable and inviting, even though it was very quiet. There seemed to be one guy doing everything that night; he opened the bar, and then poured us a glass of delicious pink prosecco, and we sat scoffing nuts and drinking before we went out to eat.

It's a 15-minute cab ride to the hotel's restaurant, TH, which was a different experience altogether. It is a bar/diner, and the thumping music was perhaps a little intrusive over a quiet dinner for two. But the atmosphere is intimate and sexy, and the interior daringly decorated in deep aubergines, with baby-blue gloss floors, backlit tortoiseshell columns, velvet drapes and stuffed mammals in tiaras. The food was to our liking so, as stuffed as the animals, we returned to the hotel for a nightcap and a good night's sleep. Next morning we rose late – nothing unusual about that. But at 11h, we wondered if we'd missed breakfast. No problem: in natural Townhouse style, food still awaited us and we weren't remotely chivvied. By lunchtime we were on the road. Now, as much as I love Italy and admire the Italian way of life, I find it frustrating that August and Mondays give the tourist such a hard time. All the shops seemed to be shut until 15h, and the church that houses da Vinci's Last Supper was closed all day. We contented ourselves with window-shopping while we waited for the shops to open. Later on, we popped into the wonderful 10 Corso Como for cocktails, before heading 'home' to Townhouse 31. ↓

A restaurateur friend from London had recommended we dine at a restaurant called Altro, on Via Burlamacchi. Low-lit corridors led us into an impressive restaurant-cum-kitchen showroom, where we sat among marble, polished steel, glass and dark wood, eating a four-course feast that couldn't be faulted. Back in our retreat, we repeated our favourite routine of sound sleep and a late start. We did nothing but what we felt like doing. Our lasting memory of Townhouse 31 is of the relaxed atmosphere and laid-back staff. A homey hideaway rather than a glitzy paradeground, it seems to reflect the genial disposition of the Italians in general, with added Milanese discretion and insight. I love the concept of discreet, polite and helpful service when you want it, and being left to your own devices when you don't. And that's Townhouse's forte.

Reviewed by Shaun Clarkson

NEED TO KNOW

Rooms 17.
Rates €240–€340.
Check-out Midday.
Room service Breakfast 07h–12h; sandwiches, snacks and drinks 07h–22h.
Facilities 24-hour internet connection; mobiles and laptops are available.
Children Very welcome. Interconnecting pairs of rooms are available, €320 for both. Babysitting can be arranged on request.
Also Breakfast is eaten downstairs on a big table, where you can chat to other guests.

IN THE KNOW

Recommended rooms It is worth asking for one of the five rooms with balconies overlooking the courtyard.
Hotel bar The Indian/Vietnamese-style courtyard and bar area has become a favourite Milanese haunt for the traditional 19h nibble and cocktail.
Hotel restaurant TH is the hotel's eccentric yet sophisticated restaurant and lounge, illuminated by an ambient colour-lighting scheme, and, on our visit, soundtracked with dance music beats. Not the place for sweet nothings, but perfect to get you into a party mood before hitting Milan's clubs. The Modern Italian menu changes every week. You'll need to get a cab there, as it is seven kilometres away on Via de Amicis (805 4041).
Top table An intimate corner, away from the main entrance.
Dress code Informal, but A-list.

LOCAL EATING AND DRINKING

Chandelier on Via Broggi (2024 0458) is a cross between religious retreat and royal palace, with red velvety decor, chandeliers of every description and dressed-up mannequins. The food is good but it's not the main attraction. **Joia** on Via Panfilo Castaldi (2952 224) is an haute vegetarian restaurant and bar attracting a cosmopolitan crowd. **L'elephante** on Via Melzo is a very hip place serving great cocktails to stylish locals (2951 8768). The cafe, bar and restaurant at **10 Corso Como** is stylish and something of a break from noisier establishments (626163). The menu focuses on light, tasty Italian dishes.

 Ten per cent off the bill in TH restaurant, and a free cocktail at aperitivo time (18h–22h). Register your Smithcard online, then show your card at check-in, to claim your offer.

Get a room! Use our free online booking service: check availability and make reservations through www.mrandmrssmith.com.

SMITH CONCIERGE Registered Smith cardholders can call +44 (0)20 7978 7333 and have Original Travel book everything from your flights to your day trips, at no extra charge.
Original idea Enjoy massive discounts on Italian fashion, on a guided tour of the most prestigious factory outlets outside Milan.

Townhouse 31 31 Via Carlo Goldoni, Milan 20129 (+39 02 701561)
townhouse31@townhouse.it; www.townhouse.it

● ROME

Rome

CITYSCAPE   ARCHAEOLOGICAL EYE-CANDY
CITY LIFE   PIAZZA PEOPLE-WATCHING

'I found Rome a city of bricks and left it a city of marble'
Caesar Augustus (63 BC–14 AD)

M T W T F **S S** M T W T F S S M T W T F S S M T W T F S S M T W T F S S M T W T
ITALIA

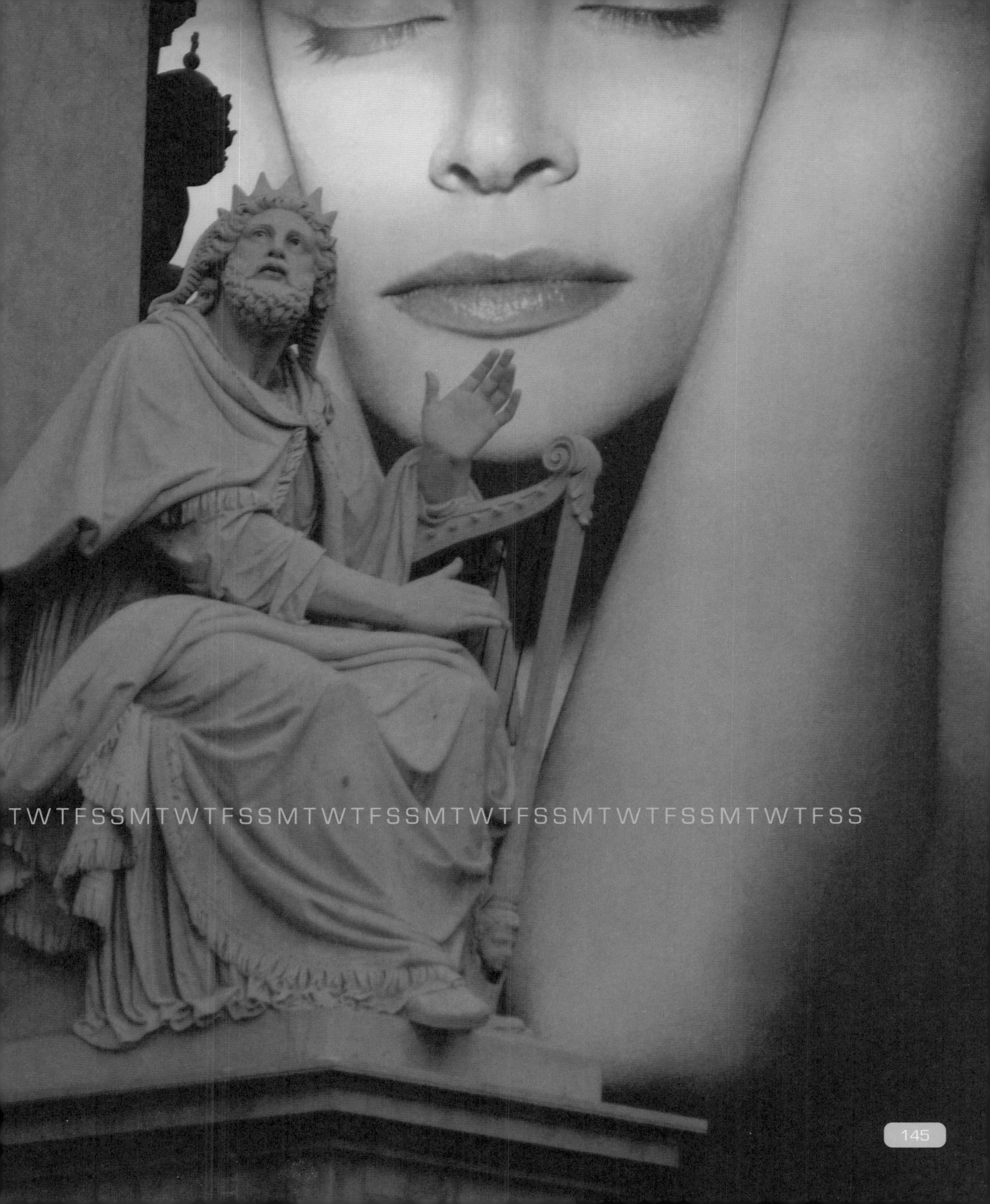

TWTFSSMTWTFSSMTWTFSSMTWTFSSMTWTFSSMTWTFSS

ROME
It's true: Rome wasn't built in a day, and it seems that every moment of its history remains visible. The vestiges of Imperial Rome stagger the imagination, and parts of the city are perfect mediaeval towns, with soaring Renaissance and Baroque architecture. With the Vatican in town, Easter and Christmas are highlights of Rome's calendar, but visitors flock all year to the Raphael frescoes and Michelangelo's *Last Judgment* in the Sistine Chapel. Was Bernini the greatest sculptor of all? Judge for yourself in the Museo Borghese. Rome is also about eating, fashion and the art of life. Romans consider the city's squares their living rooms; visitors, too, can feel at home in the buzzy Piazza Navona or Campo de' Fiori. Make like the locals and linger over delicious *cucina romanesca* – as style-conscious as the Eternal City is, when it comes to food, fashion is forgotten: pizza and pasta are at their best in traditional trattorie. And entertainment is never in short supply, whether your preference is opera or cinema, dance-music dive or jazz club. Fellini got it right about Rome: it's all about *la dolce vita*.

GETTING THERE
Planes Rome is served by two airports: Fiumicino and Ciampino. A 30-min train from Fiumicino to the centre costs €9,50. From Ciampino, at least once an hour, a public bus goes to Anagnina metro station (30 mins from centre) for €1. A taxi from either is about €40.
Trains Stazione Termini is the main station (www.trenitalia.it).
Automobiles Driving in Rome is not for the nervous. You can park in blue zones for €1/hour; daily rate for carparks is around €25. Cars with foreign plates are not allowed in the historical centre.

DO GO/DON'T GO
In the summer, the city gets sweaty and crowded; you may prefer to go in the spring and autumn.

REALLY ROME
Train as a gladiator (www.gsr-roma.com). Rent a vespa and see the sights *Roman Holiday* style.

LOCAL KNOWLEDGE
Taxis You can hail them everywhere, and taxi ranks have numbers to ring.
Tipping culture 15 per cent is usually added; small change for drinks.
Packing tips Rosary beads; a pick and shovel to unearth ancient artifacts a few metres down (the reason why the metro has never been completed).
Cuisine We loved *spaghetti all'amatriciana* (tomato and pancetta) and *saltimbocca* (veal roll with sage and butter). Thursday is gnocchi day.
Currency Euro.
Dialling codes Country code for Italy: 39. Rome: 06.

DIARY
April Good Friday: a torchlit procession from Via Crucis up the Monte Palatino re-enacts the 14 stations of the cross. Easter Sunday: the Pope's blessing from the balcony of St Peter's (www.vatican.va). **1 May** Spring music festival in Piazza San Giovanni. **May/June** Dolce Vita Jazz Festival at the Palma Club (www.lapalmaclub.it) and the Parco della Musica. **29 June** Feast day of Rome's patron saints, Peter and Paul, when the city shuts down. **September** Contemporary-photography festival FotoGrafia (www.fotografiafestival.it). Also, La Notte Bianca: all-night music, dance and theatre (www.lanottebianca.it). RomaEuropa Festival: theatre, music and dance events (www.romaeuropa.net). **25 December** Christmas blessing from the Pope, delivered at noon.

WORTH GETTING OUT OF BED FOR

Viewpoint Piazza del Campidoglio by night, for panoramas over the Forum and the Palatine.
Arts and culture Rome's importance to Western civilisation is inscribed in its imposing historical sites: the Pantheon, the Colosseum, the Forum, St Peter's and the Vatican, the Sistine Chapel. Palazzo Doria Pamphilj is a mansion housing a gallery of 15th- to 18th-century art; Villa Borghese boasts a magnificent art collection and spectacular grounds.
Something for nothing A stroll at sunset in the lush Pincio Gardens, above Piazza del Popolo.
Shopping Via Condotti, starting at the base of the Spanish Steps, is Rome's most prominent shopping street; Via Frattina runs parallel, along the same lines. Via del Corso sells younger styles. More interesting shopping can be found near Piazza del Popolo. On Via Nazionale, you'll find leather stores and a handful of boutiques. Via Sistina is good for small, stylish outlets. Porta Portese open-air fleamarket in Trastevere is the largest in Europe, open on Sundays from 05h until around 14h.
Tourist tick box The Colosseum ❑ The Sistine Chapel ❑ The Spanish Steps ❑

CAFÉS

Bar della Pace on Via della Pace (686 1216) is a social institution. For the aperitivo – a drink before dinner, 18h–21h, head down to Campo de' Fiori. **Friends** on Piazza Trilussa, and **Red**, the bar in the Auditorium di Santa Cecilia on Via della Conciliazione, are also good options.

BARS AND RESTAURANTS

On Piazza Augusto Imperatore: **Gusto** (322 6273) is a restaurant, pizzeria, wine bar and bookshop all in one, good for weekend brunch. Originally a farmhouse, **Casina Valadier** on Piazza Bucarest (6992 2090) is a café/restaurant with terraces, neo-classical columns and a beautiful garden. **Arancia Blu**, on Via dei Latini (445 4105), is Rome's best vegetarian restaurant, a rarity in these parts. Great for lunch for omnivores, too. **Il Drappo** on Vicolo del Malpasso (687 7365) is an inventive Sardinian restaurant; for pudding, try the *seadas* (cheese-stuffed fried cake in dark honey). **Camponeschi** on Piazza Farnese (687 4927) serves some of the best fish in Rome. Get seats outdoors at **Santa Lucia** on Largo Febo (6880 2427), to eat Neapolitan-leaning pasta, seafood and vegetarian dishes in a spectacular location. **Ketumbar** on Via Galvani (5730 5338) is a restaurant/bar serving fusion cuisine, with a sleek, minimalist interior – a great base for your entire evening.

NIGHTLIFE

Spago on Via Monte Testaccio is a bar/music venue/gallery space, with live music early evenings, and dancey beats later on. The terrace at **Hotel Aleph** on Via San Basilio is a popular summer drinking spot, as is the courtyard in the Hotel de Russie, where you'll find **Stravinskj Bar** on Via del Babu (32 88 81). **Supperclub** on Via de'Nari is down a narrow alley, with no sign on the door, but don't be put off – it's set in a gorgeous restored third-century mansion, with drapes and plush white beds. **Bloom** on Via del Teatro Pace (6880 2029) is an Italian restaurant/sushi bar that becomes a nightclub after dinner. Popular in summer, **Goa** on Via Libetta is a mixed/gay club that plays house, hip hop and jungle. **Art Café** on Via del Galoppatoio is another restaurant that turns into a club in the summer: door policy is strict, so it's worth booking a table for dinner. In winter, visit **La Maison** on Vicolo dei Granari.

International Wine Academy

CITY   ROME
STYLE   WINE-LOVERS' WORLD
SETTING   A STAGGER FROM THE SPANISH STEPS

MTWTF**SS**MTWTFSSMTWTFSSMTWTFSSMTWTFSSMTWT
ROMA

'If you can tear yourself away from this palatial heaven,
the most exclusive quarter of the city is at your feet'

TWTFSSMTWTFSSMTWTFSSMTWTFSSMTWTFSS

We're in the heart of Rome, standing with our backs to the Piazza di Spagna, searching for our luxury hotel, which should be exactly here, and we find – a metro station. Some mistake, surely? But no. Rome is an ancient place, specialising in the unexpected. To our right, an arched stone doorway appears, only a few steps from a hole-in-the-wall pizza place and the metro entrance – and so does Roman paradise. Glassed off from the street bustle, the tiny reception of Il Palazzetto (the building which houses the Wine Academy) leads to a remarkable wrought-iron and marble staircase (as featured in Bertolucci's 1998 film *Besieged*). The stairs wend upward to the garden restaurant, library and salon/wine bar, and further to rooms and a rooftop terrace. (A petite lift, complete with floor mosaic, is available for those who can't or won't do stairs.) As there are only four guest rooms, the place feels as if it is ours: all ours. With no signs of other occupants, it is as if we have walked into our own Roman villa. Cool.

Getting us more aquiver is Il Palazzetto's location. This island of serenity and elegance lies in the heart of the Roman tourist beast, only a few short metres from the Spanish Steps. In fact, the view from the terrace onto the 18th-century landmark is absurdly perfect – you're the envy of every tourist who looks at you as if to ask, 'How'd you get there?'. Little wonder that the Roman family who once lived here preferred it to their palazzo. The bedroom views are also ridiculously spectacular – not that you'll stare out of the windows for long. The private spaces are quiet and airy, lulling the world away. Kingsize beds are swathed in voluptuous yet unisex fabrics and the plasma TV screen is Goldilocks-size (ie: just right). The marble bathrooms seem demure. Upon inspection, they're quite naughty, with their discreetly-mirrored walls, large old-fashioned showerheads that can easily wet two, and a bath huge enough for a pair of dirty people.

Three years of refurbishment have restored the once-abandoned Il Palazzetto to a balanced, timeless style. It is not starched and traditional like its big sister, the Hassler Hotel (where you go for breakfast: no breakfast in bed here as yet, alas). Now it is home to Rome's International Wine Academy, which means there are 400 different wines available at dinner. (Fortunately, the wine tasting every evening is limited to four bottles.) The restaurant, sheltered in the covered garden, serves wildly tasty traditional dishes given a modern touch by Roman chef Antonio Martucci. And the service couldn't be more helpful or wittier. ('This is not dangerous,' says one waiter as he gestures to a bread roll – then to the latest bottle: 'This is.') So any lovers staying at the Wine Academy will be faced with the eternal question: 'Do we stay here or go out?' Choosing between the Inner Rome or the Outer Rome has never been so ruddy difficult.

If you can tear yourself away from this palatial heaven, ignoring the bottles of luscious wine in your mini-bar, the most exclusive quarter of the city is at your feet, literally. You won't even need a friendly Roman taxi. The upmarket shopping streets of Via Condotti and its environs lie on a gentle slope away from the hotel entrance. For a quick, no-frills slice with a genuine smile, Pizza Mariotti is that odd place we saw facing the hotel entrance. It turns out to be a godsend for the starving: the room is so lovely that we regularly miss lunch. Another salvation is the ordinary-looking Caffetteria DoBar on Via della Carrozze. There, kindly waiters help make embarrassing map-reading a less painful event.

Despite being told that Romans don't do pre-dinner drinks, we decide to chance it and scamper across the hotel's metal catwalk to the front of Trinita dei Monti. From there, we trot along to Hotel Aleph. This is a Philippe Starck homage with a playfully decorated bar, lined with gratis snacks. We sample a bit too much of a very delicious really-I-mustn't-but-yes-please prosecco called Deco Conti Bernardo before we stagger out to a cab. (Roman taxis are consistently great: clean, fast, professional and multilingual.) Following in Fellini's fork-steps, we go against our concierge's advice and head ↓

to Otello alla Concordia on Via della Croce, where the great director himself often dined. Alas, the place – heaving yet unremarkable – did not live up to its illustrious past, reminding us of any depressing greasy spoon off London's Old Compton Street. Both feeling like idiots for not listening to Wine Academy wisdom, we drag our sorry tails to Via del Babuino, to the beautifully minimal indoor/outdoor Stravinskj Bar, which lies within Hotel de Russie. After considerable lubrication (prosecco not as nice as that at the Aleph), we head back to the hotel.

This one-time home street of Fellini is an antique-lover's dream, but a road that loves men more than women: cobblestones seem purpose-designed to wrench off all high-heeled footwear. (As if Fellini hadn't done enough to us that night, what with his less-than-illustrious favourite restaurant. Next time, we'll listen to what the concierge says.) In the morning, we are feeling worse for wear and tear, but we sleep in soundly, not hearing a single tourist shout. We learn one thing for certain, however: when in Rome, wherever we went and whatever we did, we returned to the Wine Academy with slight regrets that we'd left at all.

Reviewed by Karen Krizanovich

NEED TO KNOW

Rooms Four.
Rates €200–€350, including breakfast.
Check-out Midday.
Room service This is not really available.
Facilities All rooms have plasma televisions with satellite and 24-hour high-speed internet connection, and the mini-bar has an extensive selection of wines.
Children An extra bed can be provided if necessary.
Also The Wine Academy runs wine courses and private wine tastings (there are two classrooms on the ground floor) as well as guided tours to Italian vineyards.

IN THE KNOW

Recommended rooms The Black Room at the top of the hotel. All come with views of the Spanish Steps.
Hotel bar The bar has a wine list with a choice of more than 400 bottles, and a roaring fire in winter. Perfect for warm weather, the rooftop bar is open Monday–Friday 18h30–midnight.
Hotel restaurant On the second floor, the hotel restaurant offers traditional Italian food with a twist, Monday–Friday 13h–15h; dinner until 22h30. You can also eat lunch and dinner in the more intimate surroundings of the library, and in the garden in the summer.
Top table In the summer, grab a place on the terrace.
Dress code Informal, but zhuzh up for dinner.

LOCAL EATING AND DRINKING

Il Prado on Via Mameli is always buzzing, owing to great food at good prices – no need to book. Also good for a quick pitstop: **Pizza Mariotti** on Vicolo del Bottino and **Caffetteria DoBar** on Via delle Carrozze. The terrace at **Hotel Aleph** on Via San Basilio and **Stravinskj Bar** in the Hotel de Russie on Via del Babuino are great spots for a drink in summer. **Reef**, also on Piazza Augusto Imperatore (6830 1430), is a popular haunt for Oriental-influenced Italian food. **Boccondivino** on Piazza di Campo Marzio (6830 8626) is all modern art and 16th-century columns, and lives up to its 'divine mouthful' name.

 A bottle of wine, selected by the director of the Wine Academy. Register your Smithcard online, then show your card at check-in, to claim your offer.

Get a room! Use our free online booking service: check availability and make reservations through www.mrandmrssmith.com.

SMITH CONCIERGE Registered Smith cardholders can call +44 (0)20 7978 7333 and have Original Travel book everything from your flights to your day trips, at no extra charge.
Original idea A guided tour of Rome by moped. You will be collected by an Italian guide, taken to the moped-hire depot, and then guided through the streets of Rome *ragazzi*-style.

International Wine Academy of Rome 8 Vicolo del Bottino, Rome 00187 (+39 06 6990878)
info@wineacademyroma.com; www.wineacademyroma.com

VENICE

Venice

'Venice is like eating an entire box of chocolate liqueurs at one go'
Truman Capote

M T W T F S S M T W T F S S M T W T F **S S** M T W T F S S M T W T F S S M T W T
ITALIA

MTWTFSSMTWTFSSMTWTFSSMTWTFSSMTWTFSSMTWTFSS

VENICE

It may seem curious in a city that sits out in the sea and is characterised by its glittering waterways, that it's walking you should prepare for when you visit. Truly one of the most beautiful cities on earth, despite throngs of tourists; it's a maze in which to lose yourself and leave the real world behind, wandering its charming, traffic-free alleys. With most of its buildings right on the water's edge, La Serenissima hides all the snap-happy sightseers well; drift along one of the hundreds of canals by gondola or watertaxi, and float back in time as you admire Byzantine, Gothic, Renaissance and Baroque architecture. Give the familiar, much-filmed Piazza San Marco a chance to sink in, then follow the locals away from the main drags to the best restaurants, hidden churches and lively markets. The nightlife culture is less than sophisticated, but with so much history to absorb, and palazzi and piazze to discover, this is a place for early nights and days spent strolling, soaking up the atmosphere of a unique environment and life on the water in the romance capital of the world.

GETTING THERE

Planes Marco Polo and Treviso airports serve Venice. From Marco Polo, take a speedboat to travel into the centre by style (€85). From Treviso, it's a 25-min taxi journey (€70); or hop on a ATVO Eurobus (about €4,30); it takes 80 mins.
Trains The station is on the Grand Canal, so jump on a watertaxi or the Grand Canal waterbus.
Automobiles Avoid taking a car; you have to park on the mainland and get a train or watertaxi.

DO GO / DON'T GO

August is hot, sticky and full of tourists. Autumn can be lovely.

VERY VENETIAN

Have a coffee in Piazza San Marco, where the first cup was served. Journey into a romantic otherworld on a gondola ride. A masked ball – find a local to take you to the best.

LOCAL KNOWLEDGE

Taxis Use waterbuses (€5 a journey). They all take the same route; the difference is how many stops they make. You can hail or call a watertaxi to access the smaller canals; it costs about €80 an hour but whisks you across the water James Bond-style in a classic wooden Riva speedboat.
Tipping culture Five to ten per cent is expected.
Packing tips Comfortable shoes; mosquito repellent in summer.
Recommended reads *Death in Venice* by Thomas Mann; *The Comfort of Strangers* by Ian McEwan; *A History of Venice* by John Julius Norwich.
Cuisine Traditional dishes include *fegato alla Veneziana* (calf's liver), cuttlefish in its ink, and seafood risotto. Wines are among Italy's best.
Currency Euro.
Dialling codes Country code for Italy: 39. Venice: 041.

DIARY

February Venice Carnival for masked mayhem (www.carnivalofvenice.com).
June The Biennale art-world extravaganza, every two years (www.labiennale. org). **July** Fiesta del Redentore: fireworks commemorating the end of the 16th-century plague. **September** Regatta Storica boat race, with magnificent gondolas and gondoliers in full regalia. Venice Film Festival on the beach (www.veneziafilmfestival.com).

WORTH GETTING OUT OF BED FOR

Viewpoint Enjoy a 360-degree look across the city from the Campanile di San Marco.

Arts and culture Venice is packed full of churches, museums and galleries. We love the Museum of Modern Art (San Stae waterbus stop) and the Peggy Guggenheim Collection in Dorsoduro (www.guggenheim-venice.it), right next to both hotels.

Something for nothing Get a taste of what it feels like to be on a gondola for next to nothing: look for the yellow 'Traghetto' signs and follow them to the water. It's a shuttle gondola service that costs 40c. If you want one to yourself, the average price is €100 an hour.

Shopping You'll find all the designer labels around San Marco, and especially on Calle Larga 22 Marzo. Boutiques and gift shops line the streets between Piazza San Marco and the Rialto. Don't buy masks in the tourist area: close to the hotels is Ca'Macana on Calle delle Botteghe, which made the masks for *Eyes Wide Shut*. For something different, buy a *forcole*, the wooden oar rest on a gondola; Saverio Pastor's workshop is on Fondamenta Soranzo in Dorsoduro (522 5699). For Murano glass, try to get to the island of Murano itself.

And... Visit the town of Asolo, among the cypress-covered Dolomite hills, or the island of Torcello, the site of the original main square. The fish market in Rialto runs Tuesdays to Saturdays. Venice has a beach: you can hire cabanas for the day, but they're not cheap.

Tourist tick box A gondola ride ❏ Ponte dei Sospiri (Bridge of Sighs) ❏ Piazza San Marco ❏

CAFES

A coffee in Piazza San Marco won't come cheap, but there's a reason why the tourists flock there – it's spectacular; and if you're lucky you'll have an orchestral soundtrack. Head to Campo Santa Margherita, where students, bohemian types and families gather to eat. **Al Marca** on San Polo is good for a pre-dinner drink if you're north of Ponte Rialto.

BARS AND RESTAURANTS

For a cosy, wine-bottles-along-the-wall kind of osteria, try **Ristorante Cantina Canaletto** at Castello 5490 (521 2661). **Trattoria alle Testiere** on Calle del Mondo Novo (522 7220) specialises in fish. At **Bancogiro** on Campo San Giacometto (523 2061), ask for a window seat. **Trattoria do Forni** on Calle Specchieri (523 2148) is very classical; book dinner in the Orient Express room. **Ristorante da Fiore** on Calle del Scaleter (721 308) is one of the best restaurants; book a month in advance. **Poste Vecie**, on Rialto Pescheria (721 822), is Venice's oldest restaurant, reached by a private bridge. **Il Refolo** is a great pizzeria near the Museum of Modern Art (524 0016), though not open all year round. **Anice Stellato** on Fondamenta della Sensa, Cannaregio (720 744) does fabulous fish with subtle spicing. **Locanda Montin** on Fondamenta di Borgo (522 7151) serves great antipasti on a vine-covered terrace.

NIGHTLIFE

Sip a bellini on the floating pontoon of **Cip's Club**, watching the sun set over the water. (Hotel Cipriani operates a free boat service to and from its private landing stage.) Try **Centrale** on Piazza San Marco, for good tunes and great cocktails. **Taverna da Baffo** in Campo Sant'Agostin stays open until 02h.

Ca Maria Adele

CITY   VENICE
STYLE   BAROQUE ELEGANCE
SETTING CANALSIDE CHARM

'Absolutely Venetian, but its African wood, polished
concrete and laid-back bohemian atmosphere mean it is
also modern and sexy'

M T W T F S S M T W T F S S M T W T F S S M T W T F S S M T W T F S S M T W T
VENEZIA

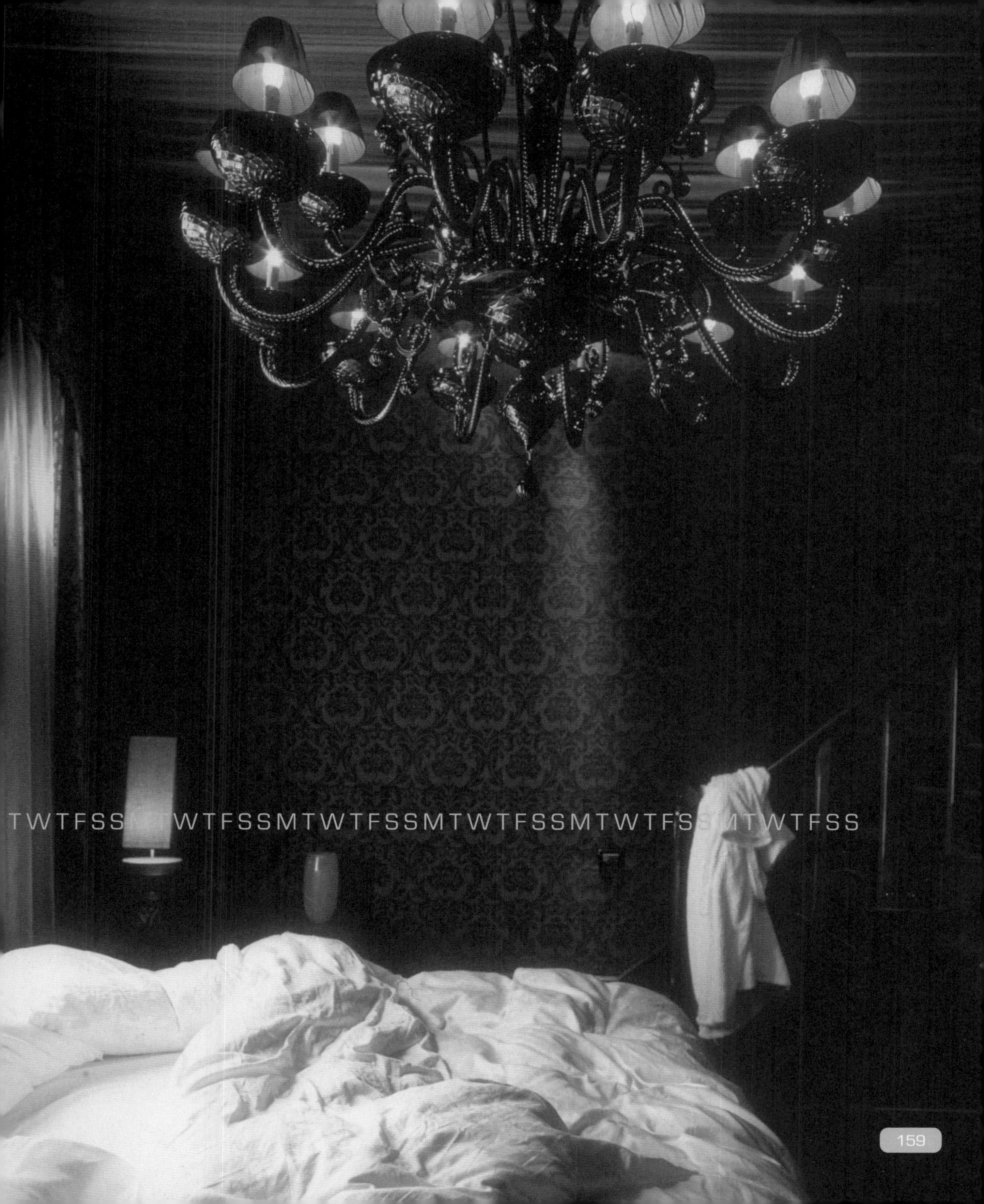

I'm lying in a Jacuzzi bath, bubbles up to my ears, glass of champagne in hand, gazing out of the window, blinking into the setting Italian sun. Just beneath my window I can hear the canal lapping at the walls of the hotel, as the bells of Santa Maria della Salute chime the hour. I know that there is a man in a striped shirt, boater and jaunty necktie pushing a gondola along the canal below, because I can hear his pole dip in and out of the water, along with his voice echoing up the walls of the narrow waterway. Really, all that's missing is the ice-cream.

The thing about Venice is this: all the clichés are true. It really is that beautiful; it really is that romantic; it really does take your breath away. And there is nowhere else like it on earth – unless you count the fake one they built in Las Vegas, but as someone who's experienced its swimming-pool waterways, fake foliage, piped synthesised Vivaldi, plastic bridges and wipe-clean surfaces, let's just say it doesn't have quite the same charm.

Hotel-wise, what you want in such an architectural museum of a city is something chic, sophisticated and as far from the madding crowds as possible (and the crowds can be quite something, especially in summer). With its huge Murano chandeliers, flock wallpaper and heavy damask fabrics, the Ca Maria Adele is absolutely Venetian, but its African wood, polished concrete and laid-back, bohemian atmosphere mean it is also undeniably modern and sexy. Located right opposite the Salute, it is in the heart of Venice's most tranquil area, the art quarter, (the Accademia and the Peggy Guggenheim Collection are both nearby), and the only tourists you are likely to come across are lost ones.

The galleries, jewellery shops and bars nearby all serve locals; forget the hotels of the masses around Piazza San Marco – the Adele is infinitely cooler. So, what I really need to make my bliss complete is a handsome Mr Smith at the other end of the bath. But I don't have one; instead, I have a very platonic Mrs Smith, and 15 years of friendship are enough for her to know she really doesn't want to share a bath with me.

Strangely, as the weekend unfolds, we realise this is not a problem. Our lover becomes Venice, which, at every twist of mediaeval passageway, every turn of canal and every step of ancient flagstone, causes sharp intakes of breath and ripples of pleasure. And there's Nicola, the ravishing owner of the hotel (fantasising about running off with him on a gondola – who, me?), who performs all the necessary duties of a dominant male: hailing watertaxis, booking restaurants, bringing us coffee/champagne/heart-melting smiles.

Indeed, the gentlemen of Venice couldn't be more delighted to find two girls wandering their city unsquired, and we ended up on a tour of Venice that you won't find in any guidebook – except, of course, this one. After dinner at Cipriani's (don't bother with Harry's Bar – we found it squalid and boring in comparison; take the private speedboat at the end of the Cipriani jetty to the hotel and have the same bellini there, among oriental gardens and flowering jasmine), our speedboat driver felt unable to let two ladies disappear off into the night on their own. Instead, he led us through the back streets of the city to Bar Centrale, which must be Venice's only hip and happening cocktail joint. They make a mean mojito, framed by blue lighting and brushed concrete and steel, and the DJ plays some surprisingly funky tunes. Then our escort recommended Piccolo's, a nightclub that throbbed into the early hours of the morning. It seemed that all Venice's gilded youth were there and, my, weren't the boys handsome? And didn't they dance well? And weren't they persuasive? ↓

Our stumbling into the hotel at 05h didn't seem to worry Nicola at all (although Mrs Smith was convinced that he looked jealous), and the big double bed with 300-threadcount sheets ensured that, by midday, we both felt much better than we deserved. The Adele serves breakfast (coffee, pastries, eggs – in a room with gorgeously ornate floor-to-ceiling windows overlooking the canal), but for serious eating in La Serenissima, you have to get out and about.

The Cipriani experience was mouthwateringly expensive, but when the food is that good it seems worth it. Much more affordable is the (again, local) Locanda Montin, a legendary artists' and poets' haunt that has a beautiful terrace covered with vines, where delicious antipasti, fish and meat are served. That Lord Byron died fat from Venetian pasta is no wonder when you discover he used to eat at the Montin.

At this point, you really must take an espresso in the Piazza San Marco, and gaze at the gold-mosaic façade of the Basilica; and you really must let one of those charming gondoliers push you about the canals, so you can lie back and gaze up at centuries' worth of architecture. And I tell you this because, if Venice is not your principal lover for the weekend, you are probably going to spend most of it flat on your back on one of the Adele's sumptuous beds, twisting the sheets around each other as the Salute chimes through the hours. And, I'm afraid, then you really would be missing out.

Reviewed by Tiffanie Darke

NEED TO KNOW

Rooms 14.
Rates From €240 (plus ten per cent tax), including breakfast .
Check-out Midday, but later on request.
Room service Only breakfast and drinks.
Facilities Private landing-stage for boats; plasma TVs and internet access in all the rooms.
Children The apartment suite has an extra room for children and babysitting can be arranged.
Also The hotel organises personal tours around the city. Choose from a boat or gondola ride to the beautiful island of Murano, or across to the Grand Canal to view the Royal Palace.

IN THE KNOW

Recommended rooms We loved the themed rooms, in particular the Sala Noir, Doge and Fireplace rooms. Room 332 and the Moorish Room have the best views.
Hotel bar You can order evening drinks in the breakfast room or the Moroccan bar on the second floor, or in summer you can have a tipple brought to you on to the terrace.
Hotel restaurant Only breakfast is served. Italian-style afternoon tea is available on the terrace, weather permitting.
Dress code As romantic as you like.

LOCAL EATING AND DRINKING

Linea d'Ombra on Ponte de l'Umiltà (520 4720) is a great local restaurant on the canal. It is the perfect plot to head to in summer as it has a lovely terrace with views across to the Giudecca; the ambience is fantastic. The array of food often includes some surprise Venetian dishes, which are sure to tantalise the tastebuds of fish lovers. **Cantinone Storico** on Fondamenta Bragadin (523 9577) is good for seafood, and has an impressive wine cellar. Definitely try and get a seat by the canal, if the weather is mild, or sit by the window in winter. Ask the waiter to tell you about the specials – and then trust his recommendations. **Peggy Guggenheim Collection Café** in the 18th-century Palazzo Venier dei Leoni is a sophisticated spot for a coffee in the wonderful garden of the museum of modern art. Elegant and peaceful, it's no wonder the art lover also chose this to be her final resting place.

 A bottle of Valpolicella on the house. Register your Smithcard online, then show your card at check-in, to claim your offer.

Get a room! Use our free online booking service: check availability and make reservations through www.mrandmrssmith.com.

SMITH CONCIERGE Registered Smith cardholders can call +44 (0)20 7978 7333 and have Original Travel book everything from your flights to your day trips, at no extra charge.

Original idea We can organise something special the whole year round, but if you fancy visiting during the Venice Film Festival, why don't you allow us to book you into a screening? We'll even arrange entry to one of the after-parties.

Ca Maria Adele Dorsoduro 111, Venice 30123 (+39 041 520 3078)
info@camariaadele.it; www.camariaadele.it

'The perfect
location,
sufficiently off
the beaten
track for you
to amble the
neighbourhood
in peace'

Charming House DD724

CITY VENICE
STYLE ICONOCLASTIC DESIGNER DEN
SETTING DISCREET IN DORSODURO

M T W T F S S M T W T F **S S** M T W T F S S M T W T F S S M T W T F S S M T W T
VENEZIA

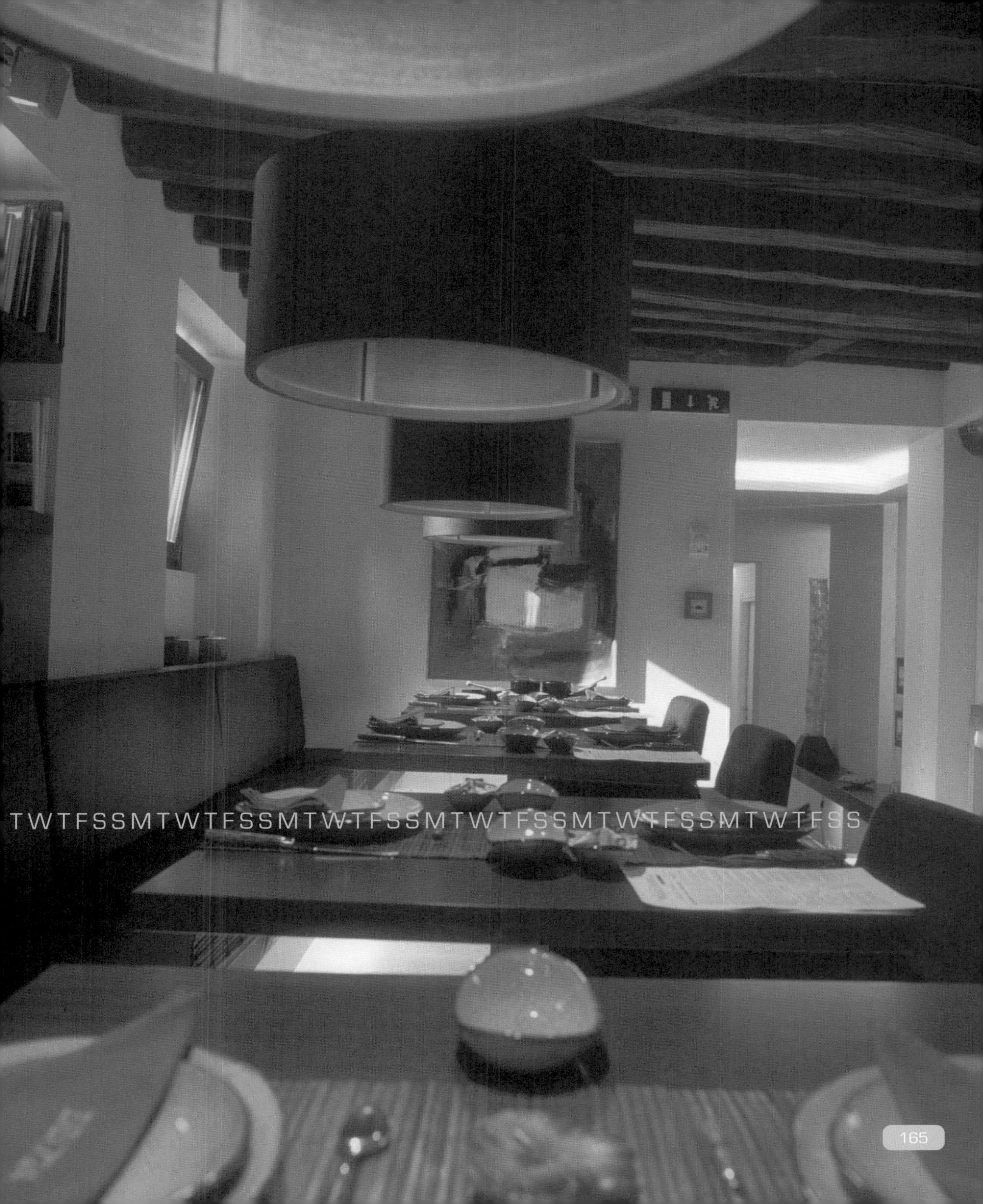
TWTFSSMTWTFSSMTWTFSSMTWTFSSMTWTFSSMTWTFSS

Arriving in Italy's most romantic city by train, we're a little concerned our trip is going to be more Venice Beach than La Venezia when we're swamped by English-speaking backpackers. It doesn't take long on the taxi boat that's going to speed us to Accademia, for the realisation to sink in: this may be a city drowning in tourists, but it is so beautiful that you barely notice.

It's with eager anticipation that we carry our overnight bags to our design-conscious abode for the weekend – but will somewhere contemporary really feel right in these pastel-hued, fairytale environs? When we find the hotel, hiding down a narrow alley in Dorsoduro, we know instantly we are somewhere really special. Making the most of every inch of space, it's the hotel equivalent of the Smart Ka. From the outside, you might expect it to be cramped, but it's a design triumph. We're led up past the only communal area (two chairs on a landing, and

a breakfast area) and into our room. DD724 may not be the only hotel in the world to feature clean lines and a brown-and-white colour palette, though it's a stroke of contemporary cool unique to these parts. What's so unexpected about the Charming House, as DD724 is also known, is that there is also an incredible warmth to the rooms. Stylish yet cosy modern furnishings are softened with touches such as the loosely knitted wool blanket knotted at the end of the bed. You glance from a widescreen TV to an open window revealing a scene that EM Forster would be inspired by. Since we booked last-minute and missed out on one of the more palatial Junior Suites, we assume our bathroom will be snug, yet it still manages to impress, right down to its own range of olive-oil products. (In a reversal of roles this trip, Mr Smith is the one to squirrel away toiletries to take home, and the aftershave balm has him cooing like a 13-year-old girl at a Rimmel stand.)

Great fun as it is settling into such an abode, it's hard to imagine anyone coming to this city to squander much of the day in their room. But early nights are de rigueur in Venice, and we know there's plenty of exploring time awaiting us tomorrow. The wonderfully helpful young lady behind the tiny front desk recommends a canalside trattoria around the corner. In Venice, recommendation is crucial. Cantinone Storico turns out to be the perfect option. The *risotto terra mare* is out of this world, and the monkfish with fresh artichokes is absolutely delicious.

By midnight, much of Venice is sound asleep, so we decide on a treat while the going's calm: a gondola trip. We head towards a waiting boat to enquire how much – €100! Eventually we barter him down to €80 for 40 minutes. Feeling as though we've got a bargain, we pile on board. It is incomparably romantic, almost haunting, as we're gently nudged along the dark, deserted canals; yet we spend the first ten minutes trying to calculate how much the gondolier must earn in a year. A friend of his calls down from a window, and they strike up voluble chat – clearly discussing whether to moor the yacht at St Barths or St Tropez this New Year's Eve. Still, it's the perfect starlit end to our night.

The next morning we're out of our room by 9h30, and first to breakfast – most civilised. Everything is laid out in ordered presentation, with a grid of little jams and a neat line of croissants on offer. Even our eggs and bacon is served in a nouvelle-cuisine manner. But the biggest impression is made by the pistachio spread. Nutella's dark-green-emulsion cousin is amazing. After such a satisfying start to the day, we leave not only contented, but, thanks again to the staff at DD724, with details of how to order *crema di pistacchio*. ↓

Our first stop is next-door: the Guggenheim Museum. Formerly the home of Peggy Guggenheim, the Palazzo Venier dei Leoni now houses masterpieces by Brancusi, Picasso, Kandinsky, Pollock and Ernst, among others. A magnificent collection in truly charming surroundings, there's nowhere like it. A browse of the gift shop, then it's time to brave the more traditional sights. En route to Piazza San Marco, it's hard to resist a fresh slice of pizza from a kiosk next to the hotel; it hits the spot and, a rare treat in Venice, it's a bargain. We now have the strength to face the hordes, and head to the epicentre. The Basilica San Marco is indeed breathtaking from the outside, but as we're not feeling up to a long wait queueing, we head to the Campanile instead. A lift takes you to the top of the tower, where a spectacular view awaits. It's a great way to get a sense of Venice's unique layout, and how far out at sea you are.

It's when you escape the mêlée of pigeons, children and many visitors, young and old, that you realise DD724 is in the perfect location, sufficiently off the beaten track for you to amble its neighbourhood in peace. After an afternoon of window-shopping, strolling and stopping off for cappuccini, we make our way towards Campo Santa Margherita. Sitting alfresco at one of the many cafés and bars, surrounded by students, artists and Italian families, we order the traditional aperitif: a spritz. Be warned, the bittersweet symphony of this Seventies-looking cocktail of Campari, white wine and soda is not for all palates. Still, our fizzy red drink is perfect for a toast, and we raise a glass to the most delightful 24 hours imaginable.

Reviewed by Mr & Mrs Smith

NEED TO KNOW

Rooms Seven.
Rates €200–€350.
Check-out Midday.
Room service Breakfast only.
Facilities LCD TVs and WiFi internet access in all rooms.
Children Rooms E and G have room for a small bed; rooms C and D can be annexed. Babysitters can be arranged. DD724 also has an apartment that's ideal for families wanting more space.

IN THE KNOW

Recommended rooms Room B has a view of the Giudecca Canal. Room G has its own small terrace for breakfast.
Hotel bar Fully stocked mini-bars in each room; no actual hotel bar, but drinks can be provided.
Hotel restaurant Only breakfast is served, but it's exceptional.
Dress code Whatever you like.

LOCAL EATING AND DRINKING

Just around the corner, **Cantinone Storico** on Fondamenta Bragadin (523 9577) serves great traditional Italian food. Book a table by the canal in summer, or the window in winter. Their seasonal specialities are mouthwatering, and if you can see the fish with fresh artichoke sauce, get it. A fantastic area to head to for lunch, dinner or a pre-dinner spritz is Campo Santa Margherita. There are tables and chairs scattered outside the many eateries on offer.
Trattoria due Torri (523 8126; closed Sundays) is nothing flash, but it's a great place to go for an inexpensive, delicious lunch or a relaxed dinner; choice is limited, but, as often, this indicates that the food is authentic/homemade. **Casin dei Nobili** (241 1841), off Campo San Barnaba (use the Ca' Rezzonico vaporetto stop), is also great for lunch, particularly if you like pizza, and a little less expensive than many other places. Sit on the terrace even if it's cloudy; if it starts to rain they just press a button and a roof appears. For late-night drinking, track down **Taverna da Baffo** (520 8862; closed Sundays) in Campo Sant' Agostin, open until 02h. It's a favourite haunt of students, but as one of the waiters rightly remarked it can really 'move'.

 Free entrance for two to the Guggenheim Collection; a DD724 T-shirt for guests who book a suite. Register your Smithcard online, then show your card at check-in, to claim your offer.

Get a room! Use our free online booking service: check availability and make reservations through www.mrandmrssmith.com.

SMITH CONCIERGE Registered Smith cardholders can call +44 (0)20 7978 7333 and have Original Travel book everything from your flights to your day trips, at no extra charge.
Original idea Take a private speedboat, *Dolce Vita* style, to Torcello Island. Here you can gaze at the 11th-century cathedral over a romantic meal at the Locanda Cipriani, where Hemingway stayed in 1949 while writing *Across the River and into the Trees*.

Charming House DD724 Ramo da Mula, Dorsoduro 724, Venice 30123 (+39 041 277 0262) info@dd724.it; www.dd724.com

MTWTFSSMTWTFSSMTWTFSSMTWTFSSMTWTFSSMTWT

MONTE CARLO

MONACO

MONTE CARLO
Columbus Hotel

TWTFSSMTWTFSSMTWTFSSMTWTFSSMTWTFSSMTWTFSS
MONACO

MONTE CARLO ●

Monte Carlo

CITYSCAPE RITZY RIVIERA
CITY LIFE IN THE FAST LANE

MTWTFSSMTWTFSSMTWTFSSMTWTFSSMTWTFSSMTWT
MONTE CARLO

'If heaven's where you go if you're good while you're on Earth,
then Monaco is where you go if you're good while you're in heaven'
American Dreams

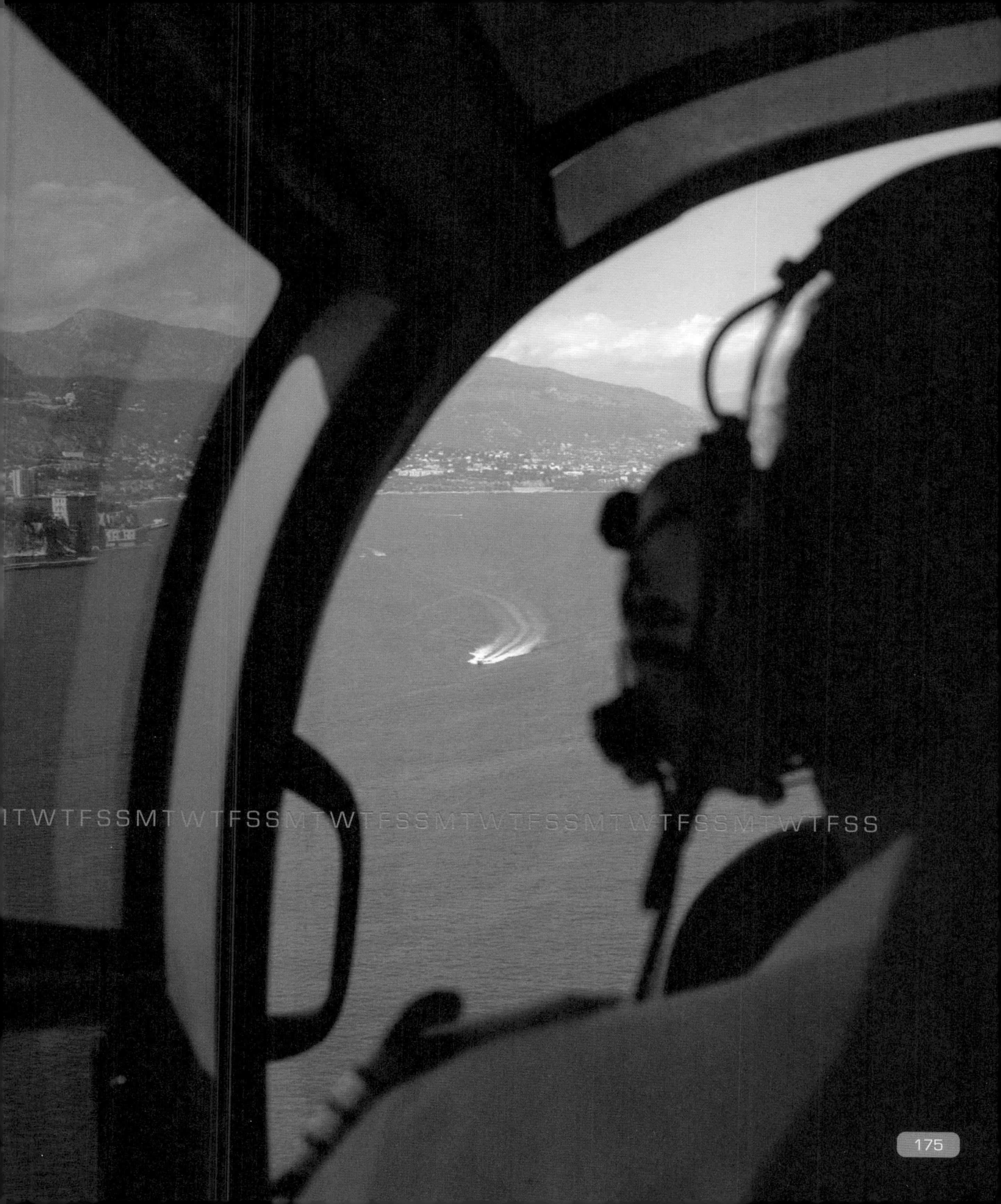

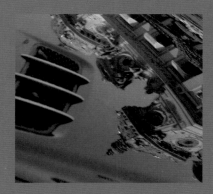

MONTE CARLO

If Monaco were in the thesaurus, it would be a synonym for casinos, luxury yachts and Formula 1. Perched along a three-mile stretch of the Mediterranean, this French-Italian hybrid is the private playground of the Grimaldi family, who are its raison d'être (should the line die out, the principality would become part of France). Safe, clean and very showy, it can be intimidating at ten in the morning when most of its inhabitants look as though they've just stepped out of a photo shoot. But, as glossy as they appear, there's no Parisian attitude – these folk are as friendly as they come. And it's not nearly as expensive as people imagine: even arriving in true Monégasque style – from Nice by helicopter – is not unaffordable. On weekends, many locals head along the coast to St Tropez, leaving you the run of the Monte Carlo Opera House and Casino, and dozens of contemporary restaurants and clubs. But it's not all bright lights, small city: the narrow cobblestone streets of Monaco-Ville on the Rock lead you through a mediaeval and Gothic past, and the 13th-century prince's palace is one of the most historic sites on the Côte d'Azur. Vive Monte Carlo!

GETTING THERE

Planes The nearest airport is Nice, about 20 mins' drive away. Hire a car, get a bus (which takes 45 mins and costs about €23 return), or grab a taxi for around €70.

Helicopters Kick off your break *Dynasty*-style and take advantage of the half-hourly helicopter shuttle service from Nice airport; it takes just six mins and costs €70 or €135 return with Heli Air (92 05 00 50; www.heliair.monaco.com), or book with Monacair (97 97 39 00).

Trains Trains run regularly to and from Nice and other French cities.

Automobiles Driving to Monaco is easy and most hotels have their own carparks, but expect to pay a daily charge.

DO GO / DON'T GO

The sun is shining and there's a buzz in the air from April to September.

MIGHTY MONTE CARLO

Watch the Grand Prix. Gamble the night away at Casino de Monte Carlo, Café de Paris, or Le Sporting (membership not required, but don't forget ID). Take a gastronomic helicopter trip to Provence, through Heli Air or Monacair (see above).

LOCAL KNOWLEDGE

Taxis Hail a taxi from anywhere in the street.

Tipping Ten–12 per cent is normal.

Packing tips Your black credit card; your best party frock.

Recommended read *Tender is the Night* by F Scott Fitzgerald;

Cuisine Monégasque cuisine is influenced by classic French, Provençal and Italian cooking: expect to eat *bouillabaisse*, tapenade, great seafood – but also haute cuisine with fine wines.

Currency Euro.

Dialling codes Country code for Monaco: 377. No city code.

Also If you want to see the Grand Prix, make sure you book at least two years in advance as most of the hotels are filled by the racing teams.

DIARY

January Monte Carlo International Circus Festival in Fontvieille Big Top.
February Primo Cup sailing competition (www.yacht-club-monaco.mc).
April Tennis Masters (www.masters-series.com/montecarlo); Spring Arts Festival. **May** Formula 1 Monaco Grand Prix (www.monte-carlo.mc/formule1); Classic Car Grand Prix (www.acm.mc). **November** National Day. **December** Dance festival at GrimaldiForum and Salle des Variétés.

WORTH GETTING OUT OF BED FOR

Viewpoint From the exotic gardens, and from the square in front of the Prince's Palace.
Arts and culture In the Fontvieille Harbour, it's worth visiting the Prince of Monaco's private collection of classic cars (www.palais.mc).
Something for nothing The changing of the guard, every day at 11h55, at Place du Palais.
Shopping The main retail area is around Boulevard des Moulins and in the Metropole Mall; folk with simple sartorial tastes may find what's on offer overly glitzy and glam. If you fancy shopping in San Remo instead, you can charter a helicopter to Italy for the day through Heli Air.
And... Treat yourself to a mud or seaweed bath at the Monte Carlo Thalassotherapy Centre and Spa (92 16 40 40).
Tourist tick box The Prince's Palace ❑ Changing of the guard ❑ Casino de Monte Carlo ❑

CAFES

Café Grand Prix on Quai Antoine (93 25 56 90); **Café de Paris** on Place du Casino (92 16 20 00), and **Le Sporting** on Avenue Princesse Grâce (92 16 20 00), where summer concerts feature stars such as Diana Krall and Julio Iglesias, and you can gamble glamorously after 22h.

BARS AND RESTAURANTS

La Chaumière on Boulevard de l'Observatoire (93 01 77 68) is set in an exotic garden, where the food is cooked on an open fire. **Le Louis XV** on Place du Casino (92 16 29 76) is right next door to the Casino de Monte Carlo. **Restaurant Monkey** on the pedestrianised Rue Princesse Florestine (93 25 60 30), is good for lunch or a low-key supper. **Le Point Rouge** on Rue du Portier (97 77 03 04) is a dressy spot for an Asian-fusion dinner. **La Rose des Vents** on Plage du Larvotto (97 70 46 96) specialises in fish and has its own private beach area – perfect for those hot summer days. **Le Saint-Benoît**, on Avenue de la Costa (93 25 02 34), overlooks the port, offers great views of Grimaldi Rock and serves French cuisine. **Sass Café** on Avenue Princesse Grâce (93 25 52 00) is sumptuous, with a red-velvet interior, and a place to be seen over French and Italian cuisine accompanied by live music. It's always packed, so be prepared to get to know your neighbours. **Zebra Square**, on the top floor of the Grimaldi Forum, Avenue Princesse Grâce (99 99 25 50), is a lounge bar and restaurant that's great for modern French tapas, pre-dinner drinks or glam late-night DJ bar activity. During high season, book a table on the balcony for a sea view.

NIGHTLIFE

Restaurant **Point Rouge** is attached to a small, intimate club, all red and black. To sit at a table you have to buy a bottle, which will set you back €210 but gives you unlimited soft drinks. Very well-known, and very expensive. The *Saturday Night Fever*-vibe of **Jimmy'z** (92 16 22 77) on Avenue Princesse Grâce is old hat for some and fun for others, especially those in a big group. **Café Style** bar, overlooking the harbour, is where the stars go.**Stars n Bars** on Quai Antoine is full of sports, movie and music memorabilia thanks to visits from pop stars and racing drivers. **Club Karement** is still one of the new kids on the block, and the spot where everyone wants to ensure their name's on the guestlist – it's where the Amber Lounge goes on, in the Grimaldi Forum on Avenue Princesse Grace.

'For every whim and want,
this jewel in the Riviera has
the answer – it fizzes with
a thousand sparkles'

Columbus Hotel

CITY   MONTE CARLO
STYLE   JET-SET SECLUSION
SETTING ON THE WATERFRONT

MTWTFSSMTWTFSSMTWTF**SS**MTWTFSSMTWTFSSMTWT

MONACO

90

Columbus Monaco, Monte Carlo, Monaco

In the polished vernacular of my chosen profession –
diamond-broking – Monaco passes for a gleaming
D-flawless. A tax-free cauldron of iniquity, set amid
the platinum shoulders of the mountains, it fizzes with
a thousand sparkles – from dizzyingly high finance to
the glamour of showbiz. For every whim and want, this
jewel in the Riviera has the answer. As our helicopter
soars over the super-yachts on the inner harbour to land
at Monaco heliport, some six minutes from Nice airport,
it's like stepping out into a billionaire's Disneyland,
Treasure Island and Pleasure Island all rolled into one.
The closed, secretive, exclusive world of diamonds
may be a glamorous one, but this is certainly not bad.

The Columbus is a five-minute air-conditioned jaunt
from the heliport, and really is in the beating heart of
the principality – although nowhere in Monaco is
exactly remote. A step away from the hustle of the
streets, it's a calm refuge, designed by Amanda Rosa
to exude funky boutique charm, with acres of brushed
suede in rich chocolate browns, blacks and creams.
Angular striping adorns the carpets and upholstery;
the stealth-wealth decor is as discreet as the staff.

'Your usual room, Mr Bond,' I think I hear; really, the
amiable concierge staff greet me with 'Mr Duttson –
so nice to have you back. Everything is taken care of.'
Ken McCulloch (of Malmaison fame) has seen to it
that he and his business partner in the hotel, racing
driver David Coulthard, employ and retain the best,
with a company mantra of 'live life, love life'. We settle
for a sea-facing room with dramatic views of the pearly
waters of the French Riviera. Our keycard registers
green and we let ourselves into our own bubble of
comfort. Ambient melodies are emanating from a
CD, beckoning us into the boutique boudoir with its
dramatic, lush bed throws and sexy red nightlighting.

Though we love our new abode, we also want to see Monaco. It's race weekend, and the atmosphere is more charged than ever: helicopters launch and soar off the huge yachts in the bay, and adventures in town call us away from the serene luxury that will serve as our rest-chamber for the next two nights.

A short walk (after one of the chocolate martinis for which the Columbus is famed) from the rear of the hotel, and we're in the marina. Here, nestling in the heart of the restaurant district is an Italian gem (a baguette diamond, if you will) called La Salière. A favourite with the in-the-know crowd, the restaurant is usually rammed during lunchtimes, but a quiet word with the Columbus concierge and we're greeted with the ubiquitous: 'No problem, sir'. You get that a lot in Monaco. After a light refuel, we find that the shopping strip is a mere stroll away. It is unequivocal in its brashness: Gucci, Prada, Dolce & Gabbana, Armani, Valentino, Versace – you get the picture.

Around the principality, eye-candy, arm-candy, yacht-candy, car-candy – in fact, just about every kind of candy you care to mention – is there to be ogled, admired and savoured. Of course, race weekend is the big one, when Rainier's roads are blocked off and the petrolheads descend for a few days of unbridled thrills and spills.

We head to the Amber Lounge, a race-weekend A-list magnet beneath the infamous Zebra Square restaurant, just minutes from Place du Casino. For three nights a year, over race weekend, it is hosted by Sonia Irvine, sister of Eddie, who welcomes in a coterie of European sports stars, dignitaries, models and glamourpusses to dance the night away. ↓

After an evening of high-octane fun, we stroll in the warm Mediterranean haze, past the starting grid etched on the main thoroughfare, revelling in the oil and burnt rubber in the air, before heading back to the safety and seclusion of the Columbus. The restaurant is in full swing, serving a mixture of Mediterranean and continental dishes; Monaco's elite, enjoying the privacy, completes the scene. A cocktail later, served with nuts (the attention to detail is remarkable), we ascend to bed.

Our heavenly room takes on a new, night-time air; preparing to snooze is a joy. We find essential oils and rich-lather soaps on the polished bathroom shelves; bear-soft towels for post-bathing bliss; and couture linen sheets that cool and pamper even the most fervent insomniac. I drift off to thoughts of the perfect pink diamond passing into the hands of a movie couple, aboard a mogul's yacht in international waters… We need all the REM we can muster to replenish our souls for another day in the screaming metropolis of the world's richest acreage.

Reviewed by Neil Duttson

NEED TO KNOW

Rooms 181; there is also an apartment available on request.
Rates €245–€590.
Check-out Midday.
Room service 24-hour menu of snacks and salads.
Facilities Outdoor pool, gym and fitness centre, boutique, candlelight turndown service.
Children Special beds and cots; babysitters and nannies on request.

IN THE KNOW

Recommended rooms Ask for a sea view.
Hotel bar The cool, modern cocktail bar on the mezzanine floor, is popular with young guests and open until the last person leaves.
Hotel restaurant Last orders: 22h30 during the week, 23h at weekends. Modern Mediterranean cuisine with lots of fresh seafood, on the outside terrace or within the chocolate-brown restaurant.
Dress code Informal for lunch, dressier for dinner.
Top table On a balmy evening, book a round table on the terrace.

LOCAL EATING AND DRINKING

On Quai Jean-Charles Rey, **Waterfront** (92 05 90 99) is a see-and-be-seen spot for modern Med food. Of course getting a table here is no easy task – make sure you nook ahead. Also on QJCR in Fontvieille, is **La Salière** (92 05 25 82) which is a top spot for Italian fare. Or, a little further along the road, try the **Ship and Castle** (92 05 76 72), just moments from the Columbus. It is an English-style pub that's open until midnight. **Zebra Square** on Avenue Princesse Grâce (99 99 25 50) is a short taxi ride away, worth a visit for the panoramic sea views and outdoor seating. Also there is the Sass Café (93 25 52 00) renowned for its Monégasque and Italian cuisine overlooking the water – and, as with most of Monaco's hotspots, it's glossy clientele.

 A complimentary bottle of house champagne on arrival. Register your Smithcard online, then show your card at check-in, to claim your offer.

Get a room! Use our free online booking service: check availability and make reservations through www.mrandmrssmith.com.

SMITH CONCIERGE Registered Smith cardholders can call +44 (0)20 7978 7333 and have Original Travel book everything from your flights to your day trips, at no extra charge.
Original idea Let us reserve a balcony or boat deck for an exclusive view of the Grand Prix. Arguably the world's most challenging motor-racing events, the Monaco Grand Prix is the last 'street course' in the Formula One calendar. The circuit runs right through the narrow winding streets of the city centre along the water's edge, the Formula 1 cars speed right by the spectators.

Columbus Monaco 23 Avenue des Papalins, Monte Carlo MC 98000 (+377 (0) 92 05 90 00) info@columbushotels.com; www.columbushotels.com

AMSTERDAM

MTWTFSSMTWTFSSMTWTFSSMTWTFSSMTWTFSSMTWT

NETHERLANDS

AMSTERDAM
The Dylan Amsterdam
Hotel Seven One Seven

TWTFSSMTWTFSSMTWTFSSMTWTFSSMTWTFSSMTWTFSS
NEDERLAND

Amsterdam

CITYSCAPE	TOWNHOUSES AND WATERWAYS
CITY LIFE	LAID-BACK LAISSEZ-FAIRE

'In Amsterdam the water is the
mistress and the land the vassal'
Felix Marti-Ibanez

MTWTFSSMTWTFSSMTWTFSSMTWTFSSMTWTFSSMTWT

NEDERLAND

TWTFSSMTWTFSSMTWTFSSMTWTFSSMTWTFSS

AMSTERDAM

The city with a village mentality, where ducks compete for canal-bank space with disoriented tourists. There is no particular must-see in Amsterdam: just take it in, one café terrace at a time, as though you've always lived there. We all know that few capitals rival this one for hedonism. The open, friendly Dutch, with their history of tolerance, know how to deliver a good time – a *really* good time. But once you've had a go at the city's vices, and dipped into the heady club and bar culture, there's plenty more to experience, such as art collections at Rijksmuseum and the Van Gogh Museum. The city's labyrinthine layout means you need to know where you're going – but that's why we're here. Jump on a tram to find apparel and antiques in the picturesque Nine Streets area; get bar-hopping in central bourgeois neighbourhoods like the Pijp or the Jordaan; hire a bike and explore architecturally interesting enclaves Zuid and the Eastern Docklands; get a dose of visual Prozac from the sunflowers and tulips in Vondel Park; or hit the beach – it's only half an hour away. It's time to graduate from the red-light district and explore one of Europe's most picturesque, liveliest cities.

GETTING THERE

Planes A taxi from the airport costs around €45. For the most laid-back ride into town, Ralph's taxi service offers a superior, leather-interiored TV-toting Merc (email ralph.q.s@worldonline.nl).
Trains A 20-minute train from Schiphol airport to the city centre costs about €30 one-way.
Automobiles Parking is hellish. Everyone uses trams or a bicycle.

TO GO / DON'T GO

Weekends are busy all year round, and September is a big time for conferences, so book ahead.

ABSOLUTELY AMSTERDAM

Hire a six-person tandem with friends (www. amsterdamactief.nl). Visit a coffeeshop – follow Brad Pitt's lead and go to De Dampkring on Handboogstraat. Enjoy an tour of the canals in a skippered 'genie boat' (a former army vessel used for towing large objects), €70 an hour for two (5327 0076).

LOCAL KNOWLEDGE

Taxis There are ranks all over, but you can usually hail; tip ten per cent. Beware of unlicensed mini-cabs.
Tipping culture The Dutch aren't big tippers; ten per cent is usually about right, and it's common to give the bartender a euro with every round.
Packing tips Bicycle clips, puncture kit, an open mind.
Recommended read *The Diary of Anne Frank*; *Tulip Fever* by Deborah Moggach; *Girl with a Pearl Earring* by Tracy Chevalier.
Cuisine Hearty, rib-sticking Northern fare, as well as herring, smoked eel, and Indonesian *rijsttafel* (rice table), an army of small spicy dishes.
Currency Euro.
Dialling codes Country code for the Netherlands: 31. Amsterdam: 20.

DIARY

30 April Queen's Day – the whole of Amsterdam is on holiday and the canals come alive. **May** National Cycling Day on the second Saturday sees thousands pedalling through town. **August** Classical concerts on the canals; Gay Pride, when the city is awash with revellers (www.amsterdampride.nl).
5 December St Nicholas Day kicks off the Christmas festivities.

°C

J 4
F 3
M 3
A 6
M 8
J 12
J 15
A 17
S 17
O 14
N 11
D 7

WORTH GETTING OUT OF BED FOR

Viewpoint Owing to topography and building-height restrictions, nothing is that high up, but your best shot is the café on the sixth floor of Metz department store on Leidsestraat.

Arts and culture Van Gogh Museum (570 5200; www.vangoghmuseum.nl), Rijksmuseum (674 7047; www.rijksmuseum.nl), the Stedelijk Modern Art Museum (573 2911; www.stedelijk.nl).

Something for nothing In April or May, take a drive out to the tulip fields and feast your eyes.

Shopping For designer labels, go to PC Hooftstraat. We prefer the Nine Streets – a grid within the canal network that is packed with boutiques and curiosity shops. We love DOM on Spuistraat, for all kinds of items you never thought you needed. Spmrkt is a warehouse of all things retro and cool: books, fashion, furniture, art. Spiegelstraat is renowned for antiques. For markets, on Saturdays and Mondays head to Noordermarkt for organic food and bric à brac, or the bigger, touristier Waterlooplein market for good second-hand clothes. Albert Cuypmarkt in the Pijp claims to be Europe's longest street market. Visit the flower market – it's the only floating one in the world – and take home some tulip bulbs. it's located on the Singel canal between the Koningsplein and the Muntplein.

And… Go with the flow in restaurants – Dutch service can be very laid-back.

Tourist tick box Van Gogh Museum ❑ Anne Frank's House ❑ The flower market ❑

CAFES

De Taart van m'n Tante on Ferdinand Bolstraat is great for tea, coffee and unusual cakes. **Moko** on Amstelveld has a great shady terrace on a picturesque square. Between April and November, on a nice day, the beach at Amsterdam is a great alternative for a drink or lunch: the best bars at Bloemendaal are the Ibiza-style **Republiek** (www.republiek.tv), and **Bloomingdale** (bloomingdale.id-t.com), owned by an Amsterdam club promoter.

BARS AND RESTAURANTS

Cinema Paradiso on Westerstraat (623 7344) is an informal, modern Italian. **Odessa** (419 3010) is a boat near the islands, which serves international fusion cuisine and tends to kick off into a party after dinner. Cosmopolitan **Brasserie Harkema** on Nes (428 2222) used to be a tobacco hall. Ask for a table on the platform. **De Kas** on Kamerlingh Onneslaan (462 4562) is a little way outside town but worth a visit, particularly if you can get a kitchen table; let the chef decide what you eat. **Bond** on Valeriusstraat (676 46 47) has plush gold Fifties decor, and is intimate and relaxed. The **Blonde Hollander** on Leidsekruisstraat (627 0521) is recommended for a truly traditional Dutch experience in hip surroundings. **Joia**, on Leidsedwarsstraat, is a cool bar. The legendary **Supperclub** on Jonge Roelensteeg (344 6400; www.supperclub.nl) is still going strong, but you may find it more fun to book dinner on its boat (www.supperclubcruise.nl).

NIGHTLIFE

Cineac on Reguliersbreestraat is a bar/club in an old theatre – the only place in Amsterdam with a no-trainers policy. **Jimmy Woo** on Leidsedwarsstraat is a glamorous nightclub where a clued-up crew go to party; there is an entry fee, but your hotel might be able to get your name put down on the guestlist.

'Conjured up from a magic hat full
of wild antiques, minimalist detail,
acres of luxury fabric and lots and
lots of money'

The Dylan

CITY   AMSTERDAM
STYLE   ORIENT EXCESS
SETTING   CALM CANALSIDE

MTWTFSSMTWTFSSMTWTF **S S** MTWTFSSMTWTFSSMTWT
AMSTERDAM

TWTFSSMTWTFSSMTWTFSSMTWTFSSMTWTFSSMTWTFSS

Hash bars, beer in McDonald's, mayonnaise on french fries… Vincent Vega didn't know the half of it. For Tarantino's burnt-out hit man in *Pulp Fiction*, the funny thing about Amsterdam was the little differences. They got the same shit over there, John Travolta explained, as we got here, it's just that there it's a little different. Wrong, dancing boy – what they got there is a lot, lot different.

Example: transport is silent: barely a car to be heard, but rather trams and bicycles whispering happy people softly around the tiny city. I say 'city'. In truth, Amsterdam is a flat Hampstead on water, where hundreds of cute little bridges play hopscotch over miles of canal. If you have a tendency to snog whenever you cross a bridge, then a weekend here means you can barely see for kissing.

But this is not Venice, where every bridge has 4,000 Japanese videoing its every move (they will eventually realise that bridges don't move), and the city is only above sea level because Pizza Express gives it 25p for every Veneziana it serves. This is a fully operational 21st-century city, where art galleries, cinemas, chain stores and boutique restaurants jostle in a joyful collaboration of 19th-century low-country kitsch and unrestrained modernism.

And it's crazy. Crazy language (like German with a mouth full of honey), crazy food (failure to plan ahead can mean existing entirely on fried cheese), crazy people (gigantic and blonde with bright pink faces, always smiling), crazy shoes (Ugg boots are the new clogs)… I promise you: windmills, brothels and practically free marijuana are simply not the half of it. Van Gogh was probably one of the sanest men in Holland.

The Dylan Amsterdam was conjured up by Anouska Hempel on the site of a 17th-century theatre, from a magic hat full of wild antiques, minimalist detail, acres of luxury fabric, and lots and lots of money. Set back off Keizersgracht, a pin-drop-peaceful canalside main drag in the very heart of everywhere you need to be, it has a cobbled courtyard with a rack of gigantic, gearless, brakeless bicycles for the use of guests. Charmingly old-fashioned, or the last word in postmodern consumer irony? It's a question you might well ask of the whole Dylan project. We turn right into a reception where two long black desks with long black benches and black cushions are lit by gargantuan black lampshades, and the walls are painted, it is said, in 25 shades of white. Good-looking staff in black designer clobber pour us champagne and check us in, and then lead us through a maze of little corridors and spiral staircases to our room.

And what a room. Ho ho ho. Whichever one you end up in, you will have the impression that a rich man's wife has gone crazy with a copy of *Wallpaper** and a limitless budget. And you won't be far wrong.

Ours was a lengthy boudoir with polished hardwood floorboards and a 20-foot ceiling. Five windows onto the courtyard were dressed with two layers of curtain: one a sort of regatta stripe, the other a mock-Burberry check, all ruched and flounced and constructed from at least three times as much fabric as is strictly necessary for light exclusion. The bed was of imperial size and four-postered with what looked like enormous ebony chopsticks. There were hazel-twig vase displays, mahogany laundry presses concealing hi-fi and video equipment, a lacquered bamboo desk, and hundreds and hundreds of cushions – the wheeze is to blend the 1990s minimalism of contemporary hotels with an ethnic opulence inspired by the spirit of the Dutch East Indies (minus the slavery). ↓

Nor does the restaurant downstairs constitute any dropping-off of standards, with a menu that hovers between Louis XVI grandeur and the supercool 'molecular gastronomy' of high modernity. Whisky and ginger shooters served in test tubes, and prawn green curry cappuccinos topped with coconut foam are followed by yellowtail hamachi sashimi with wasabi-stained flying-fish roe and, if you fancy it, a 'Fabergé egg' of chicken flesh wrapped around boiled egg wrapped around lobster. As for breakfast in bed, spreads don't come more elegant than their take on eggs Benedict: six poached eggs on a layer of smoked wild salmon on a bed of scrambled eggs encased in filo pastry with a Hollandaise sauce.

To be honest, we knew the fleshpots of Amsterdam pretty well already from years of Inter-railing and stag and hen parties, so a handful of romantic cycle rides along the canals, a sprint round the Van Gogh Museum and a couple of meals out (including kudu, springbok and crocodile satay at an Afrikaans café in the antiques district) were about the size of it. Because, you see, in a city famous for exotic sex, high kitsch and the putting into your mouth of wild and naughty things, the great thing about the Dylan is that you can do it all without leaving your room.

Review by Giles Coren

NEED TO KNOW

Rooms 41.
Rates €405–€1,495, not including tax.
Check-out Midday.
Room service 24 hours, but limited at night.
Facilities The Dylan has its own boat for canal trips; and links with a gym around the corner.
Children Facilities include special beds, cots, babysitters and childcare spa facilities.

IN THE KNOW

Recommended rooms The Manhattan rooms are fabulously over-the-top. We also loved the La Carmona rooms, in the standard range; the suites with canal views; and the loft suites for something a bit different.
Hotel bar There is a very cool mezzanine bar, good for a pre-dinner drink and canapés.
Hotel restaurant East-meets-west cuisine in an elegant environment; excellent, if not cheap, but worth the extravagance (last orders 22h).
Top table On the terrace if it's warm; otherwise, a table in the bakery overlooking the courtyard.
Dress code Dress up for dinner.

LOCAL EATING AND DRINKING

Bar Arc on Reguliersdwarsstraat (689 7070) is good for cocktails and finger food. **Brix** on Wolvenstraat (639 0351) is a cool DJ bar just around the corner, which serves a starter menu. **Brasserie Harkema** on Nes (428 2222) is a former tobacco factory – now a swish restaurant with high ceilings and wooden floors. On the main floor, you can order from a delicious selection of poultry, fish and meat dishes. There's also a cute bar with designer stools. In the open-plan red-velvet dining room of **Cineac** on Reguliersbreestraat (530 6888), the food is classy: lobster, foie gras and truffles. Take a balcony table overlooking the bar, which does great champagne cocktails. **Barok** on Wolvenstraat (330 7470) serves French cuisine with a modern twist. Funky tunes are played in its lounge/bar area. **De Kas** on Kamerlingh Onneslaan (462 4562) is situated in a converted glasshouse in a park on the edge of the city. The restaurant serves Modern European food.

A bottle of champagne in your room. Register your Smithcard online, then show your card at check-in, to claim your offer.

Get a room! Use our free online booking service: check availability and make reservations through www.mrandmrssmith.com.

SMITH CONCIERGE Registered Smith cardholders can call +44 (0)20 7978 7333 and have Original Travel book everything from your flights to your day trips, at no extra charge.
Original idea We can book you a helicopter that's normally used for ferrying oil riggers, to give you an extra-special aerial view of the city.

The Dylan Amsterdam 384 Keizersgracht, Amsterdam 1016 (+31 (20) 530 2010) hotel@blakes.nl; www.dylanamsterdam.com

Hotel Seven One Seven

CITY   AMSTERDAM
STYLE   OPULENT ECCENTRICITY
SETTING   TYPICAL TOWNHOUSE

'Huge brass beds, rich throws, suiting for curtains,
and family memorabilia give it a lived-in, personal appeal'

M T W T F S S M T W T F S S M T W T F S S M T W T F S **S S** M T W T F S S M T W T

AMSTERDAM

First, we have a confession to make: we love Amsterdam so much that we live here. But it didn't take long to convince us to relinquish our own house and take a short walk down Amsterdam's most beautiful canal, Prinsengracht, for a weekend at boutique retreat Hotel Seven One Seven. It is a very attractive old canalhouse, with no obvious 'hotel' entrance or big declaration: just a brass bell by the Amsterdam-green door. It feels like home. It looks like a home, too, which isn't too surprising, since it was a private dwelling until the owners moved out and paying guests moved in. What began as a weekend-party place turned into a business; since then, it has changed hands; its current owners fell in love with it in 1997.

The new proprietors wanted everything: the pictures on the walls, the books on the shelves, the drinks in the cabinet. The people who created its artful silk-and-tweed clutter left with nothing but a cheque and their bags. When you visit, you'll understand why this had to be the case: there's a lot of stuff in

Seven One Seven, and it's composed beautifully. And unlike the Dylan, that other style temple down the canal, this place isn't about exquisite, don't-touch perfection. You don't have to be rocking a pair of Manolos to cross its threshold: Birkenstocks or battered old Reeboks fit in just as well.

On arrival, we were met with comfort and atmosphere. In fact, we were met by an old friend, Sven – nicely in keeping with the home thing. We were given the Shakespeare Suite, which had the same warm, anti-minimalist decor as the rest of the property, and a quirky combination of contents: huge Victorian brass bed, rich throws, suiting material for curtains, an unusual parquet-topped sideboard, and family memorabilia giving it a lived-in, personal appeal. We concluded that those weekenders who got to hang out here before it became a business were very lucky people.

After a good look around, we put our feet up for tea and pastries. We had noticed that in the guest book, the ink was virtually still wet from the graffiti scrawl of a major US fashion designer – and Seven One Seven is certainly discreet enough for any passing stars. If I were here *avec entourage*, I'd go for the canal-facing Picasso Suite. Its enormously long dining table, flanked by two enormously long sofas, makes it suitable for a rock-star party – or a pair of lovebirds with 15 kids in tow, should such a Mr and Mrs Smith exist. Afterwards we headed to Christophe, our restaurant of choice for the night. Michelin-starred, it has a reputation as Amsterdam's most formal and finest dining experience, so we were conducting something of a social experiment by bringing along our gurgling and hungry eight-week-old daughter, Lola. We're hoping she won't get an appetite for solids when she sees the menu.

There has been something of a renaissance in food culture in Amsterdam; there is certainly sufficient local choice to make the lack of a restaurant at Seven One Seven neither here nor there. Although service could generally be better, quality is mostly good and, in terms of variety and experience, we'd say our home town is unbeatable: it's refreshing and progressive. Supperclub – former artist squat, now world-renowned restaurant – is more popular with the tourists than the locals, but it will feed you an amazing meal over five hours or so, as you recline on a divan. Some courses arrive on a single spoon; and they used to give you a rubber glove to eat the rabbit. 11 is another interesting place: here, you are served a four-course dinner sitting at a picnic table within huge walls that reveal a club as you finish up.

Christophe is a seemingly straighter, top-end restaurant, where the Marigolds stay strictly in the kitchen and Monsieur Michelin has given his one-starred seal of approval. We had assumed it would be very formal, if the price tags are anything to go by, but to our pleasant surprise there was hardly a suit in sight; even little Lola partaking of a little mother's milk went unnoticed. And the service is superb: the waiters were so attentive, we wouldn't have been surprised if they'd offered her an alternative. ↓

You know a good restaurant when things just roll: the silent flurry of waiters, the continuous flow of wonderful food and wines, the *Dallas / Dynasty* decor, an undercurrent of American and French accents, and Lola quietly burbling throughout. It all dashed our preconceptions of formality – but this is Amsterdam, of course. We weren't wrong about the price tag, though.

Given that we were on holiday in our home town, we made plans to visit the Noordermarkt in the morning, rather than just returning to base. It is a good – and beautiful – walk west up the canal to the market space, where Saturday morning brings vendors of organic food, bric à brac, Sixties and Seventies furniture, and the best apple pie in town (look for the queue at the café on the corner). There are bars all around, and you get a taste of authentic Dutch life that red-light-obsessed tourists can easily miss.

Back at Seven One Seven, we declined to sit on the patio off the back (it's a canal view or nothing in Amsterdam); it's more of a 'curl up by the fire' kind of place, anyway. Drinks are included in the prices, so to relax with a glass of well-rounded red in the sitting room, or kick off breakfast with a glass of champagne is more than a pleasure. The decor (Balinese mixed with African, colonial meets modern) is all the more attractive because it hasn't been designed to be marketed. It's intimate and private, and very relaxing. We'd never guessed what was behind the façade, and we're rather pleased to be in on the secret. If you like the new breed of country-house hotels in the UK, you'll love it. The difference is that rather than pushing a rock 'n' roll vibe (a professor or a sculptor would be as at home here as a superstar) Seven One Seven lets you bring your own.

Reviewed by Mark Chalmers

NEED TO KNOW

Rooms Eight, including two executive suites (four more planned for the near future).
Rates €398–€650 (plus tax), including breakfast.
Check-out No set time; check what time the room is needed by.
Room service Breakfast in bed, drinks and some snacks available.
Facilities Free mini-bar in the rooms.
Children Cots and babysitters (book well in advance) are available; an extra bed is €50.
Also Afternoon tea and pastries, and house wine whenever you like, are included in the price.

IN THE KNOW

Recommended rooms Both executive suites, Picasso and Schubert, have views of the canal. Our favourites are Tolkien, which is ultra-romantic, and Room at the Top, for its rooftop views.
Hotel bar House wine is served in the lounge at no extra cost, which more than compensates for there not being a bar.
Hotel restaurant The only food served is Dutch breakfast in the Strawinsky room or courtyard.
Top table If it's warm enough, alfresco in the courtyard.
Dress code Very relaxed; the Seven One Seven wants you to feel right at home.

LOCAL EATING AND DRINKING

Café Esprit on Spui (622 1967) is a delightful spot for a quick salad or sandwich. **Herengracht** on Herengracht (616 2482) is an art gallery, bar and restaurant, good for an aperitif or a Modern European lunch on the canal. **Metz & Co** on Leidsestraat (520 7020) is a department store with a café that's good for lunch or a coffee break with a view. The brasserie-style menu at two-floored **Morlang** on Keizersgracht (625 2681) makes it ideal for a low-key lunch or dinner. Though once you get a look at their extensive spirit selection you may find food takes second place. Make a beeline for the large canalside terrace. **Moeders** on Rozengracht (626 7957) is a fun place to go for a relaxed evening of authentic Dutch dining; get a table outside if the weather is up to it. The name means 'Mother's', which explains why the walls are covered with photographs of mums through the ages. We loved the *stamppot*, which translates as 'mashed pot'. It's is a traditional dish of mashed potatoes with vegetables, served with a Hema (famous department store) sausage, meatballs and bacon.

 Upgrade if available, and a bottle of champagne on arrival. Register your Smithcard online, then show your card at check-in, to claim your offer.

Get a room! Use our free online booking service: check availability and make reservations through www.mrandmrssmith.com.

SMITH CONCIERGE Registered Smith cardholders can call +44 (0)20 7978 7333 and have Original Travel book everything from your flights to your day trips, at no extra charge.
Original idea We'll organise a multilingual guide who's a trained art historian and can get you into private collections or the Royal Palace, even when it's officially closed to the public.

Hotel Seven One Seven 717 Prinsengracht, Amsterdam 1017 (+31 (20) 4270 717)
info@717hotel.nl; www.717hotel.nl

MTWTFSSMTWTFSSMTWTFSSMTWTFSSMTWTFSSMTWT

● BARCELONA

SPAIN

BARCELONA
Hotel Neri
Hotel Omm
Prestige Paseo de Grácia
Relais d'Orsà

TWTFSSMTWTFSSMTWTFSSMTWTFSSMTWTFSSMTWTFSS

ESPANA

BARCELONA ●

Barcelona

CITYSCAPE   MARVELLOUS MODERNISM
CITY LIFE   ENERGETIC AND COLOURFUL

M T W T F S S M T W T F S S M T W T F S S M T W T F S S M T W T F S S M T W T

ESPANA

'It presented a spectacle of democratic pleasure very unlike other
parts of the Mediterranean I had come to know'
Robert Hughes

BARCELONA is a naturally romantic, lover-friendly city. From the mountains to the beach, wide tree-lined boulevards unravel into shady squares and tiny, friendly bars, where a too-hot afternoon is never wasted. The Catalan capital sits on the shores of the Med, with a wonderful climate for exploring 2,000 years of history: follow a tour of Gaudí's achievements (La Sagrada Família, La Pedrera…) or head to one of the city's parks or beaches to bask in the sunshine. A port since Roman times, Barcelona grew more flamboyant in the 19th century, with art deco architecture to rival that of Paris; in 1992, the Olympics inspired redevelopment of the beachfront. The Spanish city with its finger most firmly on the pulse, Barcelona has always embraced style, bold design and all things new. Pockets of lively bars and restaurants around the Gothic Quarter and El Born ensure the city stays alive late into the night, as do most of her visitors, eating, drinking and partying. No wonder cava is the drink of choice – this is a place with much to celebrate.

GETTING THERE

Planes Taxis will whisk you into town in 15 mins, for €18. Buses run every 15 mins; a ticket costs about €3.
Trains A 30-min train journey into the centre from the airport costs €2; trains run every half an hour. Spain also has a reasonably priced national network. Book ahead as trains get busy (www.renfe.com).
Automobiles Driving is fine once you master the one-way system, but free parking is tricky. Daily carpark rates are about €25. Taxis are cheap, so it's not worth renting a car. The train is great for day trips.

DO GO/DON'T GO

Locals leave August to the tourists as the city can be too hot to handle.

BEAUTIFULLY BARCELONA

Rent a boat on the lake in Parc de la Ciutadella. Go to Mercat de la Boquería on Las Ramblas and get a picnic to take to the beach.

LOCAL KNOWLEDGE

Taxis You can hail one from anywhere on the street.
Tipping In restaurants and bars it's normal to tip only if the service is outstanding. Catalans leave behind a few small coins.
Packing tips Swimmers – Barcelona has its own beach. If you're vegetarian, research where you can find meat-free places to eat.
Recommended reads *The Shadow of the Wind* by Carlos Ruiz Zafon; *Barcelona* by Robert Hughes; *City of Marvels* by Eduardo Mendoza.
Cuisine Basic Catalan cuisine is a surf 'n' turf affair of seafood and meat tapas. Look out for the *menú del dia* (daily set menu) for a €10 lunch.
Also Avoid public holidays on Saturdays, as things tend to be shut. Tickets for concerts and Barça matches can be bought at ServiCaixa cash points.

DIARY

March Carnival is the week leading up to Lent and is big here, particularly in Sitges, where there are huge street processions (www.bcn.es/carnaval).
March–June Festival de Guitarra: a guitar festival with international artists (www.the-project.net). **23 April** La Diada de Sant Jordi (Saint George's day), Barcelona's Valentine's Day. **June** Trobada Castellera – the *castellers* come from all around to build their human towers in Plaça Catalunya. **November** Festival Internacionál de Jazz de Barcelona (www.the-project.net).

WORTH GETTING OUT OF BED FOR

Viewpoints From Montjuic, the hill next to the old town with a cable car to the top; Parc Güell, which was designed by Gaudí; Mount Tibidabo – take the blue tram to the foot of the hill, and then the funicular railway to the top. Or have drinks on the striking surreal roof of La Pedrera with views over the city.

Arts and culture Antoni Gaudí left an incredible legacy in Barcelona, from his undulating apartment block La Pedrera to his swan song, the Sagrada Família, still under construction. The city pays tribute to other great artists with the Museu Picasso and Fundació Joan Miró. The Museu d'Art Contemporani de Barcelona focuses on 20th-century Catalan artists. The Gran Teatro de Liceu is up there with Europe's great opera houses.

Something for nothing At the weekends, drummers play in Ciutadella Parc, where locals hang out. Las Ramblas is full of street entertainers (and pickpockets) every day. The Catalans have a tradition of building human towers, up to eight people high, during the summer months.

Shopping For designer labels, head for Paseo de Grácia. You'll find boutiques and more unusual shops in the El Born area. Our favourite shop for foodie souvenirs is Colmado Quílez Avinyó on Rambla de Catalunya. Salva G on Avinyo is a hairdressers, bar, music store and cosmetics shop all rolled into one. One of the best food markets is Bocadilla, just off the Ramblas.

And… Don't go out until after 21h as the restaurants will be dead – and most of the bars don't start humming until after 23h.

Tourist tick box La Sagrada Família ❑ Parc Güell ❑ Museu Picasso ❑

BARS AND RESTAURANTS

Stop at **La Vinya del Senyor** on Plaza Santa Maria for a glass of wine before hitting the shops in the Gothic Quarter. **7 Portes** on Passeig d'Isabel II (319 30 33) is Barcelona's oldest restaurant, and serves an authentic Catalan menu in a formal environment with a pianist from 22h30. Fish-lovers should head to traditional **La Barra de Botafumeiro** on Gran de Grácia (218 42 30). **Commerç 24** on Carrer Commerç (319 21 02) is a fashionable, modern tapas restaurant: great for dinner. **Passadis del Pep** on Pla de Palau (310 10 21) does good seafood – they call the shots on what you eat, which can be fun. **Acontraluz** is a bit out of the way, uptown on Milanesat (203 06 58), but it's a cool, contemporary restaurant with a lively atmosphere and great Mediterranean food; ask for a seat in the conservatory. Our favourite tapas bars are: **Cal Pep** on Plaça de les Olles (310 79 61), a traditional tapas bar with all the favourites – cured hams, daily specials and a bustly atmosphere in the evenings; **Cerveceria Catalana** on Mallorca (216 03 68); **Ciudad Condal** on Rambla de Catalunya (318 19 97); **Flash Flash** on La Granada del Penedès for its tortillas (237 09 90); and **Santa Maria** on Commerç (315 12 27). **Agua** on the beachfront (225 12 72) is fab for seafood, and is especially pleasant in summer if you get a table on the terrace looking out to sea; booking well in advance is advisable.

NIGHTLIFE

For after-dinner drinks, head for El Born district. Or head uptown to Carrer Maria Cubi, where there are several lively bars; our favourites are **Universal** and **Mas y Mas**. **Danzatoria** is a very beautiful, very glamorous club on Avenida del Tibidabo; entrance is free but drinks don't come cheap. **Gusto** on Calle Francisco Giner is a laid-back drinkery that gets going around midnight. If you want to mingle with Barcelona's footballerati head to **Buda Bar** on Avenida Nilópoli.

Hotel Neri

CITY   BARCELONA
STYLE   18TH-CENTURY PALACE
SETTING   SHADY SQUARE BY THE CATHEDRAL

'All you want to do is draw the drapes, sink into
the dark-grey slate bath and sip champagne'

M T W T F S S M T W T F S S M T W T F S S M T W T F S S M T W T F S S M T W T
BARCELONA

TWTFSSMTWTFSSMTWTFSSMTWTFSSMTWTFSS

Hotel Neri, Barcelona, Spain

Asking two semi-professional beach bums to review a hotel in a city centre on one of the hottest weekends of the year could have backfired. When the sun's shining, culture comes pretty low on our agenda. But, as it happened, we discovered a city and a hotel as beguiling as any beach.

The weekend began with an early flight. The idea of the same two beach bums getting to the airport super-early on a Saturday is beyond a joke; luckily, it was remarkably easy. With nothing but hand luggage, we were in a cab on our way to Hotel Neri by 11h. Located in a back street in Barrí Gotic (the Gothic Quarter, the oldest, most picturesque part of Barcelona) it's a little difficult to find, but that's a good thing. As we were to learn, this is a city that never sleeps, so our location proved a bonus when we wanted some kip; there's no chance of a hedonistic rabble partying below your window.

Too early to check into our room, we dumped our bags and found our first of many bottles of rosado waiting conveniently round the corner at a tiny café. After a lunch of some delicious garlicky prawns and a prowl around the neighbourhood streets, we got back about 15h, and were very pleasantly surprised by what the Neri had to offer. When you stumble in from the sun and heat, it's really very startling. You certainly appreciate its darkness and austerity as a welcome respite from Barcelona's busy streets. The hotel is housed in an 18th-century palace, with an extremely dramatic interior that combines striking Gothic architecture with super-modern features. It is contemporary – not in a minimalist way, but with the original features preserved and presented in a cutting-edge context. The front door is made of enormous sheets of glass and ornate metalwork, there are mad pieces of art dotted about on exposed brickwork, and gilded mirrors hang on stone walls. It all works beautifully.

Even better, the rooms are a reason to shut the door on the rest of the world. Our bedroom was sultry, spacious and sumptuously sexy. A huge bed, lots of velvet and dark silks and stacks of cushions made it hard to leave. It's the perfect place for a cheeky weekend. All you want to do is draw the drapes, sink into the dark-grey slate bath and sip champagne, or stretch out on the enormous bed and ignore whatever's on the large plasma screen in front of you. Eventually we prised ourselves out, headed up to the hotel's pretty private rooftop, and rang down to the bar for an aperitif before dinner. Below, it might have been busy all around, but cosied up on cushions, alone on a terrace nestled among age-old rooftops, we couldn't have enjoyed a more peaceful sunset.

Adjacent to the hotel is La Ribera, another of the city's oldest areas; judging by all the bright young things, it is also where the hip folk hang out. We weren't massively hungry, and wandered around until we found a fantastic tapas restaurant in a little square, where we joined bohemian thirtysomething *senyors i senyores* picking at olives and manchego cheese. With a pop of another cava cork, this Mr Smith, who lives in Africa, and Mrs Smith from South London, decided to meet in Zanzibar for another week of pleasure. But even that would be hard pushed to beat the romance of Barcelona. Everywhere you stroll, the air is alive with the sounds of buskers: opera singers, string quartets, a girl playing the harp. Sitting under the moonlight with someone you love, listening to haunting melodies picked out on a Spanish guitar, is a real life-is-sweet moment.

We weren't in the mood for anything too intrepid, so we were happy to discover how easy it is to explore Barcelona on foot. In the centre of the action, close to tourist-packed Las Ramblas, behind Avenue de Catedral, we sneaked a look at La Seu. Even Mr Smith, who had declared right at the start that he wasn't being dragged into any churches, had to concede it blew him away. You can't help but soak up Barcelona's culture – it's all around you. There are the eccentric buildings ↓

designed by Gaudí, and countless galleries and museums, many of which are within walking distance of the Neri, such as the inspirational Museu Picasso. But we suggest avoiding the best-known landmarks when the mercury is at its highest. It is worth seeing the mind-boggling craftsmanship of La Sagrada Família close up, but eschewing the queues to go up to the top we spent the rest of our morning wandering around town, eyes open to the stunning architecture.

Barcelona offers romance, decadence, heritage, a chance to party and the option of chilling. But the crowning glory for this pair? The beach. A 45-minute train ride took us to the seaside town of Sitges. The carriage was packed, but even listening to the rhythms of the Spanish chatter was fun. Serendipity had coincided our visit with a religious festival, and as we wandered down the hill, we joined a crazy procession of stilt-walkers with papier-mâché heads and voluminous costumes, all heading towards the clifftop church. We revelled in the carnival atmosphere and the sounds of accordions, guitars and windpipes, and pondered whether Tim Burton had helped out with

this particular interpretation of the nativity. We then found a spot on the sand among friendly preeners and posers. An afternoon spent lying in the sun, buying beers and snacks from the good-looking young Spaniards patrolling the beach – who could complain?

But you don't need to leave town to feel sand under your feet or frolic in the sea. A ten-minute cab ride from the hotel brings you to Barceloneta, the city's own man-made beach, flanked by lots of restaurants and bars. This discovery had us changing our return flights, booking into the Neri for another night, and extending our long weekend by another day. Our last afternoon entailed dawdling over a long, boozy seafood lunch in Port Olímpic, and more beach-based relaxation. This is a city where you can find delicious wine and tapas whatever the time, wander around or hang out until the wee hours, and finally retire to your immaculately serviced room at the Hotel Neri to get some rest before you start all over again.

Reviewed by Mr & Mrs Smith

NEED TO KNOW

Rooms 22 rooms.
Rates €215–€383 (plus seven per cent VAT)
Check-out Midday.
Room service 24 hours.
Facilities Roof terrace overlooking the Gothic Quarter, with sunloungers and bar service. Internet connection in each room; plasma TV, CD, choice of beds.
Children Very welcome.

IN THE KNOW

Recommended rooms The junior suite, with views of Plaça Sant Felip Neri.
Hotel bar Open until midnight, serving cocktails as impeccably designed as the decor.
Hotel restaurant Overlooking the square, the restaurant is set in the original stone arches of the Old Palace Neri – very romantic. It serves excellent aromatic Mediterranean cuisine until 23h.
Top table All the tables are lovely.
Dress code Fashionable, informal.

LOCAL EATING AND DRINKING

Schilling on Calle Ferran (317 67 87) is a historic café, great for breakfast or coffee. At night, it becomes a cocktail bar with music until 02h30. **Los Caracoles** on Escudellers (302 31 85) has been a big name for generations, serving international and Catalan food, specialising in snails (*caracoles*) and roast suckling pig. **Taller de Tapas** on Plaça Sant Josep Oriol (301 80 20) serves fantastic tapas with well-chosen wine, as does **Vinissim** on Calle Sant Domenec del Call (301 45 75). **Shunka** on Sagristans (412 49 91) offers excellent Japanese food. **Orígens 99.9%** on Vidrieria (310 75 31) does a modern take on traditional Catalan dishes, using organic ingredients. It's no wonder they've laminated the pages of their menus – photos of their tasty offerings must have diners drooling. Book in advance, or while you wait for a table, pick up jars of alioli and tapenade as souvenirs from their shop. Also in that area is the very traditional tapas bar **Cal Pep** on Plaça de les Olles (310 79 61). Always bustling, and fantastically authentic.

 A complimentary bottle of cava. Register your Smithcard online, then show your card at check-in, to claim your offer.

Get a room! Use our free online booking service: check availability and make reservations through www.mrandmrssmith.com.

SMITH CONCIERGE Registered Smith cardholders can call +44 (0)20 7978 7333 and have Original Travel book everything from your flights to your day trips, at no extra charge.
Original idea Platja de la Mar Bella is the city's only official nudist beach. It is also home to the water-sports centre Base Nàutica de la Mar Bella, where we can hire you equipment and arrange lessons in a wide range of activities (with your swimwear on).

Neri Hotel & Restaurante 5 Calle Sant Sever, Barcelona 08002 (+34 93 304 06 55)
info@hotelneri.com; www.hotelneri.com

Hotel Omm

CITY   BARCELONA
STYLE   ARCHITECT-DESIGNED DETAIL
SETTING ART NOUVEAU SIDE STREET

MTWTFSSMTWTFSSMTWTFSSMTWTFSSMTWTFSSMTWT
BARCELONA

'There aren't any pictures at all: the
straight lines and plain materials
are in themselves the art'

TWTFSSMTWTFSSMTWTFSSMTWTFSSMTWTFSS

Hotel Omm, Barcelona, Spain

I have to start with a confession. This Mr and Mrs Smith live in Barcelona, so a visit to a hotel on our home turf was going to have to be pretty special to make it a weekend we'd never forget. When I discovered we were to be staying at Hotel Omm, the sister to my favourite restaurant, Acontraluz, I decided it wasn't going to be a problem…

We hopped in the car, waved goodbye to thirtysomething domesticity, and made our journey across town. Finding Hotel Omm, just off Paseo de Grácia, the main avenue in the middle of Barcelona's art nouveau grid, isn't hard. In keeping with its neighbours, it's a seven-storey building with a flat front. However, this being a city touched by the hand of Gaudí, and with his apartment block La Pedrera around the corner, clearly Hotel Omm felt obliged to do something quirky. The façade of small, white rectangular slabs is tautly pulled back like a sheet of white metal and repeatedly slashed, creating slits for thin windows and small balconies protected from the full glare of the Mediterranean sun.

We'd packed light, but though the revolving door is big enough for most visitors' accessories, it was a little too small for ours. Then again, not all lovers take a pram with them on a romantic break – let alone its contents. Fortunately one of the adjacent sheets of glass slid back, to reveal a sleek minimalist reception area. No fake oil paintings or the prints of landscapes from yesteryear so popular in lobbies of swanky hotels across the world. In fact, there aren't any pictures at all. This is Omm's design and decor in a nutshell: the straight lines and plain materials are in themselves the art.

Even with a 16-month-old ankle-biter in tow, we found ourselves treated kindly from the start, and a sweet receptionist took us straight up to our room. Some couples request oysters and champagne on ice waiting for them in their room… We'd ordered a cot. It wasn't there yet but soon arrived, and managed to fit into the room's perfectly integrated minimalist wood-and-metal decor. (Something a grabbing-hands-everywhere Master Smith was having a little trouble doing.)

Everything looked crisp, yet felt comfy, and the walls, bathroom fixtures, sheets and towels were all a pristine white – a particular treat for parents of a toddler. We had an interior room, so our balcony overlooked the internal courtyard; the contrast of the scruffy rears of the buildings opposite and the elegant, modern perfection of the hotel framing them is a sight to behold. And for those who want to revel only in design-conscious bliss, there's a gauze blind, transparent enough for light to penetrate but sufficiently opaque to keep out the imperfections of the outside world.

Resisting the temptation to collapse on the bed for a siesta, we headed up to the pool bar. Wow. The pinnacle of urban living must be an elegant rooftop terrace with a swimming pool, and this was an immaculate, wood-lined haven. Looking out across the jumbled horizon of Barcelona and the gorgeous Mediterranean sky, we ordered two Spanish-strength gin and tonics to sip as we soaked up the view. As well as nuns scurrying around the convent across the road, we could see the eccentric swirls of La Pedrera's fantastical roof, one block away. To our left, the spires of Barcelona's most emblematic building, Gaudí's unfinished church La Sagrada Família, were visible in the distance. Armchair sightseers can delight in two checks in their tourist tick boxes without having to leave the comfort of their sunlounger. Perfect.

We could have happily stayed put there all day, but we mustered the energy to stumble out for a late lunch. The first restaurant we came to was just the ticket: a decent pizzeria called Samoa on Paseo de Grácia, where we snapped up an outside table. It's a colourful, retail-rich area. With our blood-sugar levels back up, Mrs Smith managed to coax me into a little shopping. But humidity and tourist levels were also up, so Omm soon lured us back, an oasis of freshness, calm and hush. ↓

We had a table (and a babysitter) booked for 21h30. The hotel restaurant is called, curiously, Moo. (Perhaps because it's so delicious, the temptation is to milk the menu for all you're worth.) It is the creation of the Roca brothers, world-famous for their creative combinations of ingredients and flavours. Their disdain for convention is, perhaps, most apparent in the spindly chocolate mixed with salt that arrived with the coffee. With each dish a half portion, we could try twice as many things. Each serving comes with a carefully selected wine: another incentive (as if you needed one) to have as many plates as possible. You find yourself ordering not just to sample the mouthwatering French-influenced food, but also for the wine that comes with it: foie gras and figs with a Pedro Ximénez, entrecôte with an Haut Medoc… We may not have left town, but our tastebuds went all over Europe.

Though we only had five floors to ascend to get to our room, the corridors were an experience in themselves. With no natural light, the charcoal-grey carpet and walls are illuminated only by a purplish glow and two phosphorescent white lines that run either side of the floor, the length of the corridor. The runway effect proved fortunate after six different wines over dinner.

Master Smith awoke a little earlier than usual, and our room was quickly transformed from a temple of calculated style to the chaos of a child's playpen. We all went for a morning swim on the roof and then down for breakfast in the open-plan bar. Could there be a more wonderful start to the day than the juice of fresh blood oranges from Sicily, delicious local breads, cheeses and salamis, exotic jams (such as raspberry and red-pepper jelly), and sandwiches of cheese and Mediterranean tomatoes that melt in the mouth? Sadly, just as we had eaten our fill, we realised that it was time to leave. We'd had a wonderful break without even leaving our everyday stamping ground. So fabulous was the aesthetic and gastronomic experience that Mrs Smith insists that we do it more often. I give in on the strength of the breakfast alone.

Reviewed by Mr & Mrs Smith

NEED TO KNOW

Rooms 59 rooms, including one suite.
Rates €290–€500, plus seven per cent tax.
Check-out Midday.
Room service 24 hours; the full restaurant menu is available when Moo is open, otherwise sandwiches and salads.
Facilities Relajaciomm is a health centre opening 2005/2006, with views of the interior garden, a rooftop swimming pool and a solarium overlooking La Pedrera. Car-parking services.
Children The restaurant is not suitable for small children; a menu at the bar caters for them.

IN THE KNOW

Recommended rooms Those looking out onto Paseo de Grácia have the best views; those facing the interior garden bigger balconies.
Hotel bars One minimalist cocktail bar/lounge, and another focusing on fine wines. OmmSessions, 23h–03h Wednesday–Saturday, often feature live entertainment.
Hotel restaurant Moo restaurant serves Catalan haute cuisine; Michelin-approved chefs Joan, Josep and Jordi Roca have two stars. The interior looks onto an enclosed bamboo forest.
Top table A corner table.
Dress code Fashionably formal.

LOCAL EATING AND DRINKING

Tragaluz on Passatge de la Concepcio (487 06 21) offers a creative take on Mediterranean fine dining, with prices to match. The menu gourmand is an excellent way to experience a showcase of its imaginative menu. Definitely try to reserve a table under the glass roof and dine beneath the stars. In summer, venture down to the beachfront for dinner at sister restaurant **Agua** (225 12 72), just as chic and modern, but a little more relaxed and buzzy. Contemporary tapas include some incredible salads and seafood dishes. In the summer, book ahead to get a table outside on the terrace, right on the beach. If you want a break from Spanish food, **Elj Apo Nés** on Passatge de la Concepcio (487 25 92) is, as the name suggests, a Japanese restaurant, open until midnight.

 A complimentary glass of Catalan cava with breakfast. Register your Smithcard online, then show your card at check-in, to claim your offer.

Get a room! Use our free online booking service: check availability and make reservations through www.mrandmrssmith.com.

SMITH CONCIERGE Registered Smith cardholders can call +44 (0)20 7978 7333 and have Original Travel book everything from your flights to your day trips, at no extra charge.
Original idea Let us steer you in the direction of some mountain biking in the hills beyond Barcelona. It's only half an hour away, and a completely different experience to life in the city.

Hotel Omm 265 Rossello, Barcelona 08008 (+34 93 445 40 00)
reservas@hotelomm.es; www.hotelomm.es

get ahead in Europe

Sit back in your stylish surrounds and let your brain soak up
this trivia, and you'll be the most erudite European in town.
If the only opera you're up on is the one with her own talk
show, and the last black-and-white film you watched was
when *Top Gun* came through on cable monochrome, it's
time to brush up on on your general knowledge of this mighty
Continent. Crack open our can of hi-brow brew and wow
barmen in elegant establishments as you wax lyrical about
local lore, or set your other half swooning with a nonchalant
reference to Puccini.

How to…

COMMUNISM TO DEMOCRACY When Russian tanks invaded Czechoslovakia to 'protect socialism' in 1968, they shut down the reform movement until the dam of resentment burst in 1989. The Berlin Wall came down and the Velvet Revolution in Prague hailed the unsaddling of totalitarianism across the ex-Soviet Bloc. On 1 May 2004, several of the new democracies joined the European Union, ending 65 years of conflict.

HE CAME, HE SAW, HE CUT HAIR Until Ticinius Mena rolled into Rome, barbers were unknown. But when this latter-day Vidal Sassoon hit town in 296BC, he had shaving in vogue faster than you can say 'short back and sides, please', and the barber shop became the place to see and be seen. And not just for the boys. Every mamma worth her toga had a hairdresser among her slaves. So highly prized were the the people of the coiff that a statue was erected in Ticinius' honour.

DO THE SARDANA Despite a Franco ban on the Catalan dance, it is alive and kicking. Fancy-footed locals step to the sounds of a *cobla* (brass ensemble), flaviol (small high-pitched flute) and tambourines.

BEHIND THE MASK In the 13th century, masks were banned in Venice but for one week a year. Otherwise men could go incognito and gamble or have their way with nuns. But at carnival, folk could be as naughty as they liked.

SOCCER IT TO 'EM Names to drop: Michel Platini and Thierry Henry in France; Franz Beckenbauer in Germany; Roberto Baggio, Francesco Totti and Paolo Maldini in Italy; Johann Cruyff and Dennis Bergkamp in Holland.

WHY 'PAPARAZZI'? The celeb-snapping journo in Federico Fellini's 1960 film *La Dolce Vita* is called Paparazzo. Crave another Fellini fact? File this: the director born in 1920 died of a heart attack on 31 October 1999, the same day as River Phoenix.

PEAKS AND TROUGHS Highest mountain: Mount Elbrus, Russia. Deepest lake: Hornindalsvatnet, Norway. Highest rainfall: Italy, followed by Germany. Most expensive wine: 1787 Château d'Yquem Sauternes.

OPERA IN A NUTSHELL
Puccini's *La Bohème* Paris, 1830: sickly seamstress ventures to the flat upstairs to get a light, and meets poet and playwright. They fall in love. Ah, but Count Paul has his eye on her. All she wants to do is help her love. Then he goes and accuses her of adultery. She croaks.
Verdi's *La Traviata* Cupid strikes Violetta and Alfredo; she abandons Paris in favour of rural idyll. Violetta however, doesn't feature in Alfredo Snr's plans. And he tells her so – she pegs it back to the capital. Unaware of dad's meddling, Alfredo storms into a soirée to give Violetta a mouthful. Pa 'fesses up, Alf says he's sorry. Too late: she's so sad she's sick. Does she make it? Nah.
Mozart's *Don Giovanni* Our man DG has a big appetite for women. For every one he seduces, a boyfriend is made jealous – eventually it's payback time. Jilted lover with a sword? Too dull. Try the ghost of an angry father. Mr Loverman gets it where it hurts: in hell.

EURO-SHAKESPEARE REDUCED
The Merchant of Venice Wealthy heiress yawns at the bachelors paraded in front of her. Enter Bassanio. Sigh. Gorgeous, but brassic. In steps Antonio, Merchant of Venice. Uh oh. Tony has cashflow problems. He turns to Shylock the loanshark. Fast forward through court battles, chicks disguised as guys, and – bravo! – a happy ending.
Titus Andronicus Rome, 1593: power, murder, seduction and deceit. Returning home victorious from a bloody war, Titus wants to retire. Instead, his sons are slain, hands cut off, tongues cut out, people beheaded and others chopped into pieces and baked in a pie. Sidney Sheldon, put that in your pipe and smoke it.
All's Well That Ends Well French belle Helena has a crush on Bertram. He's a nobleman, she's hoi polloi. Then she saves the king's life. Her reward? Any man for a husband. Helena chooses Bertie. They get hitched. That's not enough for Bert; he scarpers, leaving a list of conditions. Don't fret: the title is a clue to the outcome.

TRIVIA CORNER The word trivia originated from the Roman *trivium*, which denoted a junction of three (or more) lanes in a town. Townsfolk would gather at such meeting points, making small talk.

'The rooms are like the private quarters of a high-ranking imperial dignitary visiting the Death Star'

Prestige Paseo de Grácia

CITY   BARCELONA
STYLE   MODERN COMFORT
SETTING CLOSE TO LA PEDRERA

MTWTFSSMTWTFSSMTWTFSSMTWTFSSMTWTFSSMTWT
BARCELONA

TWTFSSMTWTFSSMTWTFSSMTWTFSSMTWTFSS

Prestige Paseo de Grácia, Barcelona, Spain

From the outset, Barcelona's Hotel Prestige has the air of a super-villain's lair. A monumental steel and glass door marks the entrance from Paseo de Grácia; dark-suited hotel staff greet you in the lobby; ceiling-high sliding mirrored panels close off your bedspace. It's modern, sleek and ever-so-slightly despotic. In a good way. Built within the Thirties' stone shell of a former office complex, it's the result of a massive and total programme of renovation, which reached fruition two years ago. Already, it's a destination in itself for European and American corporate ladder-climbers and couples who like their leisure time slick.

As we check in, we ask to have a peek at another room en route to ours; they are as you would imagine the private quarters of a high-ranking Imperial dignitary visiting the Death Star. While not

big enough to re-enact any 'rescuing the princess from the detention block' fantasies that you and Mrs Smith might harbour, the rooms on the front of the hotel are certainly airy enough, with their picture-postcard views over the Paseo de Grácia.

Once in our room, we discover original touches abound. The mini-bar, for instance (though limited), is entirely free, and we've never encountered that before, in any hotel we've ever stayed in, anywhere in the world. A complimentary stash of fruit juice, Kit Kats, Coke, water and beer, all refreshed daily – the unfortunate temptation being that you try your damnedest to finish off the lot every day, whether you want a peach juice and an alcohol-free lager or not. Welcome additions to all the extras you'd expect in a boutique hotel like this (valet parking, air-con, intelligent lighting, shoe polishing…) are Bang & Olufsen TV sets, Jacob Jensen telephones, room-based internet connections. This is a place where the management want you to feel cherished. In fact, they insist.

The communal hub of the hotel is the first-floor Zeroom – a dark-wood and leather breakfast area/bar/lounge. So multifaceted is it that it also acts as a library, celebrating Barcelona's design and cultural heritage. You can even take a piece of Prestige home with you, and the books are only a fraction of what's available to buy. Resisting the temptation to have our entire room boxed up and transported home, we tear ourselves away in search of sunshine and refreshment.

The Hotel Prestige lies smack bang in the middle of Barcelona's equivalent of Bond Street; Paseo de Grácia is a credit-card-eating luxury-brand paradise. Most of the big names have glittering boutiques on this drag, and its bars, cafés and restaurants make it a far nicer shopping environment than Regent Street. If you're looking for dirt-cheap but thoroughly respectable fashion, then Zara's three-storey lifestyle megastore offers a multitude of cool buys. Next we try Las Ramblas – Barcelona's infamous social catwalk. It's awash with tourists, but you can escape the mayhem by walking diagonally two streets away in any direction, where the modern city will dissolve into the Gothic Quarter's maze of cobbled streets lined with cool bars and shops. Exhausted by hours of exploring, we return to the hotel for a pick-me-up before heading out in search of an early dinner (our body clocks refuse to adjust to the Spanish no-eating-till-midnight schedule). The Zeroom is uncharacteristically empty, so we plump for a corner booth and spread out a map in order to plan our night's conquest of the city. We order a couple of San Miguels (on the mainland, the bottled stuff is far superior to the draught you sometimes get in bars), get out the guidebooks and fall fast, fast asleep. Sweetly, a member of staff creeps over and closes the blinds, leaving us to continue our power nap in semi-darkness. Refreshed, we head straight to 7 Portes, the city's oldest restaurant, for some top-notch seafood, namely the fantastic paella. ↓

Prestige serves breakfast until 11h, which helps soften the severest of hangovers, but diets fly out of the window as buttery chocolate cake, muffins and all manner of cooked meats and sugary cereals pimp themselves from the buffet table. Afterwards, we're faced with a dilemma – to partake of the city's enviable cultural smorgasbord or thrash the credit card to within an inch of its life? Barcelona is so chock-full of first-rate cultural fare (from the Gaudí-designed properties and fairytale-like Parc Güell to the many world-class museums and galleries) that you could fill an entire book with must-see destinations.

At the risk of delivering a cheesy tourist-board line, Barcelona can be everything to everyone, from the foodie to the culture whore to the connoisseur of the bawdy. Perhaps the only danger with Barcelona is that you might try to cram too much cultural nourishment into a weekend, and miss one of the city's enduring high points – its relaxed atmosphere. Much better to promise yourselves you'll explore the city at leisure over a multitude of visits. Our favourite way to pass the time was to pitch up at a kerbside café like Tapas Tapas on Paseo de Grácia, break out a trashy novel and get quietly and pleasantly sloshed. There's nothing like going abroad to a centre of cultural and historical excellence and then wilfully ignoring every last inch of it in favour of low-rent literature and a skinful of export-strength lager. You may feel the need to excuse yourself by explaining that you are actually 'people-watching' or maybe even 'soaking up the city's ambience' but honestly, I've always believed that most of the joy in being in one of the most relaxed cities in the world is kicking back and going with the flow. Half a dozen San Migs later, I've broken the back of my 700-page historical romp and I'm suddenly aware that this is the most fun I've had in months. The discreet charm of the Prestige has obviously located our off buttons.

Reviewed by Anthony Noguera

NEED TO KNOW

Rooms 45 rooms, some with terrace.
Rates €185–€398, plus seven per cent tax.
Check-out Midday.
Room service 24-hour light menu.
Facilities Free mini-bar, your choice of daily newspaper, 24-hour 'Ask Me' service (advice on where to shop, tickets for shows, etc), valet parking, library with music in the Zeroom. Associate services include: gym, beauty centre, babysitter and business centre.
Children Room supplement for children (two–12 years): €27 a night.

IN THE KNOW

Recommended rooms Superior double, with a terrace over looking Paseo de Grácia.
Hotel bar/restaurant The hotel bar/cafeteria serves the same menu as room service, until 23h. No formal restaurant.
Dress code City smart, or country casual. It's up to you.
Top table Next to the window with views of Paseo de Grácia.

LOCAL EATING AND DRINKING

Arc Café on Carrer Carabassa (302 52 04) is a gastro-bar with hearty Mediterranean, Asian and Caribbean food, open all day – a rare occurrence in Spain. **Orotava** on Consell de Cent (487 73 74) is a formal restaurant with baroque decor, specialising in seasonal wild game. Try the duck truffles with cava. **Menjador** on Valencia (451 14 34), close to the designer-shopping zone, is a small, busy restaurant serving Mediterranean cuisine, with a great-value *menú del día*. **Cervecería Catalana** on Mallorca (216 03 68) does some of the best tapas in town, hence it's usually packed. Hover until you can get a stool at the bar and drool over the selection of *escalivada* (sweet peppers, onion and garlic), *boccarones* (fresh anchovies) and other tasty morsels on display. **Tragaluz** on Passage de la Concepcio (487 06 21) is well-known for its imaginative Mediterranean menu and silver-service delivery enjoyed by many a visiting celebrity. We loved the six-course tasting menu featuring lobster, venison, and a mouthwatering pudding. There are three floors; try get a table under the glass roof. **Tapa Tapa** on Paseo de Grácia (488 33 69) is one of a chain, you may prefer **Taktika Berri** on Calle Valencia (453 47 59).

 A book about Barcelona and Paseo de Grácia, and a fruit basket and water in your room. Register your Smithcard online, then show your card at check-in, to claim your offer.

Get a room! Use our free online booking service: check availability and make reservations through www.mrandmrssmith.com.

SMITH CONCIERGE Registered Smith cardholders can call +44 (0)20 7978 7333 and have Original Travel book everything from your flights to your day trips, at no extra charge.
Original idea We'll arrange for you to rent a speedboat at Port Olímpic, where you can also enjoy great nightlife, with numerous bars and restaurants on offer.

Prestige Paseo de Grácia 62 Paseo de Grácia, Barcelona 08007 (+34 93 272 41 80)
paseodegracia@prestigehotels.com; www.prestigepaseodegracia.com

'Clearly, the intention is that you feel like house guests in a private home: *Gosford Park*, Catalan-style'.

Relais d'Orsà

CITY   BARCELONA
STYLE   NEO-CLASSICAL ELEGANCE
SETTING   HILLSIDE WITH A VIEW

MTWTFSSMTWTFSSMTWTF**SS**MTWTFSSMTWTFSSMTWT
BARCELONA

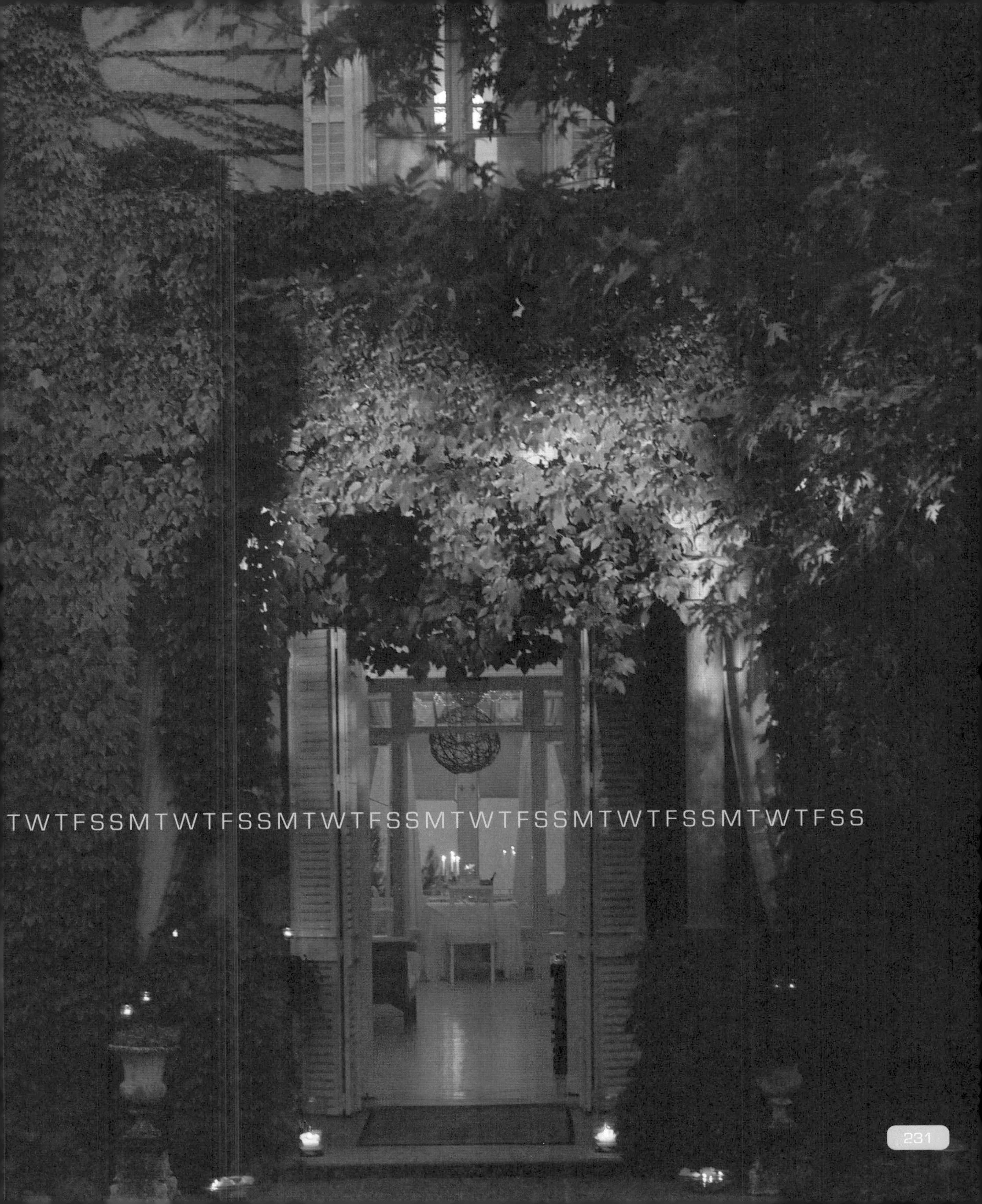

TWTFSSMTWTFSSMTWTFSSMTWTFSSMTWTFSSMTWTFSS

Relais d'Orsà, Barcelona, Spain

It's with great excitement that we show the taxi driver at the airport the address of our destination. He shrugs his shoulders. He knows all the hotels in town, but not Relais d'Orsà. 'It's only 15 minutes away,' we trill. He rings for directions. Shaking his head, he wonders if we realise that we are staying up in the mountains. We do? He sniggers that we're off to the suburbs for our weekend in the bustling Catalan capital. Much head-shaking later, after climbing the kind of winding roads that James Bond car chases are made of, he's starting to make us nervous. Then we find it. Wrought-iron gates open to reveal a magnificent mansion framed in luscious greenery. Through the front door, past billowing white muslin and open French windows, we spy a view of the Barcelona skyline laid out below. Our cabbie, poised to revel in being right, looks crestfallen. Relais d'Orsà is definitely where we want to be.

One half of the husband-and-wife team behind the hotel appears immediately to greet us. She introduces herself as Rosa, and gives us a welcome worthy of a lord and lady, especially delightful since the reality is a dishevelled post-Easyjet pair in flip-flops. Accompanied by a member of staff in a grey maid's uniform, Rosa leads us through the cosy reception room, where Billie Holiday plays softly in the background, and upstairs to our room. Clearly the intention is that you feel like house guests in a private home. *Gosford Park*, Catalan-style; we could get used to this.

Everything in Relais d'Orsà is carefully considered and just-so, from fresh flowers in imaginative vases to an antique teddy poised on a chaise longue – yet amazingly, the ambience is homely, relaxed and comfortable. As the door to our bedroom opens, a waft of vanilla hits us. Antique furniture and feminine but not fussy decor lends the room a Parisian aura. The white-tiled bathroom is elegant. Add a breathtaking view, and you have somewhere truly enchanting.

Outside in the garden, the Spanish sunshine beckons, and we spy two sunloungers with our names on. (Not literally, though with all the care and attention lavished on us so far, it wouldn't come as a surprise.) What we do find are two plump fluffy towels, which, in keeping with Relais d'Orsà's penchant for all things L'Occitane, seem to be infused with a delicious fresh scent. On the terrace, surrounded by foliage, we can't hear a thing except the chirping of cicadas; two butterflies flutter in to complete the scene. We had planned an afternoon of sightseeing and shopping, but on such a hot day we're happy to admire Barcelona here from the hills, and file all other activity under *mañana*.

As there's no restaurant in or around Relais d'Orsà to keep us in the elegant manner to which we're becoming accustomed, we opt for an excursion to a beachside restaurant, Agua, for dinner. Sophisticated but informal, it has a flavour of Californian cool. We're thrilled to get an alfresco table under the stars. A delicious

contemporary take on tapas down the hatch, we sip the last of our cava and, enjoying our romantic evening, we let our minds drift to honeymoons and wedded bliss. Then the hen-night hordes in matching T-shirts traipse past to the enormous bar next door. We leave them to compare novelty thongs while Agua's friendly staff call a cab to navigate us back to our hillside hibernicum.

Breakfast is a cornerstone of the perfect trip away, and Le Relais has the most heavenly arrangement. Just holler when you wake, and indicate where you fancy eating. (Choosing between the expansive views from the balcony and a table in the garden is as taxing as life here gets.) It's a spread fit for royalty: a platter of French cheeses, fresh pastries, fine china, and even heart-shaped pats of butter. Feet in the sunshine, a vista all the way to the sea, and freshly squeezed orange juice in hand – it's enough to make you pinch yourself. We'd stay on our first-floor terrace for ever, if the kidney-shaped pool weren't calling… ↓

Swimwear on, and toes pool-dipped, we hardly notice as our plans for museum and gallery escapades vanish. Fortunately, compensating for hours spent simply sunbathing and swimming is easy: when you do eventually motivate yourself, it's amazing how much you can achieve in an afternoon in Barcelona.

The funicular by the hotel is the smartest option into town; it leads right to the easy-to-use metro. We head straight to the open-air buses in Plaça de Catalunya for a tour of Gaudí's incredible achievements in one fell swoop. A full sightseeing circuit, from La Pedrera and Park Güell to the Sagrada Família, under our belts, we venture to Las Ramblas, but quickly escape the Oxford-Streetish melee to wander the alleyways of the Gothic Quarter. Having explored its every cobbled street, we head to the Born area. Packed with boutiques, design showrooms and buzzing bars, it encapsulates the spirit and energy that makes Barcelona such a cool city. We've had the most wonderful day and night a Mr and Mrs Smith could have; it's no wonder we make a pact in the cab back. If our room is still available tomorrow, we're not budging.

We return to El Relais and find Rosa's affable husband Francisco there to welcome us home. Admiring the moonlit exterior of our magnificent abode, we probe him about its history. Built at the turn of the 20th century by an old-fashioned family who weren't seduced by the modernist movements of the time, it's a classical holiday home in the hills. As regards the interior, Francisco reveals that Rosa has spent a lot of time in Paris and London seeking the perfect furnishings. Finally, the million-euro question: can we stay another night? We're in luck. Well, just you try to visit Relais d'Orsà without digging your heels in.

Reviewed by Mr and Mrs Smith

NEED TO KNOW

Rooms Six, including one suite.
Rates €205–€360, plus seven per cent tax.
Check-out Normally midday, but flexible.
Room service Hot and cold snacks available on request at any time.
Facilities Swimming pool, massage by prior arrangement.
Children An extra bed can be arranged for €40–€45.
Also… Getting from Relais d'Orsà into Barcelona centre is easy; the tram takes you to the metro station Peu de Funecular. Taxis from the centre of town cost €5–€10; this is probably the best way of getting home after 22h, although trains do run an hour or so past midnight.

IN THE KNOW

Recommended rooms 5 is small but very cute; 1 and 2 have fantastic views although the beds are a snug queensize. Rooms 3 and 4 face the garden and have big beds; 6 is the suite.
Hotel bar Drinks can be requested in the lounge area and patio.
Hotel restaurant A superb breakfast is prepared with fresh produce, and if you are arriving late in the evening, Francisco and Rosa will prepare something for you, provided you give them notice; otherwise, no restaurant as such.
Top table On the balcony featured in the cover image. It overlooks the whole city.
Dress code Country casuals.

LOCAL EATING AND DRINKING

There's not a lot in the immediate vicinity if you're a silver-service-craving gourmand, but if it's simple tapas you hanker after, turn right out of the hotel down to **Casa Trampa** in Plaça Vallvidrera (406 80 51). It's a traditional spot for an afternoon snack or a pre-siesta carafe of rosado. In the other direction, **Ideal** on Cami Vell de Santa Creu d'Olorda a Vallvidrera (406 90 29) is an Italian restaurant popular with families for pizza and pasta. Tables on the terrace are great for a summer lunch. **El Asador d'Aranda** on Avenida Tibidabo (417 01 15) is worth a visit not just for the finest Catalan cuisine (try lamb roasted in the oak-burning oven), but for the incredible view. Book a garden table in summer. Another lovely restaurant is **La Venta** on Mount Tibidabo itself (212 64 55), which has a formal French menu. Reserve a table on the terrace.

 A bottle of cava and fresh fruit. Register your Smithcard online, then show your card at check-in, to claim your offer.

Get a room! Use our free online booking service: check availability and make reservations through www.mrandmrssmith.com.

SMITH CONCIERGE Registered Smith cardholders can call +44 (0)20 7978 7333 and have Original Travel book everything from your flights to your day trips, at no extra charge.
Original idea We can arrange for you to have a private tour of the Fundació Gala Salvador Dalí in the nearby town of Figueres.

Relais d'Orsà 35 Mont d'Orsà, Vallvidrera, Barcelona 08017 (+34 93 406 94 11)
info@relaisdorsa.com; www.relaisdorsa.com

STOCKHOLM

MTWTFSSMTWTFSSMTWTFSSMTWTFSSMTWTFSSMTWT

SWEDEN

STOCKHOLM
Berns Hotel
Lydmar Hotel

TWTFSSMTWTFSSMTWTFSSMTWTFSSMTWTFSSMTWTFSS

SVERIGE

STOCKHOLM •

Stockholm

CITYSCAPE   FRESH-AIR FAIRYTALE
CITY LIFE   NORDIC COOL

'A peerless shopping zone, a pretty mediaeval maze, and the cradle
of a design movement that has travelled rather well'

M T W T F S S M T W T F S S M T W T F S S M T W T F S S M T W T F S S M T W T
SVERIGE

STOCKHOLM

Stockholmers are clearly proud of their home. It's famously cool, vibrant yet laid-back, and everything works beautifully – both in terms of function and aesthetics. Graffiti is classified as 'street art', frumpy clothes and clunky design are nonexistent, and the city is as safe and clean as it is hip and cosmopolitan. Stockholmers are down-to-earth and quirky-deadpan, and you'll hardly meet a local who doesn't speak English so well they can't slip words like 'otter' and 'nebulous' into conversation. A network of 14 islands on the edge of the Baltic, Sweden's capital is, in turns, a peerless shopping zone, a maze of pretty mediaeval streets, and the cradle of a design movement that has travelled rather well (H&M, Ikea, *Wallpaper** chic). Each district has its own feel, from the leafy affluence of Östermalm to the boho culture of Södermalm, and all are within walking distance of the centre. By day, you can stroll, shop, island-hop (by boat or by foot) and drink in views of sea and city; the long summer nights mean you can party and people-watch at your leisure. You'll come back poorer, but cooler and more chilled – skål!

GETTING THERE

Planes Arlanda Airport is 40km from the centre. The 45-min Flygbussarna bus service costs SEK 100. If you end up flying into Skavsta airport, a bus into Stockholm takes an hour and a half.
Trains A 20-min Arlanda Express Train costs SEK 180 and takes you into Stockholm Central Station. From here you can access Stockholm's underground, called the Tunnelbana.
Automobiles A taxi costs SEK 400. A car is only an advantage if you want to leave the city centre.

DO GO/DON'T GO

In winter, the city gets just five hours of daylight. At weekends in July, it can be very quiet as everybody heads to their summer island properties.

SUITABLY SWEDISH

Go for a sauna and massage, or hire a private Turkish bath at the Sturebadet (www.sturebadet.se). Head to the beach. In winter, go skiing in Flottsbro, or skating in Kungsträdgården Park.

LOCAL KNOWLEDGE

Taxis You can hail cabs on the street; short trips are usually inexpensive.
Tipping culture Tips are included; for good service, round up the bill.
Packing tips Deck shoes, eye-mask in summer (only three hours of darkness), contemporary-furniture wish list, duty-free booze and smokes.
Recommended reads *The Magic Lantern: An Autobiography* by Ingmar Bergman; *The Messiah of Stockholm* by Cynthia Ozick.
Cuisine The *smörgåsbord*, *surströmming* (fermented Baltic herring), *köttbullar* (meatballs). Owing to long winters, traditional dishes are heavy and rich, but modern Swedish cuisine is lighter, with more fresh vegetables.
Currency Swedish kronor; SEK 10 = about €1.
Dialling codes Country code for Sweden: 46. Stockholm: 8.

DIARY

June Midsummer skies barely grow dark, and Swedes celebrate on the weekend closest to 24 June. At Skansen, the oldest open-air museum in Europe, the festivities bring out maypoles, traditional costumes and games, and folk musicians and dancers. **July** Stockholm Jazz Festival (www.stockholmjazz.com). **13 December** St Lucia Day: Celebrations in honour of the patron saint of light, to brighten up a very dark time of the year.

WORTH GETTING OUT OF BED FOR

Viewpoint The best and most self-indulgent place from which to view the city is the restaurant Eriks Gondolen on Stadsgården (see below).

Arts and culture The Moderna Museet has a superb collection of Swedish and international art. More than 16,000 paintings and sculptures are housed in the National Museum on Södra Blasieholmshamnen. The open-air museum Skansen on Djurgården recalls the Sweden of bygone days, with flora and fauna, farms, manor-houses and craftspeople at work. The Vasamuseet: the Vasa is the world's only surviving 17th-century ship (www.vasamuseet.se).

Something for nothing Watch the changing of the guard (12h15, or 13h15 on Sundays) daily in the Outer Courtyard of the beautiful Royal Palace. Play in the snow in winter!

Shopping Biblioteksgatan, near Stureplan, has a concentration of upmarket shops. On Hornsgatan are irresistible interior design and art shops. Södermalm has many secondhand and antiques shops, as well as one-off boutiques and skater shops. For handicrafts and knick-knacks, visit the old town of Gamla Stan. Don't leave without visiting Östermalmshallen Market on Humlegårdsgatan, open until 18h Monday–Thursday; 18h30 Friday; 16h Saturday and 14h Sunday. In a characterful building next to the flower market, it's a huge delicatessen selling every type of top-quality food you can think of, with bars and restaurants to stop off in.

And... Get a boat out to the archipelago of Vaxholm in summer and have a champagne picnic (ask the hotel to pack you one). Or sail to the Royal Swedish Yacht Club (two hours from the central port) and visit the pretty beaches and harbour at Sandhamn, on the island of Sandön.

Tourist tick box The Royal Palace ❏   Skansen ❏   Vasa Museum ❏

CAFÉS

The best coffee is found in **Tintarella di Luna** on Drottninggatan, an authentic Italian café that does great paninis. If you're craving afternoon tea, we suggest the **Diplomat Tea House** on Strandvägen, for scones with jam and marmalade and sandwiches with the crusts cut off.

BARS AND RESTAURANTS

The best restaurants in Stockholm often come with bar and nightclub attached. **Hotellet** on Linnégatan (442 8900) has a bar, terrace and club. Its mezzanine restaurant does Mediterranean cuisine, and the rooftop has sunloungers. Minimalist in style, and candlelit at night. Cosy **Café Tranan** on Karlbergsv (272 8100), with its checked tablecloths, provides Swedish favourites. The traditional bar downstairs is as popular as the eatery itself. Conducive to romance by night, with its peerless views, **Eriks** on Stadsgården (641 7090) is a unique structure in the sky with two restaurants: **Eriks Grillbar** is bistro-style; **Eriks Gondolen** is more formal, serving French/Swedish dishes. **Bon Lloc** on Regeringsgatan (66 0 6060) is a foodie destination – chef Mathias Dahlgren is famed for his innovation. Stylish **Fredsgatan 12** on Fredsgatan (248 052) serves Swedish and international cuisine, and is ideal for lunch.

NIGHTLIFE

LE is the club in **Berns Hotel** on Ostgotagatan is a hip club with live music and some of the world's finest DJs; it's a magnet for the in crowd. If you're still up past 04h and crave a bit of dancing, it might be time to try and get past the bouncers at **Spy Bar** on Birger Jarlsgatan – cheesy but it can be a fun night out.

'Boutiquey but big, it was built as a restaurant in 1863 and, 14 years ago, got reincarnated as a unique hotel and entertainment palace'

Berns Hotel

CITY	STOCKHOLM
STYLE	GILDED GLORY
SETTING	HISTORIC NIGHTLIFE PALACE

M T W T F S S M T W T F S S M T W T F **S S** M T W T F S S M T W T F S S M T W T

SWEDEN

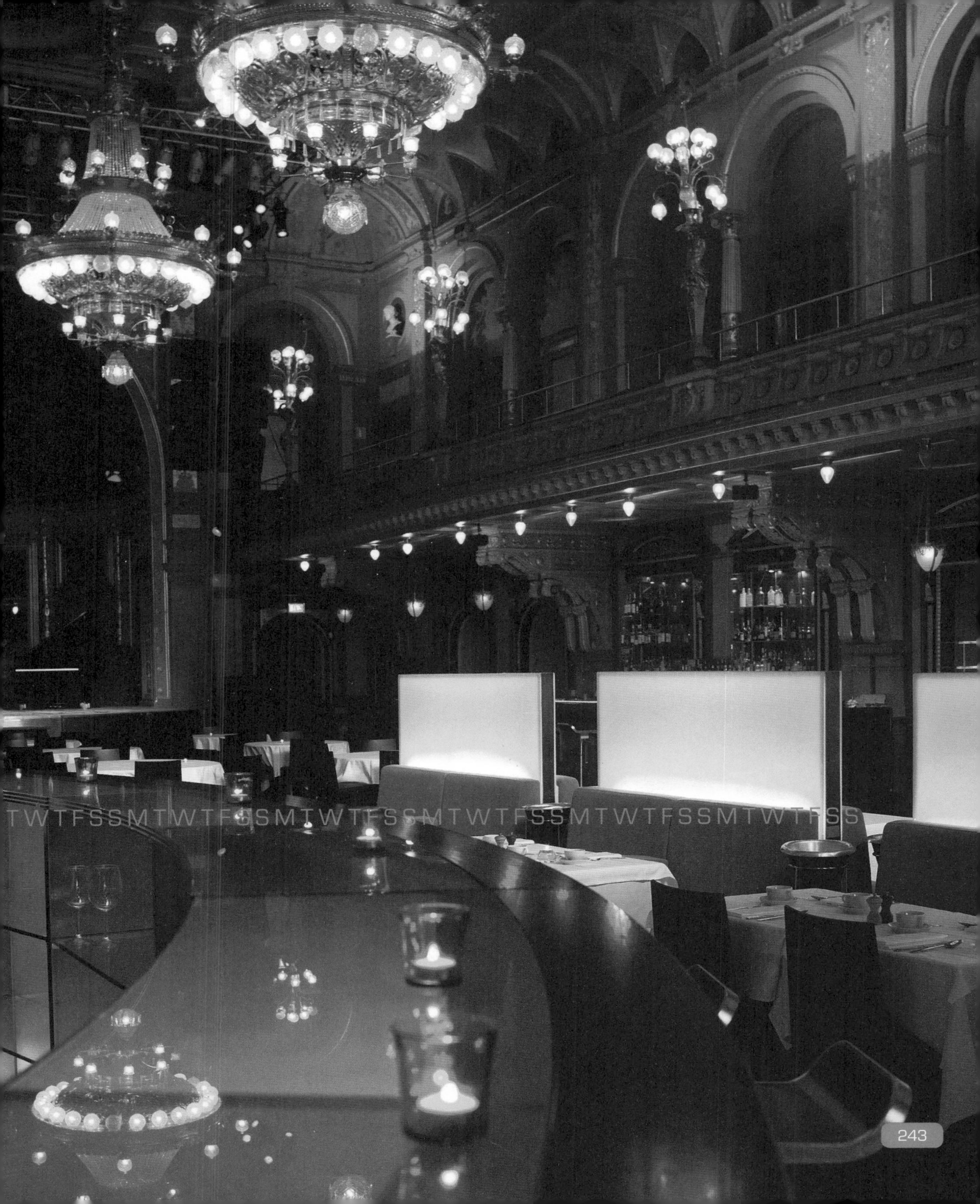

Berns Hotel, Stockholm, Sweden

We crossed the leafy square over which Berns hotel presides, and headed straight for the wrong entrance. There are two: a discreet doorway off to the right leads to reception; the exciting-looking glass structure built into the façade is where non-residents flock to drink and disport themselves in Stockholm's beloved party palace (from dinner in the restaurant to dancing in übertrendy LE). There's no lobby as such, but the main bar is big enough to hold a double-decker bus; Berns' public spaces are on a very grand scale. Hungry, we followed the advice of the beautiful people at reception and wandered up to the Sturehof, a classic brasserie situated on Stureplan, close to leafy Östermalm. There was exuberance in the air (perhaps as it was end-of-the-month payday), and we sat until 01h over five types of Baltic herring and a bottle of rosé, watching the locals go by, and promising each other to whoop it up ourselves the following night.

Boutiquey but big, with 65 rooms, Berns Hotel was originally built as a restaurant in 1863; it got reincarnated 14 years ago as a unique hotel and entertainment palace. Our room was cosy but not tiny, and we loved its style: wood panelling felt both modern and warm, and the groovy cylindrical TV console not only looked great, but also provided me with a screen for undertaking mysterious changes of attire while Mr Smith caught up with current affairs from the comfort of the bed. The modern bathroom was fine, but not as attractive as the room itself, which had the feel of a first-class cabin, without being painfully retro.

In the morning, we explored: the museum-like Red Room and Mirror Room (where we breakfasted sumptuously on, oh, the usual – gravadlax, scrambled eggs, reindeer meat), the ON-bar overlooking Berzelii Park, an upstairs bar that was to get seriously crowded later, an outdoor terrace (a summer institution), and the spectacular main restaurant, which can only be described as Conran goes to the Vienna opera.

Mr Smith, jacket junkie, was on a mission to check out
Swedish designer Filippa K, find a vintage emporium,
and have a rifle through H&M. I was happy to go along
with this, since it all had a pleasingly Scandinavian
unisex appeal. We decided to make for Södermalm, a
quirkier quarter than the superbly heeled central zone.
This took us across Gamla Stan, the mediaeval old
town, whose pretty-as-a-picture streets and squares
are the big tourist-tat-shop area. In concept boutique
c/o Stockholm on Götgatan, we browsed Myla lingerie,
vintage sunglasses, Missoni towels, Nuxe and REN
products and Lara Bohinc jewellery. In a modern mall,
Galleria Bruno, we found the best selection of It jeans
we've ever seen. Fitted out in new slinky top and manly
cropped jacket respectively, we doubled back on
ourselves for lunch at Eriks Gondolen, a bridge-like
structure high in the air, with the best views in town.

Feeling at home in Södermalm, we headed to
Bondegatan, Nytorgsgatan and Skånegatan, where
skaters, students and other species of youth hang out
in pavement cafes, bars and parks. The scene was
beginning to live up to one of my favourite Scandinavian
templates: the film *Together*, where Seventies values
and good skin meet thrift-shop chic. We had coffee in
an airy, grungey canteen called String, murmured
lovingly at some amazingly cheap leather easy chairs,
and contented ourselves with some vintage
Sanderson wallpaper from one of the secondhand
shops on Bondegatan.

We'd forgotten to book for the hotel restaurant, but the
front-desk angels saved the evening and got us a table
at the last minute. The vast gilded dining hall at Berns
Hotel is ornate, grand and lofty, and the staff (like
those in every single shop and restaurant we visited)
were sweetness itself. Mr Smith had one of the best
steaks he's ever eaten – and he's had a few – and we
drank a bottle of Crozes-Hermitage before heading
into Norrmalm. ↓

Hotellet is a packed see-and-be-seen bar, but we preferred the youthful Brasserie Godot, with its reggae soundtrack, great mojitos and bar mural. Bypassing the *Footballers' Wives* end of the nightlife scene, we went back to the Berns and were amazed to see our dignified hotel transformed into a heaving continent of dancing, drinking bodies. We sipped schnapps on the terrace, explored the different bars, and escaped by lift back to our room at some point in the small hours, Berns still pulsating away beneath us.

On Sunday morning, we could have done with some salty sea air, but decided that boarding a boat when we had a flight booked late was too ripe for farce. Instead, we walked to Djurgården and spent the rest of our city break in a facsimile of pre-industrial rural Sweden. It's great: an open-air museum, with reconstructed hovels and playfighting bears. Already sarcastic about my passion for a toy shop in Södermalm ('Oh, look, a pony with a daisy in its mouth…'), Mr Smith wondered if I was reliving my childhood. Then he discovered the elk enclosure.

Before we left for the airport we found ourselves back at the Sturehof. There's a café-society feel to the swankier parts of town, and it dawned on me that, as well as bringing out the Bond girl in me, Stockholm was close to fulfiling all the *Wallpaper**-fuelled lifestyle fantasies I'd ever nurtured. We sat among the international crowd, all cashmere and 'ciao' and tried work out a way of becoming regulars.

Of all the Stockholm clichés we were prepared for – beautiful people, sexy design, social equality, fantastic herring – not all are 100 per cent true: you'll see the occasional kink in a symmetrically beautiful face; there's some glum Sixties architecture; and while Mr Smith says he wouldn't object, apparently Swedish women have to do all the running, dating-wise. Micro-quibbles aside, Stockholm is clean, cultured and cool. And the herring rocks.

Reviewed by Mr & Mrs Smith

NEED TO KNOW

Rooms 65, including four suites.
Rates SEK 2,150–SEK 6,400 (€235–€700), including breakfast. Weekend rates available.
Check-out Midday/flexible if you ask nicely.
Room service Full menu available 24 hours.
Facilities Fruit on tap, late-night bar and club, access to a fully equipped gym at sister establishment the Grand Hôtel, a three-minute walk away.
Children Welcome, but when the bars and club get busy, it's not the best family environment.
Also A huge banquet is laid out every Saturday and Sunday for brunch, except in summer.

IN THE KNOW

Recommended rooms The Clock Suite is the biggest, with the hotel clock visible on the façade, and views over the park. Room 608 is spacious and light, and has a terrace garden. Junior suites feature interiors by Gigoretti and Thomas Sandell. Room 431 served as a dressing room for Ella Fitzgerald and Marlene Dietrich when they performed at Berns.
Hotel bars There are a number of bars, a member's club, and a terrace that gets packed in summer. The lounge bar has huge chandeliers, mirrored walls, balconies and a stage.
Hotel restaurant The baroque gilded restaurant is huge. To the right is the cocktail bar; to the left, the crustacea bar. The restaurant serves excellent fish, meat and game, sometimes to the sound of live jazz. On Saturdays and Sundays you can have brunch until 15h.
Top table An intimate corner table.
Dress code A la mode.

LOCAL EATING AND DRINKING

Berns also has **Calle P**, a glass restaurant in the park out front, especially nice in summer. Get quality fast food (Italian and Asian) to take away or eat in. A short walk north, **Riche** on Birger Jarlsgatan (54 50 35 60) is a maze-like place with a bar and two restaurants. **Teatergrillen** is a relaxed bistro; Stockholm's glitterati eat international food and drink fine wines in the bright-red main restaurant. Up the road is **Sturehof** on Stureplan (440 57 30), where you can sit out (snuggled under blankets if need be); watching the world go by over a plate of herring until late. Another bar and bistro we loved is **Brasserie Godot** on Grev Turegatan (660 06 17).

 A copy of the *Live at Berns* CD. Register your Smithcard online, then show your card at check-in, to claim your offer.

Get a room! Use our free online booking service: check availability and make reservations through www.mrandmrssmith.com.

Berns Hotel 8 Näckströmsgatan, Stockholm 11147 (+46 (0)8 566 322 00)
hotel.berns@berns.se; www.berns.se

Lydmar Hotel

CITY   STOCKHOLM
STYLE   DESIGN PLAYGROUND
SETTING BUZZING STUREPLAN

'The lobby, which doubles as
one of Stockholm's chicest
hang-outs, was packed
with fashionable Swedes'

M T W T F S S M T W T F S S M T W T F S **S** M T W T F S S M T W T F S S M T W T

SWEDEN

MTWTFSSMTWTFSSMTWTFSSMTWTFSSMTWTFSSMTWTFSS

Lydmar Hotel, Stockholm, Sweden

We'd heard so much about the hipness of the Lydmar Hotel that it came as no surprise that we had to negotiate a bouncer (the polite, benevolent kind) to make our entrance. On a Friday night, the lobby, which doubles as one of Stockholm's chicest hang-outs, was packed with fashionable Swedes. With our weekend bags containing half the contents of our wardrobes (I just can't make decisions), we were lucky to snake our way through to the reception desk without knocking anyone into their drinks.

The first thing that hit us as we walked in was the bassline: hip hop – laid-back and welcoming. (The Lydmar is also a music venue for top-class musicians and DJs.) We were slightly alarmed by the four glitter balls above our heads, but we soon realised they were not an indication of a heaving dancefloor, merely of the Swedish sense of irony.

We were given room 555 (of no interest right now, but with a significance we grasped later). Keen to drop off our bags and get back down to start our weekend, we caught the tiny lift, and were serenaded by ABC's 'The Look of Love' all the way to our floor (you can choose your preferred non-musak elevator music, from jazz to funk to reggae). The corridors are wide, noticeably dark and deliberately plain. The room numbers are conspicuously large-scale, placed proudly on the grey doors. The communal spaces give nothing away of what lies beyond them.

I should now explain that, although I was with a girl on this trip, she wasn't my girl. Owing to a bizarre course of work-related events, my wife wasn't able to join me, so I was with her best girlfriend. I should hastily add that my wife had arranged it this way: my stand-in Mrs Smith had just split with her boyfriend and needed cheering up.

There are 62 rooms at the Lydmar: those on the upper floor have all been renovated, and done up by the edgiest names in Swedish art and design. Convincing the hotel staff to let you see some of them isn't difficult (they are very proud of them). We saw 618, with funky black flowery blinds; 553, a very bright, orange room with steps leading down to a comfy sofa and huge plasma screen; and 701, where the bath is situated against a wall in the bedroom.

The main focus of our room was the huge bed, built into a raised floor. Although I didn't mention it to my stunt Mrs Smith at the time, I immediately knew what room 555 was about. It is a modern-minimalist temple; the bed is an interactive shrine; and the deities and worshippers are one and the same. I immediately missed my wife, looked at pseudo Mrs S to gauge her reaction (Shall I suggest we change rooms? Has she noticed what this room is about? Are we both grown-up enough not to get stupidly embarrassed by this really strange situation?), then pointed to the TV/DVD and sound system at the foot of the bed and said 'Cool, eh?'

After a quick change, we made our way to the bar and just soaked in the atmosphere. The cocktail menu is huge, and the bartenders know their stuff. We were hypnotised, watching them flow in time to the music as they concocted their masterpieces, cutting fruit with the understated flamboyance of sushi chefs. 'Which room are you in?' asked our ponytailed barman. I told him. He cocked his eyebrow, winked, and flashed a knowing smile. 'Champagne it is, then.' I couldn't think of a way of explaining our set-up without it all sounding a bit sordid. His smile told a thousand stories.

The Lydmar is situated in the centre of town, near Stureplan's designer shops (next door but one is an Alessi outlet), and within walking distance of Stockholm's trendy bars and clubs. On Saturday morning, after a buffet breakfast, we floated through Stureplan, cushioned by the hazy after-effects of an evening on the champagne, and over to Gamla Stan. This little island is the site of the original city, and where the official residence of the Swedish royal family is situated. ↓

By chance, we fell upon the changing-of-the-guard ceremony. Unlike their English counterparts, the sentries will engage in conversation and pose for photos. We stopped for lunch on a cobbled street, with a cellist busking melodies from *Carmen* and *Swan Lake* outside a shop selling Indian rugs, saffron-clothed dummies of Indian gods in the window. Sure enough, 20 minutes later, we heard the familiar jingles and chants of a Hare Krishna conga. It all added to the bizarre, fun hungover time we were having.

After walking through to Södermalm, an area stuffed full of cafés and galleries, and browsing the clothes and design shops on Gotgatan, tiredness overtook me, and we felt the urge to cab it back to the hotel for a bit of mid-afternoon room service (a huge club sandwich of beautifully roasted pork with a spicy mayonnaise) and a nap.

For Saturday evening, we'd booked at the well-loved Eriks Gondolen restaurant, which sits at the top of what looks like a massive crane. The food doesn't quite qualify for the prices, but the view over Gamla Stan and the water is simply breathtaking. It's a very romantic, intimate setting. As I sat there, at the height of the extended northern twilight, my mind kept wandering off to my wife; I promised myself I'd bring her here when I come back with her.

After dinner, we put our party hats on. We'd heard that the Mosebacke Etablissement was supposed to be Stockholm's coolest place. Expecting a queue, with pickers who admit only the loveliest and louchest, we were surprised when the doorman practically escorted us into the main area, where a band had been playing. The place is studenty and refreshingly unglamorous; we found ourselves dancing to the Smiths, the Cure, Duran Duran… As fun as it was, the more up-to-date tunes of the Lydmar beckoned, and we finished off the night (and ourselves) with vodka sours at the hotel bar.

Following a late brunch at Elverket on Linnégatan, where we tried to guess which of our fellow diners were thespians from the adjoining Royal Dramatic Theatre, we took a boat tour around the archipelago, and invited the brisk wet air to blow away the night before. A queasy few hours later, we went for a spot of tea at Oscars Café, a tearoom on Narvavägen with a Fifties feel.

Back at the Lydmar, we squeezed in another viewing: this time it was room 700, the biggest suite. It left us with a fitting last impression of the Lydmar. Open-plan and sumptuous, with super technology, it's the room that I will book when I return. And next time, I will be bringing my real Mrs Smith.

Reviewed by Mr & Mrs Smith

NEED TO KNOW

Rooms 62.
Rates SEK 1,280–SEK 6,500 (€140–€700), including breakfast.
Check-out Midday.
Room service Until 23h.
Children Cots are available, but be aware that the hotel's public spaces are nightlife-oriented.
Also If you arrive at night, go round to the side entrance: the reception is situated in the very popular lobby bar. The lift allows you to choose your own elevator music, from hip hop to pop.

IN THE KNOW

Recommended rooms 618 and 612 are our favourites, created by recent Swedish designer of the year Mattias Stalhbom; they are very bright with big windows and black floral blinds. 701 is the pink room, the work of another Swedish designer, Madeleine; 700 is a big open-plan suite with surround sound. Orange-and-green-themed 553 has steps leading down to a sitting area with plasma TV and leather sofa. In 555, the bed is built into the floor on a raised platform.
Hotel bar Famous for its live acts, the lobby here is a big draw, open until 01h.
Hotel restaurant The minimalist restaurant specialises in Mediterranean cuisine. Last orders are at 23h.
Top table Looking out onto the street.
Dress code Effortless cool.

LOCAL EATING AND DRINKING

Glass-fronted **Swoon** on Humlegardsgatan (070 527 54 52) offers Mediterranean and Swedish dishes. Its minimalist orange interior and alcove seating make a good lunchtime spot. **Riche** on Birger Jarlsgatan (54 50 35 60) has an international menu and a glossy clientele; on our visit we sat on a table next to Sven-Goran Eriksson. It's something of an experience: you are led through the kitchens into the red dining room. The adjacent **Teatergrillen** (54 50 35 65) is a less starry alternative, serving French cuisine among old theatre costumes. **Sturehof**, located in a trendy precinct on Stureplan (44 05 730) is an elegant brasserie serving good fish and shellfish, with a popular pavement terrrace. Within the same complex are two style-conscious drinking spots, including the dark and smoky **O-Bar**.

 They will fix guests a seasonal cocktail on the house. Register your Smithcard online, then show your card at check-in, to claim your offer.

Get a room! Use our free online booking service: check availability and make reservations through www.mrandmrssmith.com.

SMITH CONCIERGE Registered Smith cardholders can call +44 (0)20 7978 7333 and have Original Travel book everything from your flights to your day trips, at no extra charge.
Original idea What could be more invigorating than a specially arranged private guided kayaking trip around some of the 20,000 islands of the Stockholm archipelago?

Lydmar Hotel 10 Sturegatan, Stockholm 11436 (+46 8 5661 1300)
info@lydmar.se; www.lydmar.se

UNITED KINGDOM

EDINBURGH
Prestonfield
LONDON
Baglioni Hotel
The Soho Hotel
The Zetter

TWTFSSMTWTFSSMTWTFSSMTWTFSSMTWTFSSMTWTFSS

EDINBURGH

Edinburgh

CITYSCAPE **COBBLED STREETS, CASTLE VIEWS**
CITY LIFE **WIT, WISDOM AND WHISKY**

M T W T F S S M T W T F S S M T W T F S S M T W T F **S S** M T W T F S S M T W T
UNITED KINGDOM

'Friendly, open and easy to amble round, it's also
aesthetically pleasing whichever direction you turn'

257

EDINBURGH

Were Scotland's first city to have a front door, 'Welcome' would be written on the mat. In big letters. Friendly, open and easy to amble round, it's also aesthetically pleasing whichever direction you turn, with its cobbled Royal Mile, atmospheric graveyards, gracious Georgian crescents, sparkling sea views, and the dramatic backdrop of the castle. Edinburgh is delightful even when the weather isn't. If the sun is out, there are parks, botanical gardens and viewpoints such as Arthur's Seat and Calton Hill. If it's cold, the cosy pubs of Cockburn Street will have you happily cancelling other plans in favour of another wee dram. It's not all whisky and ghosts: they're a cultured lot, with an international arts calendar and more booksellers per capita than any other British city. The heart of town is George Street, where boutiques and eateries cluster. (And you don't have to feel guilty – you're celebrating local heritage; Edinburgh is the birthplace of the overdraft and the chequebook.) Beyond the crooked alleys of the centre, and the fish restaurants of up-and-coming Leith, drive a few minutes out of town, and you're tramping rugged beaches. It's hard to believe such a packed resumé could have any more surprises… but would the fact that it's built on an extinct volcano impress you?

GETTING THERE

Planes The airport is 30 mins by taxi, and costs about £20. The Lothian Buses Airlink service, which takes 45 mins and costs £3.

Trains The main station is Waverly, in the city centre; the other is Haymarket, about a mile away. GNER has a high-speed Intercity service along the East Coast; a West Coast mainline connects with the west of England.

Automobiles Edinburgh is roughly six and a half hours from London; the route from Newcastle is particularly picturesque.

DO GO/DON'T GO

If you don't like crowds, avoid August, when the Festival is on.

EXCEPTIONALLY EDINBURGH

Book a *Trainspotting* walk with expert guide Tim Bell (0131 555 2500); or do the ghost tour near the castle. Take a champagne hot-air balloon flight over breathtaking cityscape and countryside in summer, £159 for two (0131 667 4251; www. albaballooning.co.uk).

LOCAL KNOWLEDGE

Taxis You can hail a black cab from anywhere in the street, or pre-book a minicab.

Tipping culture Tipping is not expected in Scotland, but in restaurants, 12.5 per cent is considered fair. Cabs don't expect a tip, but ten per cent will earn you a smile.

Packing tips Umbrella; the weather is reliably unreliable. Your literature wish list.

Recommended reads Robert Burns poetry, Ian Rankin crime; *Glue* by Irvine Welsh.

Cuisine Good haggis is a delicacy you must try; otherwise, Scotland is famed for its game, Aberdeen Angus steak, smoked salmon and single-malt whisky.

DIARY

30 April Beltane Fire: all-night festival on Calton Hill. **June** Leith Festival, for open houses, concerts and exhibitions (www.leithfestival.com). **August** Every day has a surprise in store during Edinburgh Festival (www.edinburgh-festivals.com) as the Fringe Festival (comedy), the Book Festival, the International Film Festival and theatre productions aplenty roll into town during the month. **31 August– 1 September** Edinburgh Mela: Asian festival in Pilrig Park. **29 December–1 January** Legendary four-day New Year's Eve celebrations (www.edinburghshogmanay.org).

WORTH GETTING OUT OF BED FOR

Viewpoint From Calton Hill, watch the sun setting behind Edinburgh Castle. It takes about five minutes to climb a steep staircase at Waterloo Place, or you can drive up and park. To the east of the castle, the hill (an extinct volcano) resembling a crouching lion is Arthur's Seat.

Arts and culture The National Gallery of Scotland, the National Gallery of Modern Art and the National Portrait Gallery can all be investigated on www.nationalgalleries.org. The City Art Centre houses about 3,500 works of Scottish art, from watercolours and prints to sculpture and tapestries. See Diary for details of Edinburgh Festival.

Something for nothing Edinburgh's Royal Botanical Gardens is one of the best in the world, and contains over six per cent of all known species of plant (www.rbge.org.uk). Doors Open Day, every September, offers entry into historic buildings (www.cockburnassociation.org.uk).

Shopping Harvey Nichols and Louis Vuitton feature on St Andrew Square, while shops in the old town offer Highland dress and antiques. For whisky visit Royal Mile Whiskies on the High Street.

And… Leith, the city docks, is an up-and-coming part of town, with some great fish restaurants. The Secret Bunker is a nuclear shelter hidden under a farm for years (www.secretbunker.co.uk).

Tourist tick box Edinburgh Castle ❏ Royal Mile ❏ Arthur's Seat ❏

CAFES

Circus Café is a deli-cum-restaurant, but also a good spot for coffee, particularly on the decking on a sunny day. For afternoon tea accompanied by an harpist, head to **Palm Court** at the Balmoral Hotel on Princes Street. A great place for coffee, cake and all things nice is **Café Florentin** (0131 225 6267) on St Giles Street. **Valvona & Crolla** is a celebrated deli, and has recently opened **Vincaffe** in the designer shopping centre, on Multrees Walk.

BARS ANDS RESTAURANTS

The restaurants in the **Witchery** on Castlehill (225 5613) are extremely romantic. The restaurant of the same name is wood panelled and candlelit; the Secret Garden is airy with windows onto a terrace – both serve exceptional contemporary Scottish cuisine. **Dome** on George Street (624 8624), formerly HQ of the Commercial Bank of Scotland, serves traditional lunch and Modern Scottish dinner in a most impressive interior. The cupola in the rear room overlooks a central circular bar: the Thirties cocktail bar on one side is loud and lively; the restaurant, on the other, is more refined and elegant. **Oloroso** on Castle Street (226 7614) inhabits a highly desirable rooftop space on George Street. Lounge bar, restaurant, private dining room and terrace all in one, it serves gourmet Mediterranean food, and a fantastic selection of sherries. Window seats are best. **Rick's** on Frederick Street (622 7800) is a venue worth dressing up for by night, where super mixologists deliver award-winning martinis. At lunch, it has a good brasserie menu.

NIGHTLIFE

One of Edinburgh's most talked-about destinations is **Opal Lounge** on George Street (226 2275), 8,000 square feet of after-dark revelry, with candlelit leather-clad corners where you'll hear sweet and soulful music on chilled nights, and upbeat party tunes at the weekend. Asian-influenced eats and a 03h licence. **Oxygen** on Infirmary Street (557 9997) provides wine-bottle-sized canisters of flavoured O_2. There's also an extensive wine, beer and cocktail menu for more substantial sustenance.

'With 20 acres
of parkland,
Prestonfield
is a lush
oasis of calm
in the middle of
the most elegant
city in Europe'

Prestonfield

CITY   EDINBURGH
STYLE   SUMPTUOUS AND DECADENT
SETTING   CITY-CENTRE HIGHLANDS

M T W T F S S M T W T F S S M T W T F **S S** M T W T F S S M T W T F S S M T W T
EDINBURGH

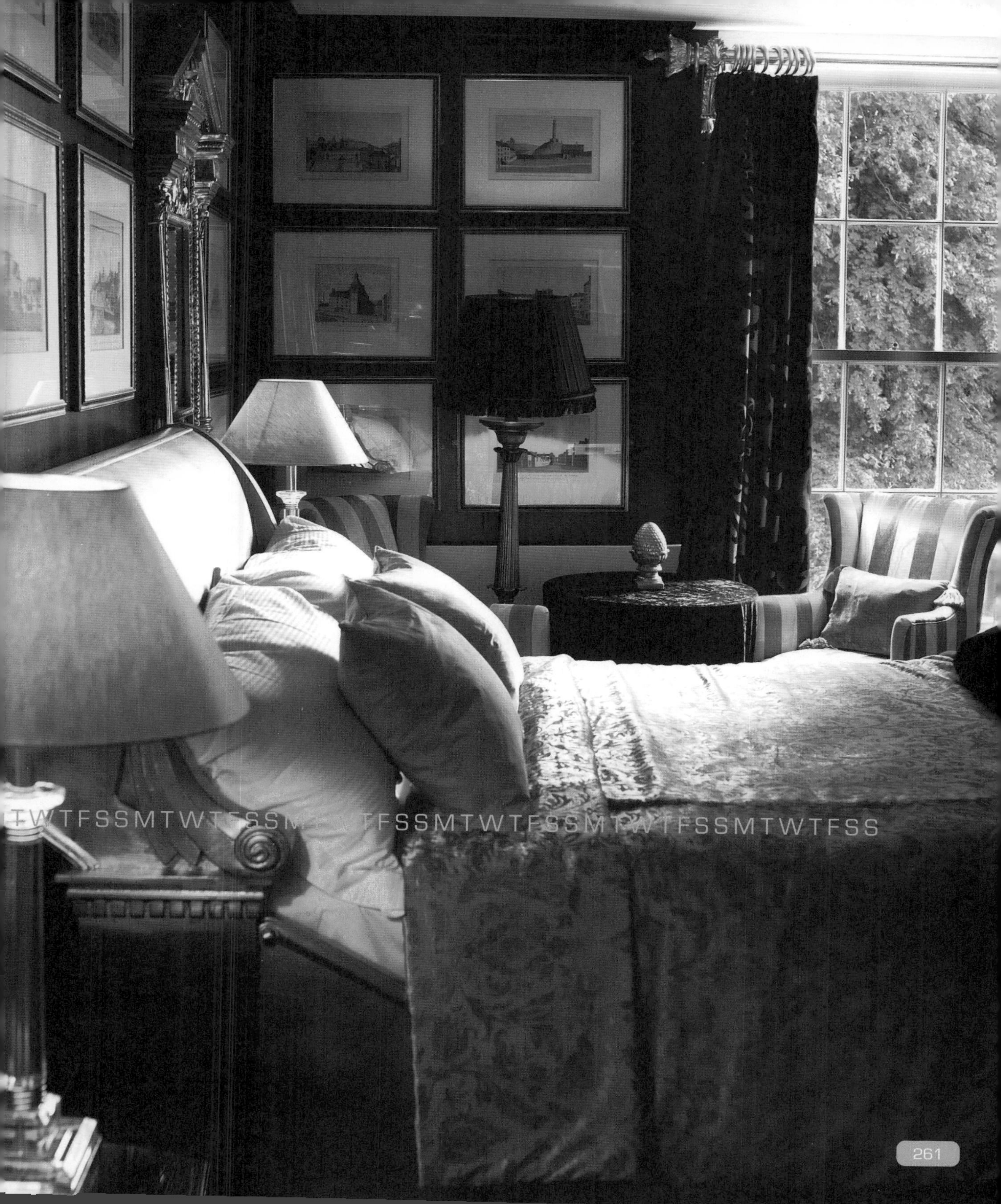

'Och, Prestonfield,' exclaims our taxi driver when we tell him our destination. 'Most beautiful hotel in the city. Very romantic.' He then launches into a long history of his own love life – a catalogue of failed marriages, costly divorces and acrimonious split-ups. 'Had I taken wife number three to Prestonfield,' he laments, 'she probably wouldn't have taken me to the cleaners.'

20 minutes from the airport and we reach the main artery of Princes Street, then, just beyond that, a long, spacious residential road. Magnificent wrought-iron gates lead to a long driveway, and finally, Prestonfield. There are few major town centres where you can find a hotel with 20 acres of parkland, a golf course and pure tranquility, but Prestonfield is a lush oasis of calm, slap bang in the middle of the most elegant city in Europe. And it has a suitably impressive entrance. To the north, Arthur's Seat rises 100 feet high; to the south, east and west, it is green and grassy as far as the eye can see,

with Highland cows grazing just feet from the grounds while a cluster of peacocks goosestep their way around the gardens. The moment we come to a halt, a smartly kilted doorman welcomes us to Prestonfield. But for the Australian accent, we could have been transported to 17th-century Scotland.

The exterior of Prestonfield is simple and understated – it's your average 28-bedroom country manor, if 28-bedroom country manors can ever be average, but inside, it has been designed with an outright disregard for minimalism. It's like the Cluedo house brought to life, with huge, luxurious stately rooms, and immaculately attired staff uttering the kind of speech usually restricted to novels: 'Shall sir be taking tea before retiring?' You half expect the eyes of the portraits lining the hallway to flicker from side to side, a bookshelf to spin around revealing a secret passageway, or Miss Scarlett to appear, candlestick in hand, screaming 'murder' inconsolably. Of course, it's

actually a very peaceful and relaxing retreat, with all the drama confined to the decor. Swathes of woven fabric wallpaper, plush curtains, an incredible collection of antique furniture, intricately carved ceilings, ruby, gold and jet-black colours – it's pure modern decadence.

Our bedroom is snug, but very sexy. There's a big puffy bed with crimson coverings, ornate lampshades, and an antique chest revealing the kind of mod cons you expect from more contemporary luxury hotels. There's a Bose stereo, a big flatscreen television, and a DVD player – not that we're planning to stay in and watch films. There's also a complimentary bottle of Pol Roger champagne, which, needless to say, doesn't stay unopened for long. The bathroom is also on the small side, but the deep-massage shower more than compensates, and feeling fully refreshed, we book dinner at Rhubarb, the hotel's own restaurant (so named because Prestonfield was the first estate in Scotland to propagate the vegetable when it was introduced from China).

After a glass of champagne on a black crocodile-skin banquette in the Yellow Room, a black-kilted porter leads us to our table next door, where we have mesmerising views of the colourfully lit parkland outside. The deep-red walls are adorned with the house's ancestral portraits, which have hung in the room since they were painted. Regional Scottish ingredients feature prominently on the menu (Borders lamb, Lindisfarne oysters, Scottish salmon and Isle of Skye scallops) and the wine list is particularly impressive. A dreamy, melt-in-your-mouth experience ensues, the conversation flows, the wine quickly disappears, and the hours slip away. Instead of coffee, we opt to end our night with a mint tea (forcing the waitress out to the herb garden in the dark) in the Tapestry room, the balcony doors wide open. ↓

Breakfast is big and very Scottish – you choose from a full-fat fry-up, kippers, or the continental buffet. Greedily, we choose a bit of everything and return to the bedroom for a snooze, before heading into one of our favourite cities. The Old Town and the Royal Mile are punctuated with mediaeval buildings of every shape and size, and the new town is a picture of Georgian elegance. Overlooking it all is the castle – Edinburgh's number-one tourist attraction. To capture the splendour of the skyline, we head for the clean-cut contemporary surroundings of the Tower restaurant on the fifth floor of the Museum of Scotland. The food is fantastic, but we refrain from overeating, having squirrelled away a spread for late-afternoon snacking in the Princes Street Gardens in the middle of the city. It is a great place for a picnic; the vista takes in the cathedral and the ever-present castle, and there's lots of space to spread out a tartan blanket. As the sun sets beyond the hills, the buildings take on an amber glow, and the city lights spark to life, giving the ancient Scottish stones a whole new fantastical aspect. To our delight, the castle, beautifully illuminated, is further animated with bursts of fireworks marking the end of one of the concerts that are a regular occurrence at the National Heritage site.

We head for pre-dinner drinks at one of the scores of basement bars that line the city centre's streets. Opal Lounge is at the top of its class. It's open until 03h, but we have other plans – Oloroso. One of the best new-wave gourmet restaurants in town, it's famed for its modern Mediterranean menu and its showcasing of sherry as a modern, metropolitan tipple. Satisfied we've sampled sufficient of both, we tumble into a taxi home. Back at the hotel, as we tuck ourselves into the crisp white linen, I reach for the phone and do the one thing that will make the next morning a little less painful. I order a late check-out before we disappear into a blissful sleep. 'Will sir be wanting anything else?' Only another few days at Prestonfield…

Reviewed by Jeremy Mascarenhas

NEED TO KNOW

Rooms 24.

Rates £195–£250, including Full Scottish breakfast.

Check-out Midday.

Room service 24-hour, but there is a reduced menu after midnight, serving smoked salmon sandwiches, cheese and biscuits, steak, Caesar salad.

Facilities Air con, high-speed internet access, Bose sound system, DVD player, plasma TV.

Children Welcome up to the age of 12: a bed can be provided in your room for no extra charge, but there is a charge for the third breakfast.

Also The hotel has three rooms for private dining: the Garden (seats 50); the Stuart Room (seats 16); and the Italian Room (seats 28).

IN THE KNOW

Recommended rooms Top-floor rooms are very romantic, with combed ceilings, and walls upholstered in aubergine silk toile, and great views looking on to the park land.

Hotel bar There are four main bars in the hotel, all with open fires: the Yellow Room has black crocodile leather banquettes. The candlelit Tapestry Room has a 17th-century plaster ceiling and terrace. Settle into an antler chair and enjoy one of the 100 malts on offer in the Whisky Bar. 17th-century hide panels from Córdoba in Spain, line the walls of the Leather Room.

Hotel restaurant At Rhubarb, chef Kenny Coltman creates modern Scottish food with the best seasonal produce from Scotland's finest regional suppliers: Lindisfarne oysters, Isle of Skye scallops and Black Gold beef. Opulent gold, red and black rooms, open 12h–15h and 18h–23h.

Top table Table 5, next to the window.

Dress code Low-key luxe.

LOCAL EATING AND DRINKING

Oloroso on Castle Street (0131 226 7614), with an a la carte and grill menu is great for lunch or dinner. **Atrium** on Cambridge Street (0131 228 8882) serves Mediterranean food mixed with contemporary Scottish cuisine. **Montpeliers** on Bruntsfield Place (0131 229 3115) is a bar/restaurant that does the best breakfast. Bar open until 01h. Top floor of the Museum of Scotland is **Tower Restaurant** on Chambers Street (225 3003), with castle views. The inspired Scottish menu features the best seasonal ingredients (oysters, seafood, game, Angus beef).

 All guests get a bottle of Pol Roger, but you'll also be collected from the airport at no extra charge. Register your Smithcard online, then show your card at check-in, to claim your offer.

Get a room! Use our free online booking service: check availability and make reservations through www.mrandmrssmith.com.

SMITH CONCIERGE Registered Smith cardholders can call +44 (0)20 7978 7333 and have Original Travel book everything from your flights to your day trips, at no extra charge.

Original idea We can take you on a special tour of the Pentland Hills, south west of the city.

PRESTONFIELD Priestfield Road, Edinburgh (+44 (0)131 225 7800)
info@prestonfield.com; www.prestonfield.com

● LONDON

London

CITYSCAPE PRETTY, GRITTY AND GREEN
CITY LIFE CULTURAL KALEIDOSCOPE

'I can't think of anything more
exhilarating than a trip to London'
Virginia Woolf

M T W T F S S M T W T F S S M T W T F **S S** M T W T F S S M T W T F S S M T W
UNITED KINGDOM

LONDON'S four corners offer everything you could possibly want, but they require careful navigation. Head north to Hampstead Heath, south to Borough Market, upriver to Kew Gardens or down to Tower Bridge, and you'll find entertainment in abundance, indoors and out, come rain or shine. There are glorious green parks for perambulating, historic streets and squares for exploring. Monuments galore; museums stacked with world treasure; galleries showcasing the up-and-coming; stages where the big names tread; the music industry's vanguard, busy in the clubs. London does every kind of cool, from the now-boho quarter of the Victorian East End to the walkways of a redeveloped South Bank, where Tate Modern and the London Eye loom. And gone are the days when eating meant disappointing pub grub; this is a city that's emerged as a food capital of the world. Thanks to 34 Michelin-starred restaurants, and chic cocktail bars, you'll sup like royalty. A multi-ethnic English eccentric, the British capital lets you eat and shop your way around the globe by bus or by tube. Whether you want your food frill-free or fashionable, your lifestyle designer or cheap 'n' cheerful, London's got it, and she flaunts it.

GETTING THERE

Planes London has several airports. Heathrow is at the western end of the Piccadilly Line on the Tube, or 15 mins from Paddington on the Heathrow Express train (£13 one-way). Gatwick is to the south; frequent trains from Victoria cost £12 one-way. City airport is east, in the Docklands; north of London are Luton (35 mins from Kings Cross by Thameslink, about £12 one-way), and Stansted (45 mins to Liverpool Street by train, about £14 one-way). A taxi from any will cost you dearly.
Trains International trains come into Waterloo; from there take the Tube (the London Underground) to anywhere in the city.
Automobiles On weekdays 07h—18h30, there's a Congestion Charge of £5 to drive in central London (www.cclondon.com). Parking is easy but costly.

DO GO/DON'T GO

London empties out in August, but tourist sites still get crowded. Spring and summer can be lovely, even if the weather is reliably unreliable.

LITERALLY LONDON

Take a soapbox to Speakers' Corner on a Sunday and have your say, or go horse-riding (7262 3791) – both Hyde Park. Visit a tailor on Savile Row; we like Maurice Sedwell (7734 0824).

LOCAL KNOWLEDGE

Taxis You can hail black cabs anywhere, or ring Zingo (08700 700700) from your mobile, and the nearest one will find you. Avoid unlicensed mini-cabs.
Tipping culture Ten per cent is standard, but many restaurants now add a discretionary 12.5 per cent, so be careful not to tip twice.
Packing tips A pocket *A–Z* with a Tube map will stop you getting lost.
Recommended reads *London Fields* by Martin Amis.
Cuisine You name it… but jellied eels, pie and mash (try F Cooke on Broadway Market, E8) and the Full English breakfast are trad London fare.
Currency Pound sterling.
Dialling codes Country code for the UK: 44. London: 020.

DIARY

Late March Oxford and Cambridge Boat Race (www.theboatrace.org).
Mid-April London Marathon (www.london-marathon.co.uk). **Late May** Chelsea Flower Show (www.rhs.org.uk/chelsea). **Late June** Wimbledon LTC (www.wimbledon.org). **July–September** The Proms (www.bbc.co.uk/proms). **August bank holiday** Notting Hill Carnival. **September** Open House Weekend (www.londonopenhouse.org). **Mid-October–early November** The London Film Festival (www.lff.org.uk). **5 November** Bonfire Night, aka Guy Fawkes.

WORTH GETTING OUT OF BED FOR

Viewpoint Book a ride on the London Eye, the South Bank's big wheel (www.londoneye.com). Or go for a drink in **Oxo Tower** near Blackfriars Bridge (7803 3888), or **Vertigo 42** on Old Broad Street (7877 7842), a champagne and seafood bar 590 feet above pavement level.

Arts and culture Tate Modern and Tate Britain house British and international art collections (www.tate.org.uk). The Victoria & Albert Museum has fantastic permanent and cutting-edge displays of craft, design and textiles (www.vam.ac.uk). At Somerset House, there are open-air rock, pop and classical concerts in the summer; ice-skating in winter (www.somerset-house. org.uk). Grab a copy of weekly listings magazine *Time Out* for more information about what's on, or visit www.ticketmaster.co.uk to book everything from theatre to gigs.

Something for nothing The Changing of the Guard, at Buckingham Palace, 11h30 daily in summer. If it's sunny, head to a green space (www.royalparks.gov.uk). If not, lots of museums are free: try the Photographers' Gallery (www.photonet.org.uk), or the Serpentine (www.serpentinegallery.org).

Shopping The designer-label zones are Sloane Street and Knightsbridge and Bond Street and South Molton Street. Markets abound in London: Camden gets packed on Sundays with students and tourists hunting for novelties, second-hand clothes and clubwear; over east, Spitalfields Market sells funky babywear, cool T-shirts, artworks and organic food; get up early for Columbia Road Flower Market at the top of Brick Lane (itself a teeming Sunday-morning institution); for organic food and great tasting opportunities, Borough Market is open Fridays 12h– 18h and Saturdays 09h– 16h; Portobello Market in Notting Hill, on Fridays and Saturdays, mixes antiques, vintage and directional fashion and food.

Tourist tick box Buckingham Palace ❑ The London Eye ❑ Tower of London ❑

CAFES

The rooftop café at **Alfies Antique Market** on Church Street, Marylebone, for a Full English or afternoon tea alfresco. Admire Sir Norman Foster's Great Court in the **British Museum** on Great Russell Street. **Bar Italia** on Frith Street is famous for serving the best cappuccini, day and night.

BARS AND RESTAURANTS

For great grill food in buzzy surroundings, try the **Electric Brasserie** on Portobello Road (7908 9696). **Mirabelle** on Curzon Street (7499 4636) is an elegant stop for great French food. Former car showroom, the **Wolseley** on Piccadilly (7499 6996) serves European food all day long, and **J Sheekey** on St Martins Court (7240 2565) is renowned for its fantastic seafood. **CVO Firevault** on Great Titchfield Street (7580 5333) is a drinking/eating space beneath a fireplace shop; roaring hearths make it perfect in winter. We adore modern Asian **Hakkasan** on Hanway Place (7927 7000) and its dim sum sis **Yauatcha** on Broadwick Street (7494 8888). Make a trip to Shoreditch for the eccentric interior and French cuisine of **Les Trois Garçons** on Club Row (7613 1924), then pop to **Loungelover** on Whitby Street (7012 1234) for cocktails.

NIGHTLIFE

Cargo on Shoreditch's Rivington Street offers live bands, cutting-edge DJs, a friendly bar and tapas. **Aura Kitchen and Bar** on James's Street (7499 6655) serves Pacific Rim for dinner, then transforms into a club where party folk flash their cash. With Moroccan cushions, Chinese daybeds and cosy corners, popular **Chinawhite** on Air Street (7343 0040) is a decadent den.

'The kind of luxury preferred by Rome's beautiful people and image-obsessed Milanese'

Baglioni Hotel

CITY   LONDON
STYLE   ITALIAN ELEGANCE
SETTING   PARKSIDE KENSINGTON

MTWTFSSMTWTFSSMTWTFSSMTWTFSSMTWTF**SS**MTW

LONDON

TWTFSSMTWTFSSMTWTFSSMTWTFSSMTWTFSSMTWTFSS

Baglioni, London, UK

Just east of Kensington High Street, opposite Hyde Park, the Baglioni offers a location as desirable as London has to offer. The room we stay in gives us the best view imaginable: not over the park, which some enjoy, but across to the Thistle Hotel – the sort of establishment I usually stay in. I imagine its residents dreaming of one day making it across the road.

My knowledge of London hotels doesn't extend much beyond the Park Lane strip where I perform as a comedian – a corporate sphere apart from the intimacy of the Baglioni. Speaking as someone whose only Italian trips have been for skiing, this temple to restrained extravagance offers the kind of luxury preferred by Rome's beautiful people, or perhaps the image-obsessed Milanese. And now us.

The hotel doesn't have the glitzy façade that some insecure five-star hotels cling to. There are none of the flags or huge signs sported by the neighbouring hotels. Clearly, Baglioni's clientele is sufficiently in the know to

be aware of its presence, because the Georgian building, although respectable and impeccable, doesn't allude to the over-the-top grandeur that awaits inside. A cascading water feature, stone floors and oversized gold vases spilling enormous white roses create a suitably classy entrée to our new world of care-free indulgence. I feel myself happily slotting into this new lifestyle (at least until the morning, when we'll be asked to leave, albeit politely). Back to a life of using towels for weeks, and trying not to cry as the kids continue on their mission to devalue our home.

It seems fitting in such opulent surroundings, that the staff are also beautiful. My wife and I are accompanied to our bedroom by one of the polished receptionists, via a lift with its own plasma TV. Did this imply that the elevator is going to take an especially long time? Fortunately not, and within seconds we're outside room 307. (Maybe they just ordered too many plasmas.) By now fully acclimatised to the luxury that characterises the Baglioni, we expect our room to be exquisite.

It doesn't come as a surprise, then, when it is exactly that. Purple and gold is the daring colour scheme for the fabrics and carpet, which doesn't stop at the floor – nothing as humdrum as wallpaper at the Baglioni. (Outside very secure prisons and police stations, I imagine, this quality of hotel is the only place where padded rooms and bulletproof glass – a feature of the VIP suites – are appropriate.) In the plasma-screen department, my over-ordering theory is borne out; we get two. I race to check out the ensuite. It's stunning: marbles, slates and chromes, and a pair of beautiful his 'n' hers copper bowls, with an array of luxurious hair and body products on offer. I react badly. 'Bloody hell! Mrs Smith, check this out! This is much too beautiful a place to have people doing what people do in bathrooms,' I shriek. Our managerial escort excuses herself (perhaps twigging we're not the most sophisticated guests to cross the hotel's threshold) and informs us that our butler will be up shortly to demonstrate the espresso machine. I think better of mentioning the fact I'm more of a Rosie Lee man; it would seem sacrilegious in this temple to Italian elegance.

An hour or so into our stay, and all the facilities that the room has to offer have been well and truly tested. Shortly after, another member of staff calls round to see if she can turn my bed down. But it's a special night for this couple; I explain that I'm hoping there won't be anything turned down in my bed tonight, thank you. (The kind housekeeping lady returns later to make our room immaculate again, and light candles throughout.)

Even though the Natural History Museum and the V&A are a stroll away, we've opted for pure R&R during our South Ken one-night stand. Watching one of their Hollywood classics is just as commendable as viewing any number of Assyrian bas-reliefs and, what with a sortie into the park for a stroll along the Serpentine, come the evening, we've worked up quite an appetite.

As swanky as the hotel restaurant is, with its central glass bar and sumptuous dining space, all velvet armchairs and black Murano glass chandeliers, the chef of Brunello is facing a very real challenge. I am a dedicated Italian-food sceptic, having only experienced ↓

lower-rung establishments where the dishes are dressed up with glugs of oil and delivered with dubious accents. Imagine my delight when I am brought my starter: a warm mushroom salad with aged balsamic vinegar and shaved Parmesan. A lifetime of overcooked ravioli is forgotten in moments. It is so delicious that I consider cancelling my halibut in favour of another. My knowledge of wine extends to knowing that it comes in two colours, but I like an impressive list. (Little comes in at under £30; judging by the gloss of our fellow diners, that isn't usually a problem.) After dinner, we fancy a nightcap, and we have been recommended the cocktails in Isola, a two-minute cab ride towards Knightsbridge. But given our exquisite surroundings and the impermanence of this lifestyle, it seems crazy to leave, so we stay in the bar, sipping martinis made with gold.

As tempting as it is to spend a lazy morning taking advantage of acres of comfortable bed, or exploring Ken Gardens, we have to be up at 07h to catch a flight. We're the first breakfasters of the day. Then it occurs to me: Baglioni residents don't work – they lounge and shop.

And the nearby retail temple that is Harvey Nichols is, like them, still sleeping. Who could blame anyone for wanting to stay cocooned away in this urban palazzo? Ultra-modern and super-cool, it plays out like a scene from an advert pushing aspiration and success. I feel tempted to give my fellow residents a congratulatory pat on the back for having made it. I suspect I'm the only one who even knows there's a hotel chain that shares its name with a prickly Scottish plant.

As we leave the hotel, reality feels harsh, unpolished, inelegant. We make for the Tube; we're not on expenses any more. Shut-eye in such a wonderful environment has been an eye-opener. Thanks to the Baglioni, we've had a taste of the high life, and the wife has loved every minute. She remarks that we should use our home town more adventurously, and stay in hotels like the Baglioni regularly. I'll have to become funnier, I tell her. 'Yeah right,' she sighs. Note to self: just how many reasonably amusing gags equal another night at the Baglioni?

Reviewed by Dominic Holland

NEED TO KNOW

Rooms 68, with 53 suites, including three executive suites and two presidential suites.
Rates £190–£1,900 (plus VAT).
Check-out Midday.
Room service 24 hours. When the dining room is open, the restaurant menu is available.
Facilities Plasma TVs, free use of their extensive film and music library, spa and gym.
Children Special beds, cots, and babysitter service all available.
Also Butler service is included.

IN THE KNOW

Recommended rooms The open-plan Junior Suite 107 has high ceilings, a large walk-in wardrobe, two plasma TVs, a bathtub and walk-in shower.
Hotel bar and restaurant Italian fine dining and superb martinis are to be had in opulent Brunello or on its terrace. Last orders 22h45; the bar closes at 01h. Private dining possible for up to 60.
Members' club Sixty has a capacity of 150; DJs play hip hop through to house, 19h–02h.
Top table To the side of a window overlooking Kensington Gardens, or next to the fireplace.
Dress code Dripping in designer: Italian labels, preferably.

LOCAL EATING AND DRINKING

Refuel after a hard day's shopping, on well-presented Modern British and European dishes at the **Fifth Floor** in destination department store Harvey Nichols on Knightsbridge (7235 5250). Gourmets will love the daily-changing set menu in the pretty white interior of **Clarke's** on Kensington Church Street (7221 9225). Long-time favourite with ladies who lunch, **San Lorenzo** on Beauchamp Place (7584 1074) is Italian, cosy and surprisingly low-key. Lovers of Japanese cuisine should put **Zuma** on Raphael Street (7584 1010) top of their list; book ahead. **Lonsdale House** on Lonsdale Road (7727 4080) is a stylish backdrop for elegant tapas-sized dishes and incredible cocktails. **Pétrus** at the Berkeley on Wilton Place (7235 1200), for Marcus Wareing's exceptional French cuisine. Get past the CCTV door inspection at **Apartment 195** on King's Road (7351 5195), and relax in a sexy nocturnal environment. **Boujis** on Thurloe Street (7584 6678) is a bijou bar where the fashionable flock. **Kensington Roof Gardens** on Kensington High Street (7937 7994) boasts a restaurant, a club and an acre and a half of tropical greenery.

 A complimentary cocktail for each guest. Register your Smithcard online, then show your card at check-in, to claim your offer.

Get a room! Use our free online booking service: check availability and make reservations through www.mrandmrssmith.com.

SMITH CONCIERGE Registered Smith cardholders can call +44 (0)20 7978 7333 and have Original Travel book everything from your flights to your day trips, at no extra charge.
Original idea Hire a private butler for a picnic in Green Park, Hyde Park or St James' Park – all within skipping distance of the most of the city's biggest attractions.

Baglioni Hotel 60 Hyde Park Gate, Kensington, London SW7 (+44 (0) 20 7368 5700)
info@baglionihotellondon.com; www.baglionihotellondon.com.

'Local folk flee editing suites and photography studios for after-work tipples at the long pewter bar'

The Soho Hotel

CITY   LONDON
STYLE   MODERN BRITISH WIT
SETTING   CENTRAL SECRECY

M T W T F S S M T W T F S S M T W T F S S M T W T F S S M T W T F **S S** M T W

LONDON

The Soho Hotel, London, UK

When the offer arose to experience one of the capital's most desirable hotel debutantes, I can't resist – especially since it's but a stumble from this couple's Covent Garden office. But don't let beaded curtains and neon adults-only signs creep into your imagination at the mention of Soho – Kit and Tim Kemp's transformation of a former carpark at the end of a cul de sac couldn't be any further from that ever-fading image. And though, just like the namesake districts in Manhattan and Hong Kong, it's as bustling as neighbourhoods come, this chic-sleep sister to the Covent Garden Hotel is a bubble of cool calm amid a storm.

As we veer off Wardour Street and head towards a twinkly-lit porch, a sharply dressed doorman is waiting to welcome us to us to this extraordinary urban Neverland. A 10-foot-tall porcelain Botero cat sculpture, oversized plant pots and a clash of driftwood and neon-tinted Perspex are a refreshing alterative to the marble and brass lobbies of most hotels in this postcode. (And the pebble-adorned pillars must have fans of home makeover shows scribbling in their notepads; in-favour-of and otherwise.) The only reminder at check-in of the hotel's all-but-airbrushed motoring past, is a collage of Botero's puss, comprised of tax discs and Monopoly board strips.

It's only 18h on a weeknight, but the tea-light-dotted lobby, and Refuel, the hotel's bar and restaurant, are already buzzing. This is an establishment where the watering hole and eatery have independent allure; local folk flee editing suites and photography studios for after-work tipples perched at the long, pewter bar, under the deco-style auto-themed mural. As we pass Refuel's glass front, we can't resist craning to spy which famous faces are among the chattering masses tonight. (I spot a big-name DJ, and Mr Smith clocks an award-winning director.) A magnet for movers and shakers, the pony-skin seats of the screening room downstairs regularly hold the derrières of most high-falutin', and a daringly decorated cocktail lounge and function room hosts endless star-studded launches. (And should guests who are less keen to see and be seen want to escape the media mêlée, there's an elegant all-white, pink-lit library, and lime- and fuchsia-accented drawing room on the ground floor to retreat to.)

The Soho Hotel is much bigger than you'd imagine, and we're grateful for a friendly escort through the pretty paisley corridors. Our spacious deluxe digs are sunny and cheery – even though outside, the weather is anything but. The fresh country-manor kiss to the decor of faded painted rustic furniture, and pastel- and bright-coloured prints, bedspread and curtains are, rather uniquely, the stuff that both *Country Living* and *Elle Deco* dreams are made of. Sadly the photo-shoot feel doesn't last, as I decide to unpack and get changed for dinner. (This Mrs Smith has a knack of transforming a showroom-perfect setting into a movie scene depicting a locale that's just been turned over in a hunt for a top-secret microchip.) Clothes shucked and cosmetics strewn, and I'm prancing around, clad only in shoes, when the doorbell rings. I lunge into the respectable roomy marble bathroom and grab one of the cotton-wool-soft Henry VIII-dimensioned robes. ↓

Settling down with his room service-delivered Tanqueray and tonic, I wonder if Mr Smith has noticed my fresh purchase from around-the-corner shop Agent Provocateur. It proves challenging even for a beribboned cleavage to compete with such a perfectly mixed G&T and the enormous olives delivered with it. At least the guy sitting at his computer in the building over the road (provided he is extremely long-sighted), can appreciate my cabaret. Shame he's not looking. I abandon my burlesque show and suggest we head down for dinner. At the mention of which, my chap's mouth is at long last watering.

It is when Mr Smith glimpses the wine list when I finally get the boggle-eyed, raised-eyebrows response that I'd hoped my lacy smalls might have achieved. 'They do each one by the glass,' he puffs, excited that he can have a Chablis with his foie gras parfait, a Mendoza with his Aberdeen Angus beef fillet, and a muscat with tarte tatin. Plans of visiting one of the many cocktail joints within stumbling distance start to fade, usurped by the desire to spend as much of our stay in situ. After a fireside nightcap from the honesty bar in the drawing room, we return to a boudoir fresh from a magic turndown service. All traces of my Tasmanian devil tendencies have been tidied away, and rather wonderfully, mineral water and an aromatherapy spray labelled 'sleep well' have appeared on the bedside tables. The sheets have been folded back invitingly. Mr Smith collapses on the bed, smiling. 'I've never known a post-work night out like it,' he sighs. 'And one I could get used to,' I think to myself…

Reviewed by Mr & Mrs Smith

NEED TO KNOW

Rooms 91.
Rates £235–£2,500 (plus VAT), including breakfast.
Check-out Midday.
Room service An extensive 24-hour menu.
Facilities High-speed internet access, CD/DVD, valet service.
Children Families are welcomed.

IN THE KNOW

Recommended rooms Rock stars opt for the sprawling terrace suite, with its views over Soho's rooftops, but we love the deluxe rooms on the fifth floor, especially 509.
Hotel bar and restaurant Whether you want an aperitif or a full-on banquet, Refuel offers modern international cuisine, with cosmopolitan food platters also available to pick at with your drinks, throughout the day.
Top table By the rack of plants, which separates the restaurant from the bar.
Dress code Soho sophisticates.

LOCAL EATING AND DRINKING

Stop for tea and cakes down the road, at **Yauatcha** on Broadwick Street (7494 8888), or book a table downstairs for delicious dim sum. Perch on a stool in the tiled former-fishmonger interior of **Randall & Aubin** on Brewer Street (7287 4447) for seafood or a grill. Dinner at **The Ivy** on West Street (7836 4751) promises showbiz faces among your fellow diners. The real reason to book well in advance, though, is for the surprisingly reasonable classic British dishes, among oak panelling and stained glass. **J Sheekey** (7240 2565) is another favourite specialising in seafood and Modern British dishes. **Sketch** on Conduit Street (0870 777 4488) is celebrated for its extravagant, futuristic yet elegant design, and offers haute cuisine, brasserie fare, or fab patisserie in its tearoom.

 A bottle of champagne on the house. Register your Smithcard online, then show your card at check-in to claim your gift.

Get a room! Use our free online booking service: check availability and make reservations through www.mrandmrssmith.com.

SMITH CONCIERGE Registered Smith cardholders can call +44 (0)20 7978 7333 and have Original Travel book everything from your flights to your day trips, at no extra charge.
Original idea Hire a guide to direct you to the best cultural exhibits in London, for a tailored museum experience among the world's most diverse collections.

The Soho Hotel 4 Richmond Mews, London W1 +44 (0)20 7559 3000
soho@firmdale.com; www.firmdale.com

'Cutting-edge design, with
clever and ironic contrasts
and clashes of modern styles'

The Zetter

CITY	LONDON
STYLE	SLICK WAREHOUSE CONVERSION
SETTING	OFF-CENTRE CLERKENWELL

M T W T F S S M T W T F S S M T W T F **S S** M T W T F S S M T W T F S S M T W T
LONDON

MTWTFSSMTWTFSSMTWTFSSMTWTFSSMTWTFSS

The Zetter, London, UK

It's with nostalgia that we wander up Clerkenwell Road towards the Zetter. Clerkenwell has come a long way since the Sixties. My father studied at the art school here, and his strongest memory of the area is of the all-pervading aroma from the local tobacco factory. Years later, I attended the same college, but by then all the factories were empty; by the time Mrs Smith attended, a decade later, Clerkenwell was firmly established as a thriving and fashionable London arrondissement – the cigarette fumes now emanating from the many bars and clubs.

We've had the Zetter described to us as an 'urban inn'. It is housed in a Victorian warehouse building that blends in so well with its surroundings that it seems more likely to be a top-end design company. We almost pass right by, then, just as we're trying to work out how to get in, a glass door glides open. We get the feeling we've been let into a secret lair rather than just an exclusive hotel…

Having sworn I'd avoid using the much-abused word 'cool', what can I say? That's exactly what the Zetter is. It's a hotel that's all about cutting-edge design, with the clever and ironic contrasts and clashes of modern styles that you'd expect from an establishment embodying London's eastside renaissance. The flamboyant pink chandelier that greets you in the lobby is a statement of intent, and the bold thinking continues throughout the building. Just off the lobby is a small bar that smacks of Seventies Austrian chalet; wood panelling, floral chairs and cork stools make us smile.

The staff are genuinely warm and charming, and there's an informality that we find immediately relaxing. But as we rise in the lift, Mrs Smith is most excited about the small touches. As a graphic designer, she appreciates the work of Precious McBane, a playful mix of the contemporary and the classic, used in our quirky key fob and the number on our door, a rooftop studio. (It's well worth the extra to go high: not only do you get your own balcony, but also views over the London skyline.)

The room is modern and full of light, yet cosy. The fittings are minimal, but ornate flourishes include a *Z* logo embroidered on an orange blanket, and a delightfully absurd standard lamp. The bathroom has a nautical theme, with a porthole that looks out onto our olive tree on the balcony patio. And, fittingly for Clerkenwell, land of the digerati, the Zetter comes out tops on technology too; there's nothing you can't access from your TV, be it the internet, a library of 4,000 songs, or extensive local information. Who needs a butler when you've got this?

What's so special about our room is that it feels like a dream studio apartment. Not folk who like everything to match, we love furnishings like this: surprising, original and a little cheeky. It's the sort of place former geeks with something to prove should come to, and take some photos of themselves 'at home' to post on friendsreunited.com: the 21st-century equivalent of turning up to a school reunion in a flash motor – the thought of anyone belonging in these surrounds would

give them insta-cred. Our favourite touch, oddly, isn't anything costly or showy; it's actually the water. To our amazement, the handsome bottle that stands before us is full of aqua that's been pumped from springs 1,500 feet below us. Sure, you wouldn't expect EC1 to be giving the Swiss Alps a run for its H_2O, but before you wince at the thought of sipping from East End sewers, let us add that this is an area whose name is derived from the Clerks Well, which in centuries past was revered for its health-promoting qualities. Anyway, nutritious or not, London water has never tasted this good.

After such a salubrious start to our stay, we head off for a few aperitifs. On our way out we discover the hotel's most striking piece of design – its back stairway. We're overwhelmed by the raucous carpet and vivid walls: decoration at its boldest. The fact that the red gloss walls clash with Mrs Smith's outfit is all that prevents us from taking a photo. Our first stop in the outside world is Exmouth Market – a ↓

strip of boutiques, bars and eateries that is, unusually for London, mainly alfresco. As we walk past a few old haunts, memories of misspent afternoons flood back, and I can't help keeping an eye out for one of my alcoholic lecturers. Convinced we spy one at the bar of an old boozer, we decide to have a butcher's at Medcalf instead. (An appropriate rhyming-slang slip, as that's exactly what it used to be.) It's now a laid-back bar/restaurant, as is customary for this terrain.

Continuing on the meatery-turned-eatery theme (when you're Eastside, part of each hip hang-out's charm is often its previous incarnation, carnivorous or otherwise), we think it fitting to head to our namesake-for-the-night, Smiths of Smithfields, a former meat warehouse turned into four floors of restaurants and bars. It's Saturday night, and Clerkenwell is livening up, though it's not too heaving. (Local workers party hard on Friday nights, whereas the rest of the weekend is more relaxed.) After rum cocktails in the huge embrace of Smiths' red-leather banquettes, we stroll back to the Zetter's beautiful high-ceilinged restaurant, with its huge 180-degree curved windows overlooking a cobbled square.

After dinner we have the best intentions of reliving our student days on a nearby dancefloor (several clubs are within walking distance, and Hoxton is a brief cab ride east), but four courses of delicious Modern Italian have put paid to that, and our room with a view is too tempting. As we bemoan our bodies not being as young as they were, we return to find that the hue of the pink fluorescent light in our bedroom's ceiling is wonderfully flattering, and feel sufficiently rejuvenated to trawl the TV for music to have a nightcap to (admittedly opting for less BPMs than we might once have done).

If we didn't go to bed with ringing in our ears, we're only too delighted to wake up to it; there aren't many sounds in London more romantic than the bells of St Paul's on a Sunday. Just as I comment what a unique memory our leisurely breakfast on the balcony will make, I notice Mrs Smith smuggling a rather-more-real souvenir into her bag. Once I've convinced her to not pinch the offbeat ashtray, we reluctantly head down to check out. Though we might be leaving the Zetter empty-handed, we don't leave empty-headed. It has left a vibrant stamp on our consciousness of London. 'Maybe it was something in the water,' smiles Mrs Smith.

Reviewed by Mr and Mrs Smith

NEED TO KNOW

Rooms 59, including seven rooftop studios.
Rates £125–£305.
Check-out Midday.
Room service 24 hours, with restaurant menu until 23h, when a snack menu starts.
Facilities CD/DVD, with 4,000 tracks on demand, vending machines, high-speed internet access, airport transfers and limo service, massages can be arranged.
Children Are welcome; childminding service available.
Also Hot-water bottles available (with hand-knitted covers).

IN THE KNOW

Recommended rooms A rooftop studio: two are extra spacious with large private terraces and views of Sir Norman Foster's skyscraper, the 'Gherkin', and St Paul's Cathedral.
Hotel bar Part of the Zetter restaurant, with modern decor, it serves cocktails until 23h.
Hotel restaurant Beautifully lit and fabulously designed; the Modern Italian menu is versatile, but especially good for brunch. Lunch 12h–14h30; last orders 23h.
Top table Ask for a table in the window.
Dress code Informal for lunch; smarter for dinner.

LOCAL EATING AND DRINKING

Head east for super-cheap Vietnamese on Kingsland Road; or cruise Brick Lane for curry (**Café Naz** is always reliable). Exmouth Market is a great lane of shops and eateries. We love **Moro** (7833 8336) for Spanish and North African tapas and grills; **Exmouth Grill** (7837 0009) where you tailor fish or meat dishes by choosing sauces. **Medcalf** (7833 3533) was a butcher's, now a buzzing diner and drinkery. From foie gras to smoked eel, **Club Gascon** on West Smithfield (7796 0600) serves Michelin-starred French fare; **St John** on St John Street (7251 0848) puts colour in the cheeks of carnivores with earthy British cooking. A former working man's café, the **Quality Chop House** on Farringdon Road (7837 5093) has hard benches but great food. Pub/club/ restaurant **Smiths of Smithfields** on Charterhouse Street (7251 7950) is ideal for brunch. **Match Bar** on Clerkenwell Road (7250 4002) provides cocktails over the road from the hotel.

 A ten per cent discount off the bill in the Zetter restaurant is offered to all Smith cardholders. Guests staying overnight also receive a complimentary cocktail upon arrival. Register your Smithcard online, then show your card at check-in, to claim your offer.

Get a room! Use our free online booking service: check availability and make reservations through www.mrandmrssmith.com.

SMITH CONCIERGE Registered Smith cardholders can call +44 (0)20 7978 7333 and have Original Travel book everything from your flights to your day trips, at no extra charge.
Original idea The finest views from a natural environment can be had from Hampstead Heath or Greenwich observatory. We'll take you north or south in a chauffeur-driven limousine.

The Zetter 86–88 Clerkenwell Road, London EC1 (+44 (0)20 7324 4444)
info@thezetter.com; www.thezetter.com

travel tips

1. Tell your bank you're off on your travels, so that it doesn't freeze your credit card if it spots unusual spending patterns when you go shopping.

2. When you change money, it is useful to get a few local coins for trolleys, transport and tips.

3. Check the forecast before you pack, so that you have the right wardrobe for the weather.

4. Just take the essentials. That way you can carry your bag on the plane as hand luggage, so there's no risk of losing it, or wasting undue time hanging around the baggage belt.

5. If you have too much stuff to fit into carry-on luggage, tie a ribbon around the handle of your suitcase so that you can spot it quickly – you'd be amazed how many bags look alike.

6. A great idea is also to divide your clothes and your partner's between your cases, so that if one bag is lost, your weekend won't be. Or keep a few crucial items in your hand luggage, just in case.

7. You might benefit from calling the airline to reconfirm your reservation and, if possible, to book seats at the front (less affected by turbulence/quicker to disembark) and specify dietary requirements (not only can vegetarian meals be better, but you also get served first).

8. It's worth trying to remember to take your own large bottle of water on the plane… the air gets really dry and it can feel like an eternity before the drinks trolley comes round.

9. Why not skip jostling taxi queues at arrivals by phoning ahead to order? Better still, ask your hotel to arrange a pick-up service – they may even provide one. If you forget, try grabbing a cab that's dropping off outside departures – there's no queue and it's often cheaper.

10. Change your bedlinen and leave the house tidy before you go, rather than leaving in a tumult of last-minute packing, so returning home will be a treat, not a painful crash back down to Planet Reality.

talk of the town… need to know

	SPANISH	ITALIAN	FRENCH	GERMAN
Hello	Hola	Ciao	Bonjour	Guten Tag
Goodbye	Adios	Arrivederci	Au revoir	Auf Wiedersehen
Please	Por favor	Per favore	S'il vous plaît	Bitte
Thank you	Gracias	Grazie	Merci	Danke
Excuse me	Perdona	Scusi	Excusez-moi	Entschuldigung
OK	Vale	Va bene	OK	Machen wir
Where is…	Donde está…	Dov' è…	Où est…	Wo ist…
Can I have the bill please?	La cuenta, por favor	Il conto, per favore	L'addition, s'il vous plaît	Die Rechnun bitte
How much does this cost?	¿Cuanto vale?	Quanto costa questo?	Ça côute combien?	Wieviel kostet das?
A bottle of chilled champagne please	Una botella de champán enfriado por favor	Una bottiglia di champagne raffreddato per favore	Une bouteille de champagne fraîche svp	Eine Flasche eisgekühlten Champagner bitte
I love you	Te quiero	Ti amo	Je t'aime	Ich liebe Dich

SWEDISH	ESTONIAN	DUTCH	CZECH
God dag	Tere	Hallo	Dobrý den
Adjöken	Nägemist	Dag	Nashledanou
Snälla	Palun	Alstublieft	Prosím
Tack själv	Tänan	Dankuwel	Děkuji
Ursäkta	Vabandage	Sorry	Pardón
Visst	Teeme nii	OK	OK
Var ligger…	Kus on…	Waar is…	Kde je…
Kan jag få pröjsa är du snäll? Notan tack!	Palun arve?	Kunt u mij de rekening geven alstublieft?	Mohu poprosit o účet?
Hur mycket kostar den här?	Kui palju maksab?	Hoeveel kost dit?	Kolik to stojí?
En flaska kyld champagne tack	Üks pudel külmat champagner	Een fles gekoelde champagne alstublieft	Prosím, láhev vychlazeného šampaňského
Jag älskar dig	Ma armastan sind	Ik hou van jou	Miluji tě

talk of the town… in the know

	SPANISH	ITALIAN	FRENCH	GERMAN
Mr & Mrs Smith	Señor y Señora Garcia	Signor e Signora Rossi	Monsieur et Madame Dupont	Herr und Frau Schmidt
Take me to your leader	Lléveme a su líder	Mi porta al suo capo	Portez-moi à votre chef	Bringen Sie mich bitte zu Ihrem Anführer
Do you know the way to San Jose?	¿Usted sabe llegar a San Jose?	Conoscete la strada al San Jose?	Savez-vous comment arriver à San Jose?	Kennen Sie den Weg nach San Jose?
Taxi!	¡Taxi!	Tassì!	Taxi!	Taxi!
Please call off your violin player	Por favor dígale a su jugador del violín que pare	Gli dica al violinista di andarsene	Dites, s'il vous plaît, au violoniste de quitter le camp	Bitte stellen Sie dieses Gedudel ab
Follow that car!	¡Siga ese coche!	Segui quella macchina!	Suivez cette voiture-là!	Folgen Sie diesem Wagen!
What will make me drunk? Quickly?	¿Qué me va a emborrachar? ¿Rápidamente?	Cosa mi rendera ubriaco? Subito?	Qu'est-ce qui me rendra ivre? Rapidement?	Was macht mich betrunken? Schnell?
No, I have not stolen your dressing gown	No, no he robado su albornoz	No, non ho rubato la vostra vestaglia	Non, je n'ai pas volé votre robe de chambre gestohlen	Nein, ich habe Ihren Morgenmantel nicht
Shaken, not stirred	Sacudarido, no revuelto	Agitato non mescolato	Agité, pas remué	Geschüttelt, nicht gerührt
Help!	¡Ayuda!	Aiuto!	Au secours!	Hilfe!
All we need is radio ga ga	Lo único que necesitamos es radio ga ga	Tutto ciò che ci serve è radio ga ga	Tout ce qui nous faut est radio ga ga	Alles was wir benötigen ist radio ga ga

SWEDISH	ESTONIAN	DUTCH	CZECH
Herr and Fru Andersson	Proua ja Härra Tamm	Meneer en Mevrouw Jansen	Pan a Paní Novak
Ta mig till er ledare	Palun, viige mind teie juht	Breng me naar de leider	Zavedťe mě k vašemu vedoucímu
Kan du vägen till San Jose eller?	Kas teie tunnete teed San Jose?	Weet jij de weg naar San Jose?	Znáte cestu do San Jose?
Taxi!	Taxo!	Taxi!	Taxi!
Kan du be violin-spelaren dra åt pepparn	Palun kutsuge oma viiulimängija äär	Kun je alsjeblieft die violist hier weghalen	Prosím, odvolejte vašemu houslistu
Förfölj den där bilen!	Soitke selle auto järele!	Volg die Auto!	Následujte tento vůz!
Jag vill bli aspackad? På stubben?	Kuidas ma saan ruttu purjuks?	Wat zou me snel dronken voeren?	Co mě rychle opije?
Nej, jag har inte snott din badrock	Ei, ma ei ole varastanud teie hommikumantlit	Nee, ik heb je peignoir niet gestolen	Ne, neukradl jsem váše aty (župan)
Skakad, inte rörd	Raputatud mitte segatud	Geschud, niet geroerd	Rozmixovat, ale nemíchat prosím
Hjälp!	Appi!	Help!	Pomoc!
Allt vi behöver är radio ga ga	Kõik kus meil vaja on radio ga ga	Het enige dat we nodig hebben is radio ga ga	Vše co potřebujeme je radio ga ga

(useful numbers)

AIRLINES

Air Berlin (08707 388880; www.airberlin.com).
London Stansted, Manchester and Southampton to
airports throughout Germany, Italy, Netherlands, Spain.
Air France (08453 591000; www.airfrance.com).
Birmingham, Edinburgh, London Gatwick and Heathrow,
Manchester and Newcastle to Paris.
Alitalia (08705 448259; www.alitalia.com). London
Heathrow to all international airports in Italy.
Basiqair (020 7365 4997; www.basiqair.com/en).
London Stansted to destinations including Amsterdam,
Barcelona, Milan, Stockholm, Venice.
BMI Baby (08702 642229; www.bmibaby.com).
Birmingham, Cardiff, Edinburgh, Glasgow, London
Gatwick and Stansted, Manchester, Nottingham,
Teesside to Amsterdam, Paris, Prague.
British Airways (www.britishairways.com;
08708 509850). Various airports all over the UK to
all our European destinations.
British Midland (08706 070555; www.flybmi.com)
London Heathrow, Manchester and Teeside to
Hamburg, Milan, Nice, Paris, Stockholm, Venice.
CSA Czech Airlines (08704 443747;
www.czechairlines.co.uk). Birmingham, London
Gatwick, Heathrow and Stansted, Manchester,
Edinburgh and Glasgow to Prague.
EasyJet (08717 500100; www.easyjet.com). East
Midlands, Liverpool, London Gatwick, Luton and Stansted
and Newcastle to Amsterdam, Barcelona, Edinburgh,
Milan, Nice, Paris, Prague, Rome, Tallinn, Venice.

Estonian Air (020 7333 0196; www.estonian-air.com).
London Gatwick to Tallinn.
Finnair (08702 414411; www.finnair.com). London
Heathrow to Helsinki, which is an 18-minute helicopter
ride with Copterline from Tallinn (www.copterline.com).
FlyGlobespan (0131 312 2402;
www.flyglobespan.com). Edinburgh and Glasgow to
Barcelona, Nice, Prague, Rome, Venice.
Iberia (084 8 509000; www.iberia.com). Birmingham,
London Heathrow and Manchester to Barcelona.
Jet2.com (08712 261737; www.jet2.com).
Leeds Bradford to Amsterdam, Barcelona, Nice, Paris,
Prague, Venice.
KLM (08702 430541; www.klm.com). Birmingham,
Cardiff, Glasgow, Humberside, Leeds, London City
and Heathrow, Manchester, Newcastle, Norwich and
Teesside to Amsterdam.
Lufthansa (08708 377747; www.lufthansa.com).
London Heathrow and Manchester to Hamburg.
Monarch (08700 406300; www.flymonarch.com).
Luton and Gatwick and Manchester to Barcelona.
My Travel Lite (08701 564564; www.mytravellite.com).
Birmingham to Barcelona.
Ryanair (08712 460000; www.ryanair.com). From 18
airports in the UK and six in Ireland to Amsterdam,
Barcelona, Hamburg, Paris, Italy, Spain, Sweden. But be
warned: some airports are a long way from city centres.

Skyscanner Enter your flight requirements into
www.skyscanner.net and it searches all airlines at once
(including budget ones) giving you a range of prices.

CAR HIRE

Budget (www.budget.com; 08701 565656).
Hertz (www.hertz.co.uk; 08708 448844).
Europcar (www.europcar.co.uk; 08706 075000).
Avis (www.avis.co.uk; 08700 100287).
Easy Car (www.easycar.com; 09063 333333).
Calls are charged at 60p a minute from a land line.

TRAINS

Eurostar (www.eurostar.com; 08705 186186).
Seat 61 (www.seat61.com/europe.htm). Gives
helpful information on travelling to Europe by train,
including where to buy tickets, train times and fares.

BOOKS

Amazon (www.amazon.co.uk).
Stanfords (020 7836 1321; www.stanfords.co.uk)
is a specialist retailer of maps and travel books.
Grant & Cutler (020 7734 2012;
www.grantandcutler.com). Foreign language
bookshop with mail order.

MAPS

Mappy (www.mappy.com) will help you plan
a route across Europe, including journey time,
distance and tolls.
Map Vista (www.map-vista.com) provides online
street maps for every European city.

**All phone numbers are for the UK, unless an
international code is given.**

DIAMONDS

 Duttson & Company
(020 7349 7803; www.duttson.com).
Unlike many in the business, Neil Duttson is
a first-generation, self-taught diamond man.
A lifelong passion for stones led him to study
with the HRD, Diamond High Council and the
International Gemmological Institute before starting
out on his own. With a stellar client list that would
make Anna Wintour arch an eyebrow in interest,
he's kindly offering Smith cardholders ten per cent
off the purchase of a diamond for an engagement
ring. 'Treating a customer differently, seeing them
enjoy the experience and knowing that their
engagement ring is exactly what they always
dreamed of, is just as much a thrill to me as selling
a gem with a million-dollar price tag.' He will also give
Mr & Mrs Smiths-to-be a free wedding band with the
purchase of a diamond, and five per cent off pieces
in Duttson Rocks Arm Candy, his spectacular
bracelet range.

LINGERIE AND MISCHIEF

Smith **Myla** (08707 455003; www.myla.com).
Present your Smith card at one of Myla's four
London shops and receive a ten per cent discount.
King's Road: 74 Duke of York Square, SW3. Notting
Hill: 77 Lonsdale Road, W11. Mayfair: 4 Burlington
Gardens off Old Bond Street, W1. South Kensington:
166 Walton Street, SW3. (Please note: this offer is
only available to cardholders who visit a Myla shop. It
does not apply to mail order, website purchases or at
any Myla concessions within department stores.)

So, who are Mr & Mrs Smith?

Right from the start, we knew it was important to give you an honest account of what you can expect when you visit a *Mr & Mrs Smith* hotel. In order to give you the real insider information, we selected a panel of people who we feel are credible, and who can see in the dark when it comes to style, fun and originality. They all reviewed the hotels anonymously, so there was no special treatment. What you read is what actually happened on their *Mr & Mrs Smith* trip. The reviewers' only obligation was to go with a partner and bring us back the kind of honest account you would expect to get from your best friend.

THE BAR CONNOISSEUR

Jeremy Mascarenhas has been publishing the *London Bar Guide* since the explosion of designer bar culture in the Nineties. His time is now split between managing the company, travelling the country to view the latest spaces and consulting brands on new trends in the bar world. Having launched the annual *London Restaurant Guide* venues and with two more titles on the way in the new year, he craves more than anything a day off – a Sunday morning in bed watching *Hollyoaks,* if the truth be told.

THE CLUB OWNER

Rory Keegan is the founder and creator of Chinawhite and Taman Gang in London, and the Mao Rooms in Ibiza. He spends his time designing nightclubs throughout the world and is currently engaged in creating a club in Moscow. In past lives he has been involved in fine art at Sotheby's, microlight planes in Wales, feature films in LA and theatre in the West End of London. His big hit was *Les Liaisons Dangereuses*, reputedly inspired by his rather strange personal life.

THE COMEDIAN

Dominic Holland is an award-winning stand-up comedian. He writes a regular column in *The Guardian* and has published two novels, *Only in America* and *The Ripple Effect*. His acclaimed BBC Radio 4 series, *The Small World of Dominic Holland*, is being developed into a television series that Dominic hopes will hit our screens sometime during his lifetime. He is married with three children and one more on the way.

THE CREATIVE

Formerly an architect and installation artist, **Mark Chalmers** is creative partner at global ad agency StrawberryFrog, and has worked on international campaigns for brands such as Sony-Ericsson, Ikea and MTV. He attempts to balance the sometimes unpleasant trait of being one of those people who makes you buy things by doing yoga. Mark lives in Amsterdam with his photographer wife Carmen and their daughter Lola Love. Having recently been locked out of his hotel room naked, he promises in future to keep a copy of *Mr & Mrs* close at hand at all times, if not always for intended use.

THE DIAMOND DEALER

Neil Duttson is at the forefront of the diamond Industry. He is leading a trend in bespoke setting: buying the gem on behalf of the client and then involving them at every stage of creating the jewellery, giving the piece a little more personal history. Before immersing himself in the closed world of diamonds, Neil organised events worldwide, from classic English weddings to hotel launches on the east coast of Africa.

THE DJ

Rob Wood is a man of many hats. When he is not a music journalist, he works as a DJ or consultant. Having been managing editor of *Jockey Slut*, he now writes for *XL8R*, *Fact* and *Hotdog* magazines. In between that he plays at the Big Chill, the White House, Plan B or Fabric and gives music-related advice to record labels and brands. His wife and fellow reviewer, Amber, runs the stylish *bargrooves* series of grown-up house music compilations and is a self-confessed interior-design and hotel fanatic.

THE MAGAZINE EDITORS

Editing *The Sunday Times Style* magazine takes **Tiffanie Darke** from catwalk shows in Milan to spas in the Maldives, and allows her to sample an international bacchanalian feast of what the world considers hip, happening, pleasurable and modern. Nice work if you can get it. Tiffanie is qualified to recognise the potential of hotel rooms; she has written extensively about matters of the bedroom, both for national newspapers and in two novels she has published, including the very entertaining *Marrow*, a tale of food and sex in the kitchens of London's celebrity restaurants.

After coming to the attention of the music press for his fanzine, **Anthony Noguera** edited various music magazines in the Nineties before joining *Sky* as a senior features writer in 1993. He joined *FHM* as features editor in 1995, and went on to be editor. Under him, it became the best-selling monthly in British history; it also gave Jennifer Lopez her first-ever cover story. He has won EMAP Editor of the Year and the same award from British Society of Magazine Editors. Anthony moved to *Arena* as editor-in-chief in October 2001.

Matt Turner is editor of the leading hotel-design magazine, *Sleeper*. He studied journalism in Liverpool in the early Nineties, but spent most of his time in nightclubs. He joined *Night* magazine as a trainee, and within three years took the top spot. Over the next five years, he travelled to clubs around the UK and to party capitals around the world, staying in hotels of all shapes and sizes. In September 2002, he was appointed editor of *Sleeper*. He now spends more time checking out contemporary hotels than ever, but gets a lot more sleep than he used to.

Lucy Yeomans began her career in 1993 in Paris, where she was at the helm of an English-language lifestyle monthly. She also freelanced for *Harpers & Queen* and *The Sunday Times*. Returning to the UK, she was appointed features editor of *The European* and moved to *Tatler* in 1997 as features editor, becoming deputy editor a year later. On her first day as features director of British *Vogue*, she was offered, and accepted, the position of editor at *Harpers & Queen*. That was in November 2000; since then, Lucy has transformed *Harpers* into one of the most chic and talked-about magazines on the market.

THE FASHION DESIGNER

Stella McCartney graduated from St Martins College in 1995 and went on to be creative director of the house of Chloé for four years. In 2001 Stella launched her own fashion label in partnership with the Gucci Group, and showed her first collection in the autumn of 2001 in Paris. She has since designed the costumes for Madonna's Reinvention tour, Annie Lennox's summer concert tour and the wardrobe for Gwyneth Paltrow and Jude Law in the film *Sky Captain and the World of Tomorrow*. She co-wrote her review with her husband, Alasdhair Willis, former publisher of *Wallpaper** and now head of creative consultancy Announcement.

THE FOOD CRITIC

After spells as an elf in Harrods' Santa's Grotto (when he dandled the future king of England on his knee) and employment as a barman, a hospital porter and a shirt-salesman in Paris, **Giles Coren** got a job as a secretary at *The Daily Telegraph*, in 1994. He writes The Intellectual's Guide to Fashion in *The Sunday Times Style* under the pseudonym Professor Gideon Garter and has been restaurant critic of *Tatler* and *The Independent on Sunday,* and diary editor and parliamentary sketch-writer of *The Times*. He ghost-wrote bestselling *Against The Odds – The Autobiography of James Dyson*, and his first novel, provisionally titled *Winkler's Fear of Trains*, comes out in 2005.

THE GALLERY OWNER

Alexander Proud founded Proud Galleries after incarnations as an antiques dealer, an oriental-gallery owner and an internet pioneer. He made his reputation with shows such as 'Destroy – the Sex Pistols'. Subsequent shows, including Rankin's 'Nudes' project, have cemented the position of Proud Galleries as one of the most exciting photographic galleries in Europe. He sits on the panels of various photographic bodies and is a guest commentator for the BBC. Then 2001 saw the launch and success of Proud Camden Moss, and further launches are planned in Brighton, New York, Paris and Tokyo. Soon after his trip to Tallinn, he married his Mrs Smith, the *Guardian Guide*'s Danielle Rigby.

THE HOTEL CONSULTANT

For **Guy Dittrich**, becoming a hotel marketing consultant is the culmination of a career path that began in London at PriceWaterhouseCoopers and led to an operations role with PRCo, a public-relations company specialising in luxury hotels. From there it was but a short step to a three-year stint as UK MD of Design, the specialist hotel marketing company for contemporary hotels. Born and raised in Zimbabwe, Guy now lives in Munich, from where he also writes about hotels for *Condé Nast Traveller*, *Wallpaper**, *The Guardian* and *The Observer*, and has a regular column for *Sleeper*.

THE HOTELIER

Since March 2004, **Paul de Zwart** has been at the helm of Dhillon Hotels; the fruits of his labour won't be seen until 2005, but he assures us it will be well worth the wait. Prior to this post, he dedicated two years to developing a pan-European hotel/art retreat business. Before that, from its launch in 1996 until 2002, he was vice president and general manager of the *Wallpaper** group, including the eponymous magazine, and the creative advertising agency Wink Media. Before that he worked for Urban Productions, where he honed his events-management skills and his passion for hospitality.

THE INTERIOR DESIGNER

With a BA in fine art and a series of successful exhibitions under his belt, **Shaun Clarkson** gained attention for his outrageous sculptures and installations. He went on to apply his talents to more commercial ends, namely drinks brand promotion and event art direction and, most notably, the interior design of bars, clubs and restaurants. Shaun is best known in the UK for creating London venues including the Atlantic Bar & Grill, Jerusalem, Denim, Pop, Bartok and the Cheyne Walk Brasserie.

THE JOURNALIST

Karen Krizanovich grew up watching movies and riding horses in the rural outskirts of Chicago, Illinois, USA. Trained as a philosopher, she is currently juggling writing about films with producing. Honestly, she doesn't want to direct. Traveling and being nosy is her obsessive hobby. Favourite place? Wherever she hasn't been before.

THE MTV EXECUTIVE

Gemma Richards has been working in the music industry for 12 years; she started off putting on parties and club nights while at university, and then, four years later, was installed behind the scenes at Kiss FM. Since 1997 she's been at MTV Europe, where she runs the sponsorship and client service team.

THE PR

With her trademark vigour, energy and dynamism, American-born **Jori White** founded her own consultancy and, a decade on, Jori White PR is one of the UK's leading lifestyle PR agencies. Her high-profile client list includes *34* magazine, Zuma, the Cinnamon Club, London's Courthouse Hotel Kempinski and, of course, *Mr & Mrs Smith*. Jori's name has become synonymous with success and style, and throughout the years she has hosted many glamorous attention-grabbing launches including those for Sir Michael Caine and Sir Roger Moore.

THE RESTAURATEUR

Founder and chairman of Gruppo Ltd, **Oliver Peyton** has worked in the hospitality industry for the past two decades. As a drinks importer, Oliver masterminded the UK distribution for Japanese beer Sapporo, and turned the previously obscure Absolut into an übercool vodka. The first of his award-winning restaurant ventures came in 1994 with the Atlantic Bar & Grill. He has followed that with gastronomic successes Coast, Mash, Isola, the Admiralty in Somerset House and now a British café, Inn the Park, in St James's Park.

THE STYLIST

For the past 12 years, **Jason Alper** has been brushing shoulders of celebrities from the film and television world. Quite literally – he's a costume designer and stylist. Most recently, he has been responsible for creating all the costumes for Ali G and all of Sacha Baron Cohen's other characters, for HBO stateside. When he's in London, he works with Cat Deeley on *CD:UK*, as well as styling commercials and promos. Jason has presented fashion pieces for daytime TV, and has been appearing on *The Collections* for VH1.

THE MR & MRS SMITH TEAM

James Lohan is one half of the couple behind *Mr & Mrs Smith*. James' first company, Atomic, created the infamous Come Dancing parties and club promotions. (One of his London parties, in 1998, was voted 'number-one place to be in the world' by *FHM*.) He built on this success with Atomic Events and Atomic Promotions with Ben Sowton, producing events for clients such as Jack Daniel's, Finlandia vodka and Wonderbra. He then went on to co-found the White House bar, restaurant and members' club in Clapham. Launched in March 2000, it is one of London's hippest establishments. Since the conception of the book, James has visited 400 hotels, the dirty stop-out.

Tamara Heber-Percy, co-founder of *Mr & Mrs Smith*, graduated from Oxford with a degree in languages, then left the UK for a year in Brazil, where she launched a new energy drink. Since then, she has worked as a marketing consultant for international brands such as Ericsson, Honda, Unilever and Swissair. Her last role in that field was in business development for Europe, the Middle East and Africa at one of the UK's top marketing agencies. She left the corporate world in 2002 to head up her own company – an exclusive introductions agency – and to launch *Mr & Mrs Smith*.

Bloom are the creators of the *Mr & Mrs Smith* brand and designers of the book, and are one of the UK's freshest design agencies. Founded in 2001 by three of the youngest heavyweights in the industry – Gavin Blake, Ben White and Harriet Marshall – it is responsible for inspirational brand designs for some of Europe's and the USA's leading consumer brand companies. The house style is bold, iconic and distinctive, and their attitude open and irreverent. The Bloom team on *Mr & Mrs Smith* are partner Ben White, senior account manager Oona Bannon, design director Jason Badrock, designer Emily Wood and production director Tim Reynolds.

Almost a decade ago, editor **Juliet Kinsman** was at the helm of dance-music magazines. Since she traded dancefloors for do-not-disturb signs and designer dining, her job lets her spend a lot more time in bed for work; and as editor of the *London Restaurant Guide* she has enjoyed eating her way around town. From strip clubs to celeb weddings, she has covered it all for *Time Out*, *InStyle*, *Marie Claire*, *The Face*, *OK!* and the BBC, among others, and a spell reviewing hotels and restaurants for TV gave her a behind-the-scenes look at what goes into making a great place to stay.

Co-editor **Sophie Dening** got a taste for room service during her innocent years, when she took time off school to tour Europe with her opera-singer mother. As soon as she was old enough to appreciate luxury, she ran away to Morocco backpacking, but has since reaccustomed herself to elegant hotels. She graduated from UCL in 1997 and worked in book publishing before becoming a sub at *Tatler*, where she witnessed elegant eccentricity on a daily basis. Since 2001, Sophie has been chief sub-editor at *Harpers & Queen*; she lives in Hackney and holidays in the South of France, Bangkok and the Scottish Highlands.

In 1990, publishing director **Andrew Grahame** launched the country's first corporate-fashion magazine. After moving into fashion shows, exhibitions and conferences, he transferred his talents from business clothing to business finance, launching *Small Company Investor*. He started a promotions company in 1993 with clients such as Sony and Virgin, and after a spell as a restaurant/bar/club owner in Chelsea, Andrew decided to try out tourism in 1997, creating the award-winning London Pass and New York Pass, which give visitors access to the cities' attractions. Andrew has now promised to concentrate on hotel-book publishing.

Renowned for his meticulous, creative, yet relaxed approach to his work, **Adrian Houston** has photographed famous personalities and unusual landscapes, as well as shooting big advertising campaigns. He has photographed faces such as the Dalai Lama, Sir Ranulf Fiennes, Luciano Pavarotti and Jim Carrey, and his images have appeared in Vogue, GQ and *The Sunday Times*. Adrian has commercial clients throughout the world, and has created his best work in some of the world's most unexplored locations; the Discovery Channel recently featured him on their Discovery People series.

Having grown up in the south of Spain, production manager **Katy McCann** moved to Madrid after graduating from Manchester University. There she pursued a career in journalism, to become editor of the largest English publication in the city, *InMadrid*. Drawn back to London by the English weather, she was tracked down by the *Mr & Mrs Smith* team to help work on the European Collection, which fits in perfectly with her love of travelling, her multilingual skills and her hope of opening up her own hotel some day.

Edward Orr has been working in investment banking, and managing companies in their early stage for more than ten years. As a result he has had to stay in many hotels across five different continents… and he just doesn't like them. This qualifies him not just to look after the finances of *Mr & Mrs Smith* but also to have penned one of the team reviews and confirm that *Mr & Mrs Smith* hotels really are special enough to be a treat for even the most jaded corporate traveller.

originaltravel
THE BIG SHORT BREAK

We have teamed up with Original Travel to offer Smith
cardholders the ultimate in concierge services. Once
you have registered your card, get in touch with them
to book your European city break. At the end of each
review, they have suggested an Original idea, just to give
you a taste of the kind of activities they can arrange.

telephone: +44 (0)20 7978 7333
website: www.originaltravel.co.uk

Why they're Original

With a collection of inspiring, original and exclusive
trips within easy reach of the UK, Original Travel has
redefined the concept of the short break. They are
delighted to present their exciting range of Big Short
Breaks in Europe, Africa and the Middle East. Each
of their destinations has been specifically chosen
to minimise the amount of days required off work,
while maximising the potential for outstanding and
original experiences. All of their trips are offered on
a completely exclusive basis, and you can choose from
70 holidays set out in six categories. They propose an
itinerary for each holiday, but each trip can be tailored
to your requirements, however specific. Their dedicated
team of reliable staff all have first-hand experience of
the destinations and are ready to help you design your
ideal short break.

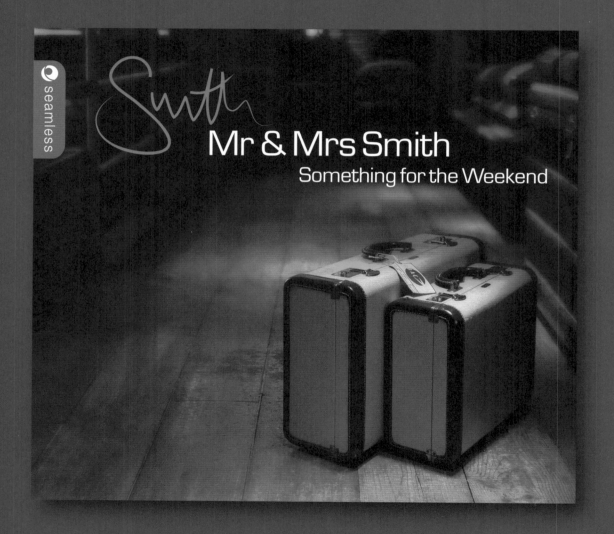

Mr & Mrs Smith – Something for the Weekend

With Mr & Mrs Smith hotel guides, our aim is to provide everything
you need to ensure the best escape possible. Working with a team of
opinionated thirtysomethings at Smith HQ, we went about the challenge
of putting together a collection of music. After many heated debates, broken
Britney singles, and vinyl Frisbeed across the office, we arrived at our first
compilation: an uplifting mix of tunes, old and new, to put a smile on your
face, perfect for your car stereo or your hotel room – in short, something for
the weekend. To achieve this, we collaborated with someone who has more
musical knowledge than all of us put together (and a record collection that
required building an extension): Rob Wood, ex-managing editor of *Jockey
Slut* magazine, and all-round DJ supremo, playing at clubs and festivals
across Europe, from Fabric to the Big Chill. We then needed a label
to produce the CD, and our first choice was Seamless Recordings
who produce the very cool *bargrooves* series.

Volume one travels from disco and soul to jazz-funk, Balearic house, Britpop
and beyond. A mix like no other, and one that we hope you'll enjoy listening to
as much as we enjoyed putting it together. Stay tuned for volume two…

Saint Etienne Nothing Can Stop Us Now
Ralph Myerz & The Jack Herren Band Think Twice
Rune Lindbaek Junta Jaeger
Randy Crawford Cajun Moon (Long Trip version)
Rae & Christian Spellbound
McKay Tell Him
Faze Action Broad Souls

Chungking Les Fleur
Max Sedgley Happy
Chris Rea Josephine (French edit)
Lambchop Up With People
RSL Wesley Music
Primal Scream Come Together

[applause]

thank you

Thanks once again to the savvy, hard work, creativity and explorations of our team: Andrew Grahame for his inspiration; Juliet Kinsman and Sophie Dening for their exceptional way with words; Edward Orr for keeping our finances on track; Katy McCann and Laura Mizon for their multilingual smarts and invaluable research; Aline Keuroghlian our inspired PR & marketing director; Adrian Houston for his mesmerising photography, and to his assistant Tom Mattey, and Hasselblad cameras; Bloom Design for their vision, brand genius and creativity, with special thanks to Ben White, Oona Bannon, Jason Badrock, Cluny Brown, Emily Wood, Harriet Marshall, Linda Fisher, Tim Reynolds and John Cox; Jori White; Fadi Shuman and his fantastic team at Pod1 for our beautiful website; Ben Sowton and Amber Spencer-Holmes at Seamless Recordings and Rob Wood for making our CD *Something for the Weekend*; Nick, Alastair and Tom at Original Travel and Travel Intelligence for making all your travel dreams come true; Hallmark for getting this to you; Hugh, Carol and Veronica at Portfolio Distribution, Luci Heyn and Norma Weir at Imago, and all of our reviewers for sharing their tales; thanks to all our stockists; Graham and team at Trichrom Ltd for printing the book and Tsunami Creative.
A big thank you to Myla, British Airways, Phase One, Hamburg Tourist Board, Tai, and IP Bartenders for their cocktail recipes; and last, but by no means least, huge thanks to anyone else who has supported us or helped make this book happen including: Tillie Allen, Kay Bischoff, Chiara Bocchini, Ori Kafri, Sara Capuano, Sara Carneholm, Mark and Carmen Chalmers, Emma Charles, Laura Clarke, Nicole at Dial a Flight, Harry Downes, Ally Ireson, Divya Kohl, Zrinka Kulusic, Jeremy Kinsman, Hannah Lohan, Annabel Mackie, Chris Mair, Scott Minshall, James Mollison, Alex Morris, Tony Mulcahy, Luis Nascimento, Mark Redgrave, Danielle Rigby, Edmund Sumner, Cristiano Spiller, Concetta Testa, Alasdhair Willis; and of course all those 'other halves' who accompanied our reviewers, or helped with content.

Mr & Mrs Smith

index